2001

Religion & Society

Religion & Society

The Role of Compassion, Selfless Service, & Social Justice in

Five Major Faith Traditions

An Anthology
Compiled by

Lucinda Allen Mosher

THE COUNCIL FOR RELIGION IN INDEPENDENT SCHOOLS
BETHESDA, MARYLAND

Founded in 1898, the Council for Religion in Independent Schools serves as a national, ecumenical resource to assist independent schools to promote the spiritual and ethical development of young people; to establish and nurture a climate in which religious inquiry and expression are encouraged; and to develop programs and curricula which insure that service, truth, equity, and goodness are an integral part of a student's learning.

Cover design: Leigh Axton Williams

Am I supposed to look after my brother?
— *Genesis 4:9b* CEV

 yup!

Contents

Forward

This anthology was born the morning I was asked to develop a new course for the coming term at Pomfret School, on whose faculty I served for nineteen years. To be called *Religion and Society,* it would combine community service with study of the way such service is motivated by several of the world's religions, thus interweaving an academic approach to the teaching of religion with experiential learning. The result was a course which Pomfret's chaplain, the Reverend Bradley C. Davis, has described as one which "encourages the sane application of religion to life among all of our students who value their respective religious or philosophical traditions. Our conviction is that true religion (or true philosophy, for that matter)—when rightly applied—has everything to do with compassionate service among the needy within the human family." Put another way, whereas courses in history ensure that students are well aware of the conflicts created throughout in the world in the name of religion, courses such as *Religion & Society* are important to the curriculum as a vehicle to persuade at least some students that the legacy of religion is not strife, but compassionate service as well. Considering that Pomfret School's Statement of Purpose includes a mandate to foster respect for religion, such a course teaches that compassionate service is a distinctive and respectful characteristic of all major religions.

The purpose of the course which spawned this anthology was, therefore, to introduce or reinforce the experience of giving service, to help students analyze their own feelings about compassionate service and the recipients of that service, and to guide them in a comparative study of the religious motivations for undertaking such service. It makes sense to offer a course that stresses the interrelatedness between religion and society—one which focuses not merely on theory, but on application as well. One hopes that students who participate fully in a combination of hands–on experience and guided reading will become both religiously thoughtful and politically aware. One hopes, as Chaplain Davis puts it, that they will "discover the rich diversity of motivations for service that have existed for millennia in many cultures. Perhaps the experience will be rich enough that the giving of service will become a perennial part of the lives of these young people."

The decision to create this anthology arose from the need to organize, under one cover, readings on service and compassionate action from five world faiths. Hinduism, Buddhism, Judaism, Christianity, and Islam form the skeleton; therefore, it includes five chapters of primary sources: excerpts from the sacred literature of each tradition which demonstrate the scriptural basis for compassion, service to humanity, and social justice. Likewise, it contains five chapters on applications—explanations of the unique vocabulary of compassion and service as well as examples of such. These come from such divergent sources as scholarly books and journals, biographies, and the popular press. Locating—then securing permission to use—interesting, challenging, relevant readings, then solidifying what could be used has been a complex task. Indeed, many excellent readings could not be included. Therefore, while this anthology is extensive and varied, it does not claim to be exhaustive.

Editorial decisions in presenting the chosen material strove to make it readily accessible to our readership. Therefore, scholarly apparatus—especially the bracketing of words and phrases—was deleted in most cases. Most of the selections have been abridged; however, in most cases, elipses have likewise been omitted. When absolutely necessary, obscure vocabulary has been replaced by a more commonplace synonym. These readings span many centuries of authorship and at least one hundred years of translation; therefore, there has been no attempt to apply any corrective for language which might now be considered sexist.

A project of this magnitude could not have been completed successfully without help in many forms; the list of people to whom I owe debts of gratitude is a long one. Over the three years that I taught this course for Pomfret School, my students—among them representatives of every faith considered in this anthology—helped me screen a wide variety of material; likewise, my dear friend and colleague at Pomfret, the Reverend Bradley C. Davis, whose vision this book was initially, did much to bring shape and motivation to the project. Their patience with a work in progress was deeply appreciated. Thanks must also go to my mentors at Hartford Seminary: Professors Ibrahim Abu-Rabiᶜ, Miriam Therese Winter, and Willem Bijlefeld; to the Reverend Leigh Axton Williams (my colleague in the General Theological Seminary doctoral program) who designed the cover; to Arumugaswami (Managing Editor of *Hinduism Today*), and Ibrahim Hooper (Council on American–Islamic Relations), for critiquing specific chapters; to Kathleen Atwood (Director of Pomfret School's Dupont Library) and her assistant, Anne Wolchesky, and likewise, the staff of the Hartford Seminary Library, all of whom doggedly helped me with research. Thanks is also extended to Dr. Shaik Ubaid (Secretary General of the Islamic Circle of North America), and Umar al-Qadi (President, Mercy International), and Dr. Ali Antar (Central Connecticut State University), for their assistance. My deepest gratitude, however, goes to two people without whom this anthology could never have achieved its final form: James M. Goodmann, Assistant Director of the Council for Religion in Independent Schools, who patiently and persistently served as the copy editor of the project; and my husband, Barrie S. Mosher, who not only donated his skill as layout editor but also provided support and assistance in ways beyond number.

Ultimately, what will be the value of this anthology? Certainly, it can provide reading resources for any course—in preparatory school or beyond—which deals with issues of religion and compassionate action. It will likewise be an excellent supplement to a World Religions course textbook. Most importantly, this collection of material provides an avenue for an encounter with crucial issues; therefore, I join with my former colleague, Brad Davis in hoping that "from grappling with what certainly appears to be a universal imperative, students will come to terms with what has been called the moral argument for the existence of God."

The Feast of All Saints, 1996

Lucinda Allen Mosher
New York City

Preface

Modern academic research on the relationship between religion and society abounds in almost every country in the world. Often, social scientists, especially in the West, have studied the social and political dimensions of religion while paying only scant attention to the spiritual, mystical, and theological sides of religion. Indeed, there are few studies that attempt to strike a balance between the two approaches: the objective social science approach, and the intimate spiritual approach. In this new work, Lucinda Mosher tries to do both. She has compiled a great deal of classical and modern writings from various religious traditions. In essence these writings are preoccupied with the same central problematics that are expressed differently by different scholars and mentalities.

In surveying the material, one is struck by the similarities, for instance, between the Hindu concept of suffering and the Islamic one, especially in Shi'ism and Sunnism. Likewise, one is struck by the similar meaning of *jihād* in Islam and early Christianity when many Christians were forced into martyrdom as a means of preserving their religion. In such a selection of important articles, the author is aware of the historical significance of the articles selected, the pivotal role they play within their own tradition, and their relevance to today's religious quest.

Social justice, as a concept and way of life, forms the basis of every religious tradition. This is as clear in Judaism as it is in Islam or Hinduism or Christianity. Besides being a major concept, social justice has been a dynamo that propelled many believers to action, conditioned their mentalities, and crowned their religious endeavor. One might argue that social justice, besides being a theological issue in all of these traditions, has also been an ideological issue leading to uprisings and revolutions. The case of Iran in 1979 is just one illustration. Social justice leads to martyrdom as well as to great social movements and revolutions. In that sense, the author invites us to look seriously at the ramifications of social justice in world religions and the impact it might have had on inducing social and historical change.

Lucinda Mosher is to be commended on this timely selection. I think that students of comparative religion, sociology and anthropology of religion, and

modern religious movements will find this work inspiring. One hopes that thi
work will be followed by similar works of more analytical nature.

—Ibrahim M. Abu-Rab:
Professor of Islamic Studies and Christian–Muslim Relation
Hartford Seminar·
Hartford, Connecticu

Chapter One

Hindu Sacred Writings and Compassion

It is often said that Hinduism—an umbrella term for a wide variety of beliefs and practices—has as many versions as there are practitioners in India! Hinduism can be personal or transcendental; a path of sensuous experiences or a path of renunciation of the comforts of life; seemingly polytheistic or avowedly monotheistic with its plethora of gods being understood as icons: windows on the one Ultimate Reality. In fact, the term "Hinduism" itself has been imposed on this ancient faith by Westerners. It is more appropriately called "Sanatana Dharma"—eternal law or eternal religion—a term under which may be collected the many variations of belief rooted in study of and reverence for the ancient texts known as the Vedas.

The language of Hindu sacred literature is Sanskrit. While this literature stems from an incredibly long oral tradition, written scriptures are an integral part of Hinduism. It understands these sacred writings to be beginningless and authorless—and thus free from human error. The *rishis*—learned sages—who transmitted this literature are therefore mere vehicles of the Divine. These writings contain all the information necessary to achieving enlightenment—the Hindu parallel to the more western notion of salvation. Furthermore, it is believed that once enlightenment is achieved—not a common or easy task—a Hindu can actually outgrow the need for scripture.

Rig Veda

Literally meaning *body of knowledge*, the Vedas are collections of hymns dating from as early as 6500 BCE. They were transmitted orally before being committed to writing, a process which lasted perhaps as long as nine hundred years. The best known of these collections is the Rig Veda—a collection of 1028 metrical hymns.

He who gives liberally goes straight to the gods; on the high ridge of heaven he stands exalted. —*Rig Veda 1.125.5*

The gods surely did not ordain hunger alone for slaughter; various deaths reach the man who is well fed. The riches of the man who gives fully do not run out, but the miser finds no one with sympathy.

The man with food who hardens his heart against the poor man who comes to him suffering and searching for nourishment—although in the past he had helped him—he surely finds no one with sympathy.

The man who is truly generous gives to the beggar who approaches him thin and in search of food. He puts himself at the service of the man who calls to him from the road, and makes him a friend for times to come.

That man is no friend who does not give of his own nourishment to his friend, the companion at his side. Let the friend turn away from him; this is not his dwelling-place. Let him find another man who gives freely, even if he be a stranger.

Let the stronger man give to the man whose need is greater; let him gaze upon the lengthening path. For riches roll like the wheels of a chariot, turning from one to another.

The man without foresight gets food in vain; I speak the truth: it will be his death. He cultivates neither a patron nor a friend. The man who eats alone brings troubles upon himself alone. —*Rig Veda 10.117.1-6*

Upanishads

These influential Indian philosophical writings contain both poetry and prose, mostly in dialogue format. Their early formation spans the period from approximately 1450–1250 BCE; they took written form between 1500–600 BCE. Included within them is a story known as *The Three Da's,* a tale assumed to stem from the beginning of time itself. By explaining the origin of Hinduism's principal virtues: *damyata, datta,* and *dayadhvam* (restraint or self-control, giving, and compassion), this dramatic sequence demonstrates the very basis of the Hindu ethic.

The Lord of All Creatures—that is, *Prajapati*—had three kinds of offspring: gods, men, and *asuras*—which we might call demons. All of them lived with their father, *Prajapati,* as students of *brahmacarya*—that is, sacred knowledge.

After having lived this life of a student of sacred knowledge for some time, the gods addressed their father. "Speak to us, sir."

The Lord of All Creatures answered them with just one syllable, *"Da."* "Did you understand?" he asked them.

"We understand," they replied. "When you said *'Da,'* you actually meant, *'Damyata:* Restrain yourselves.'"

"Yes!" exclaimed the Lord of All Creatures, "you understand!"

Next, the men addressed him, "Speak to us, sir."

To the men the Lord of All Creatures also spoke but one syllable, *"Da."* "Did you understand?" he asked them.

"We understand," said the men. "When you said *'Da,'* you actually meant, *'Datta:* Give.'"

"Yes!" said the Lord of All Creatures, "you understand!"

Last, the *asuras*—, that is, the demons—said to him, "Speak to us, sir."

To the *asuras* the Lord of All Creatures also spoke but one syllable, *"Da."* "Did you understand?" he asked them.

"We understand," said the demons. "When you said *'Da,'* you actually meant, *'Dayadhvam:* Be compassionate.'"

"Yes!" said the Lord of All Creatures, "you understand!"

This same lesson is boomed time and again by the thunderous voice of divine Ultimate Reality: *Da! Da! Da!* (which means: restrain yourselves; give; be compassionate.) Everyone should practice these same three virtues: self-restraint, giving, compassion. —*Brihadāranyaka Upanishad 5.2.2*

Mārkandeya Purāna

Purāna means "religious lore", and is meant to be chanted to music. There are eighteen major examples of this genre of folk literature. The following comes from perhaps the oldest example of this genre. It is attributed to the ancient sage, Mārkandeya, who wandered inside the body of the god Vishnu, thus, trekking throughout the entire world. Four characters appear in the drama given below: King Vipascit, who is described as "a peerless perfect man" by the narrator; an officer of Yama, the god who cares for the dead and provides for their needs; Dharma, the personification of the eternal law and, thus, Ultimate Reality itself; and Indra, the king of the gods, also their warrior, and the god of rain.

Vipascit:"Ho! servant of Yama! Say, what sin have I committed, for which I have incurred this deepest hell, frightful for its torments? Known as King Vipascit, I protected the earth with uprightness; I let no fighting rage; no guest departed with averted countenance; nor did I offend the spirits of the ancestors, the gods, ascetics, or my servants; nor did I covet other men's wives, or wealth, or aught else belonging to them. How, then, have I incurred this very terrible hell?"

Yama's officer:"Come then, we go elsewhere. You have now seen everything, for you have seen hell. Come then, let us go elsewhere."

Thereupon the king prepared to follow him; but a cry went up from all the men who dwelled in torment: "Be gracious, O king! stay but a moment, for the air that clings to thy body gladdens our mind and entirely dispels the burning and the sufferings and pains from our bodies, O tiger-like man! Be gracious, O king!"

Vipascit: Neither in heaven nor in Brahma's world do men experience such joy as arises from conferring bliss on suffering creatures. If, while I am present, torment does not hurt these men, here I will remain, firm as a mountain."

Yama's officer:"Come, O king; we proceed. Enjoy the delights won by your own merit; leave here the evildoers to their torments."

Vispascit: "As long as these beings are in sore suffering, I will not go. From my presence the denizens of hell grow happy. Fie on the sickly protection—begging life of that man who shows no favor to one distressed, even though he be a resolute foe! Sacrifices, gifts, austerities do not work for the welfare of him who has no thought for the succor of the distressed. To grant deliverance to these men excels, I consider, the joy of heaven. If many sufferers shall obtain happiness while only I undergo pain, shall I not in truth embrace it?"

Dharma: "These evil-doers have come to hell in consequence of their own deeds; you also, O king, must go to heaven in consequence of your meritorious deeds. I lead you to heaven; mount this heavenly chariot and linger not; let us go."

Vipascit: "Men in thousands, O Dharma, suffer pain here in hell; and being in affliction they cry to me to save them; hence I will not depart."

Dharma: "O king! Your merit is truly beyond reckoning. In evincing now this compassion here in the hells, your merit has amounted even higher. Come, enjoy the abode of the immortals; let these unfortunates consume away in hell the sin arising from their own actions!"

Vipascit: "Whatever good deeds I possess, O Lord of the Thirty Gods, by means thereof let the sinners who are undergoing torment be delivered from hell!"

Indra: "So be it, O king! You have gained an even more exalted station: see too these sinners delivered from hell!" *—Mārkandeya Purāna 13-5.*

Śrimad Bhāgavatam

Scholars disagree about the age of the Bhāgavata Purāna, but the oral tradition was given written form in the 9th century CE. This lengthy Sanskrit epic by an unknown author is written in the style of South Indian Hindu religious poets known as Ālvārs. Because it is widely cherished, this collection of "religious lore of the gracious Lord" has had a significant impact on Vaishnavite Hinduism—those whose devotion is centered on Vishnu. In the story below, which comes from the portion entitled "The Dynasty of Bharata," Ultimate Reality is personified as Rantideva, whose acts serve as a model for us all. Each guest who visits Rantideva is this story represents a different level of society: *brāhmana,* the priestly caste; *sūdra,* the caste of manual laborers; and *candāla,* the outcastes or Untouchables. The version given here utilizes translation and commentary by A. C. Bhaktivedanta Swami Prabhupada.

Rantideva was one who saw every living entity in relationship with the Supreme Personality of Godhead, and therefore he completely engaged his mind, his words and his very self in the service of the Supreme Lord and his devotees. The Supreme Personality of Godhead, being extremely pleased with Rantideva, entrusted him with very confidential service.

Rantideva is famous in both this world and the next, for he is glorified not only in human society but also in the society of the gods. Rantideva never endeavored to earn anything. He would enjoy whatever he got by the arrangement of providence, but when guests came he would give them everything. Thus he underwent considerable suffering, along with the members of his family. Indeed, he and his family members shivered for want of food and water, yet Rantideva always remained sober. Once, after fasting for forty-eight days, in the morning Rantideva received some water and some foodstuffs made with milk and *ghee* [clarified butter], but when he and his family were about to eat a *brāhmana* guest arrived. Because Rantideva perceived the presence of the Supreme Godhead everywhere, and in every living entity, he received the guest with faith and respect and gave him a share of the food. The *brāhmana* guest ate his share and then went away.

Therefore, having divided the remaining food with his relatives, Rantideva was just about to eat his own share when a *śūdra* guest arrived. Seeing the *śūdra* in relationship with the Supreme Personality of Godhead, King Rantideva gave him also a share of the food.

When the *śūdra* went away, another guest arrived surrounded by dogs, and said, "O king, I and my company of dogs are very hungry. Please give us something to eat." With great respect, King Rantideva offered the balance of the food to the dogs and the master of the dogs, who had come as guests. The King offered them all respect and homage.

Thereafter, only the drinking water remained, and there was only enough to satisfy one person, but when the King was just about to drink it, a *caṇḍāla* appeared and said, "O King, although I am lowborn, kindly give me some drinking water."

Aggrieved at hearing the pitiable words of the poor fatigued *caṇḍāla*, Mahārāja Rantideva spoke the following sweet words. "I do not pray to the Supreme Personality of Godhead for the eight perfections of mystic yoga, nor for salvation from repeated birth and death. I want only to stay among all the living entities and suffer all distresses on their behalf, so that they may be freed from suffering. By offering my water to maintain the life of this poor *caṇḍāla*, who is struggling to live, I have been freed from all hunger, thirst, fatigue, trembling of body, moroseness, distress, lamentation and illusion."

Having spoken thus, King Rantideva, although on the verge of death because of thirst, gave his own portion of water to the *caṇḍāla* without hesitation, for the King was naturally very kind and sober. Gods like Lord Brahmā and Lord Siva, who can satisfy all materially ambitious men by giving them the rewards they desire, then manifested their own identities before King Rantideva, for it was they who had presented themselves as the *brāhmana, śūdra, caṇḍāla* and so on. King Rantideva had no ambition to enjoy material benefits from the gods. He offered them veneration, but because he was a devotee of Lord Vishnu, Vāsudeva, the Supreme Personality of Godhead, he fixed his mind at Lord Vishnu's lotus feet.

—*Śrimad Bhāgavatam Canto 9, Chapter 21*

Mahābhārata

Literally, "The Great Story of the Bhāratas," this semi-historical story is the national epic of Hindu India, and includes many lessons in righteous behavior. Scholars believe that this epic existed as oral tradition long before it took written form sometime between 500–300 BCE. With over 100,000 verses, the *Mahābhārata* is well over ten times as long as the Christian Bible, and is especially revered as scripture by Vashnavites and Smārtas. Perhaps the most widely read, best known portion of the Mahābhārata—in fact, of all Indian religious literature—is the *Bhagavadgītā.* Its title means "Song of God" or "a song of instruction by the Supreme Ultimate Reality" expounding on liberation through devotion to God.

A primary character in the *Bhagavadgītā* is Arjuna. Seemingly the third son of Pāndu and Kuntī, he is in reality the offspring of Indra—king of the gods, and is receiving instruction from Lord Krishna.

At the beginning, mankind and the obligation of selfless service were created together. "Through selfless service, you will always be fruitful and find the fulfillment of your desires": this is the promise of the Creator.

Every selfless act, Arjuna, is born from the eternal, infinite Godhead. God is present in every act of service. All life turns on this law, O Arjuna. Whoever violates it, indulging his senses for his own pleasure and ignoring the needs of others, has wasted his life. But those who realize the God within are always satisfied. Having found the source of joy and fulfillment, they no longer seek happiness from the external world. They have nothing to gain or lose by any action; neither people nor things can affect their security.

Strive constantly to serve the welfare of the world; by devotion to selfless work one attains the supreme goal in life. Do your work with the welfare of others always in mind. It was by such work that Janaka attained perfection; others, too, have followed this path.

What the outstanding person does, others will try to do. The standards such people set will be followed by the whole world. There is nothing in the three worlds for me to gain, Arjuna, nor is there anything I do not have; I continue to act, but I am not driven by any need of my own. If I ever refrained from continuous work, everyone would immediately follow my example. If I stopped working I would be the cause of cosmic chaos, and finally of the destruction of this world and these people.

The ignorant work for their own profit, Arjuna; the wise work for the welfare of the world, without thought to themselves. By abstaining from work you will confuse the ignorant, who are engrossed in their actions. Perform all work carefully, guided by compassion. —*Bhagavadgītā 3.10-26*

No one who does good deeds will ever come to a bad end, either here or in the world to come. When such people die, they go to other realms where the righteous live. They dwell there for countless years and they are reborn into a home which is pure and prosperous. —*Bhagavadgītā 6.40-1*

Giving simply because it is right to give, without thought of return, at a proper time, in proper circumstances, and to a worthy person, is enlightened giving. Giving with regrets or in the expectation of receiving some favor or of getting something in return, is selfish giving. —*Bhagavadgītā 17.20-21*

Chapter Two

Readings on Hinduism and Social Action

The Hindu world view is rooted in the concepts of samsara and karma. Samsara is the endless cycle of birth, death, and rebirth; only when a soul has matured sufficiently can it break out of the cycle and achieve Moksha, thus merging with Ultimate Reality from which it came in the first place. Meanwhile, one's experiences in each lifetime are determined by karma: "you get what you deserve, and you deserve what you get."

Hindu practice or discipline—yoga—takes many forms. Two have special relevance to social action. Karma yoga—the path to God through work—is service devoid of self-interest, service on behalf of others. Bhakti yoga is the path to God through devotion—through love. This love for God may be translated into action on behalf of others.

Swami Vivekananda, the Ramakrishna Movement, and Hindu Social Work
Jan Peter Schouten

Vivekananda—which, Schouten explains, means "the bliss of discriminating between reality and illusion"—is the name by which the great teacher Narendanath Dutt came to be known. (His name is also sometimes transliterated as Narendra Nath Datta.) Embracing an understanding of Hinduism which emphasized service to humanity, Swami Vivekananda made worldwide lecture tours which did much to popularize Hinduism in the West and to establish the Vedanta Society.

The biggest and most influential Hindu monastic organization that is engaged in social work, is the Ramakrishna Movement. The movement consists of two institutes, the Ramakrishna Math and the Ramakrishna Mission. The Math is a monastic order which—besides engaging in religious activities—is active in the social field. The Mission has as its members monks of the Math as well as lay people, and the aims of this society are in the fields of social care and religious propaganda. The organizations are closely connected. Not only is much of the work in the Mission done by monks of the Math, but moreover the Governing Body of the Mission consists of Trustees of the Math.

The movement has its origin in the life of Sri Ramakrishna Paramahamsa (1836–1886), a mystic who taught the oneness of all religions. Before he died Ramakrishna entrusted the guidance of his disciples to his favorite pupil Narendra, whose monastic name was Swami Vivekananda.

Swami Vivekananda (1862–1902) was the most brilliant reformer in nineteenth–century Hinduism. He was a good organizer and moreover had a strong social feeling. This led him to design a monastic organization based on a combination of contemplation and social service. During one of his early journeys through India, Vivekananda became acquainted with the life of the people in his country and was deeply struck by their great poverty. His travels culminated in a meditation on a rocky island near Cape Comorin. There, on the utmost southern point of India, he saw his mission clearly: "We have to give back to the nation its lost individuality and *raise the masses*."[1]

The Ramakrishna Movement grew particularly strongly in its first decades. Important projects were the founding of an Institute of Culture in Calcutta and a big hospital in Vrindaban. The main center of the Movement is the monastery at Belur near Calcutta, which was founded in 1899. At the monastery, the Movement has set up extensive juvenile work; here, the religious education is not always the main purpose but it always plays a role.

The social work of the Movement is quite impressive, as evidenced by the wide range of activities documented in the annual report of 1975. First of all the Movement gives occasional help on a large scale; in 1907 the Ramakrishna Movement had already set up relief projects for famine-stricken areas. Nowadays there are relief projects for floods, drought, scarcity and fire.

Among the continuous social assistance programs the medical work is of the utmost importance. The annual report mentions thirteen hospitals with 1588 beds, where 46,451 patients were treated. An even more important contribution to public health is the outdoor dispensaries, often situated in regions where there is no medical care at all. There are sixty-five such dispensaries which registered 3,657,791 cases in the year under review; in addition there are five mobile dispensaries which treated 90,123 cases. The organization has also a sanatorium for tuberculosis patients, 101 milk distribution centres and even a veterinary section. For some years the Ramakrishna Mission has also been engaged in its own medical research.

The work of the Ramakrishna Mission does not lead directly to social change. However revolutionary the ideas of Swami Vivekananda might have been, his followers do not show very much of that spirit. As a principle, the Movement does not play any political role. But even within its own institutions there is little impetus for social change. The Ramakrishna Math and Mission are well managed and successful institutions for humanitarian work, but in the process of institutionalization the initial elan has faded away.

Our main interest is how this humanitarian work could develop in a Hindu surrounding and how it is justified with arguments from Hindu scripture and tradition. A first answer to that can be found in the writings of the founder of the movement, Swami Vivekananda. He never unfolds a systematic social theory, but from his numerous speeches and letters one can see a clear vision of social life.

A first element of this vision is Vivekananda's concern for the misery of the poor masses. When he writes about his travels through India, he bursts out:

> A country where millions of people live on flowers of the Mohua plant, and a million or two of Sadhus and a hundred million or so of Brahmins suck the blood out of these poor people, without even the least effort for their amelioration—is that a country or hell? Is that a religion, or a devil's dance?[2]

One cannot conclude from this that he considers the repression of the poor as a necessary social consequence of Hindu philosophy. In another letter he writes: "No religion on earth preaches the dignity of humanity in such lofty strain as Hinduism, and no religion on earth treads upon the necks of the poor and the low in such a fashion as Hinduism." Religion itself cannot be blamed for anything, he concludes, but it is the Pharisees and Sadducees of Hinduism who invent all kinds of methods of repression. In a letter to his friends he even dares to write: "Kick out the priests who are always against progress, because they would never mend, their hearts would never become big." So something has to change in India and more than once Vivekananda states frankly: "We do stand in need of social reform." The necessary reforms are amelioration of the position of women and uplift of the masses.[3]

For Vivekananda the most important means to achieve social change is education. But Vivekananda is realistic enough to realize that he cannot give such education to people who are hungry, so he stresses constantly that the people must get enough food.

Vivekananda has given Hinduism a new dimension: spirituality that aims at social service and the welfare of all. It has often been presumed that he borrowed this notion from Christianity. But it is dangerous to draw conclusions too rapidly. His religion-colored social concern could have been borrowed from Christianity, but in his writings there is not a single indication in that direction. On the contrary, Vivekananda tries constantly to legitimate his views with arguments from the Hindu lore. In this respect there is no Christian influence. But there is something else: Vivekananda's ideal of a monastic order that combined spirituality and social work. Undoubtedly the idea of a lay organization for social work, the later Ramakrishna Mission, is due to his American experiences. We thus conclude that modern Christianity's principal influence on Vivekananda was in the form of organizational ideas.

Thus, the Ramakrishna Movement is a good example of an organization that renders social service from a religious inspiration. The numerous activities of this monastic institution prove that in Hinduism a serious concern for the poor is not absent. The Ramakrishna Movement was built up by Swami Vivekananda. His concern for the downtrodden in his country is still fascinating after a century. His reinterpretation of the Hindu tradition, the "practical Vedanta," has changed the image of Hinduism. He was the first who fought for the poor in India, legitimating his actions with the Hindu lore. The impact of his ideas has been enormous.

Karma Yoga and Hindu Ethics
Carl T. Jackson

Jackson mentions monism—an important term in the Hindu understanding of the nature of God and of humanity. Monism explains that the creature—humanity—and the creator—Ultimate Reality—are of the same substance; the creature and the creator differ only in degree of maturity.

If Vedanta has supplied the theoretical foundation for the Ramakrishna movement, yoga may be said to embody its practical teaching. Self-liberation as defined by Vedanta represents the goal, but yoga as explained by Swami Vivekananda has offered the means to that end. As in the case of Vedanta, the movement has simplified and adapted the yogic teachings for a Western audience. Ramakrishna writers have defined "yoga" variously as the "act of yoking or joining," or as "union of the individual soul with the Godhead," or again, as the "method by which such union is achieved."

The four major types of yoga available to a Ramakrishna student are karma, bhakti, jnana, and raja yoga. Swami Vivekananda was one of the earliest Hindu teachers to explain the four types of yoga in a language that Westerners could comprehend. Originally presented as lectures in New York, Vivekananda's exposition has since become authoritative for most followers. According to movement literature, each of the four types has its own distinctive characteristics.

Karma yoga, referred to as the "path of selfless work," is recommended as the yoga best suited for people of active temperaments. In karma yoga work in the world becomes the preferred path to salvation, a conception that squares poorly with the common Western belief that Hinduism emphasizes repudiation of the world. Movement writers claimed that the karma yogi remains *in* the world but not *of* it, seeking to convert every action into a form of worship. The ideals are renunciation and selfless service in God's name; what one renounces is not the action itself, but desire for the fruits of action. Ramakrishna writers insist that no one needs to convert to Hinduism in order to benefit from its disciplines and, apparently, this is believed to be especially true of karma yoga. Few American followers of the Ramakrishna movement have indicated interest in karma yoga, despite the fact that its emphasis on worldly activity would seem likely to appeal to a typical Western seeker.

Though the Vedanta message presented in the West by the Ramakrishna movement clearly drew deeply from the well of classical Hinduism, it also diverged sharply from Hindu orthodoxy. The movement's positive view of science offers one of the best indications of its nontraditionalism. A concern with questions of ethics and social responsibility marked a second divergence from traditional Hinduism. The writings of Ramakrishna swamis are notable for the attention they devote to the subject. Swami Nikhilananda's chapter "Hindu Ethics" in *Hinduism: Its Meaning for the Liberation of the Spirit* provides an excellent example. Presenting a fairly detailed account of the origin and nature of Hindu ethics, the swami emphatically insisted that an ethical outlook provided the "steel-frame foundation of the spiritual life." In explaining the common Western misunderstanding of Hinduism's moral outlook, the swami noted that ethical sensitivity had not so much been absent but had assumed a different form in Hinduism than in the West. While the West stressed social ethics, Hinduism had emphasized the ethics of the individual.

Swami Prabhavananda claimed that, in truth, Hinduism offered a superior foundation for ethical action, thanks to its "doctrine of unity" set forth in the *Upanishads,* which offered the "only basis" upon which true ethical life could be lived. He contended that Hinduism offered greater justification for moral behavior than other religions. He wrote: "'Love thy neighbor as thyself,' say the *Upanishads,* and after them both Buddha and Christ." Why should one love one's neighbor? A Hindu understood "Simply because he *is* yourself."[5] Only a monist could have made such an assertion. Few other Hindu movements, ancient or modern have devoted so much attention to ethical questions.

However, the Ramakrishna movement's clearest break with traditional Hindu views was its advocacy of humanitarian aid, an extension of its ethical emphasis and a policy reflected in its heavy involvement in Indian educational, medical, and welfare projects. Once again, Swami Vivekananda seems to have been the decisive influence. Where Ramakrishna tended to show little sensitivity to and, on occasion, outright contempt for humanitarian efforts, Vivekananda proclaimed that Hinduism should be based both on *"renunciation"* and *"service."*[6] Renunciation has always been a central goal in Hinduism; however, emphasis on service is something new.

Vivekananda's successors have clearly accepted his service ideal, making humanitarianism one of the Ramakrishna movements's identifying characteristics. In some cases, the swamis called not merely for humanitarian aid but for more thoroughgoing social revolution, occasionally sounding almost socialistic in their condemnation of economic exploitation.

At the same time, one must not go too far. However known for their humanitarian work, leaders of the Ramakrishna movement have always argued that such activity must be viewed as secondary to individual self-liberation. In this regard, Swami Prabhavananda observed that "none of the monks of the Ramakrishna Order regards himself as a humanitarian." He insisted that the monk's one goal in life was to know God, and that "worship and meditation" offered the "means to that end."[7] Supporters of humanitarian aid to others, the swamis have been unwilling to justify humanitarian work for its own sake. In this respect, the Ramakrishna Order has remained true to the spirit of traditional Hinduism.

The Wisdom of Gandhi: Comments on Religion and Society
Mohandas K. Gandhi

Mohandas Karamchand Gandhi lived from 1869–1948. At once a consummate politician and a revered spiritual leader, he merited the honorific *Mahatma*—great soul. He modelled and popularized social action grounded in nonviolence, courage, and truth in his drive for civil rights for people of color and political autonomy for India. He led the movement for Indian independence from Great Britain, as well as for internal social change. He sought to improve the situation of India's Untouchables, whom he preferred to call *Harijans*—Children of God. He strove to make India economically independent by encouraging cottage industry and the use of domestic products. His demands for tolerance for all—regardless of religion, caste, or race—ultimately resulted in his assassination. The interplay between religion and society threads its way throughout Gandhi's writings, from which three excerpts are included here.

Religion and Social Service

The following is taken from a response to questions posed in January, 1935, by Sir S. Radhakrishnan.

My religion is Hinduism which, for me, is the religion of humanity and includes the best of all the religions known to me. The bearing of this religion on social life is, or has to be, seen in one's daily social contact. To be true to such religion one has to lose oneself in continuous and continuing service of all life. Realization of Truth is impossible without a complete merging of oneself in and identification with this limitless ocean of life. Hence, for me, there is no escape from social service; there is no happiness on earth beyond or apart from it. Social service here must be taken to include every department of life. In this scheme there is nothing low, nothing high. For all is one, though we *seem* to be many.

Morality and Society

In January and February, 1907, Gandhi wrote a series of articles for Indian Opinion, in which he summarized the 1889 work, *Ethical Religion,* by American philosopher and ethicist, William MacIntyre Salter, the founder of the Society for Ethical Culture. These articles were brought together in book form in 1922. Here is an excerpt from Gandhi's sixth chapter.

So long as man remains selfish and does not care for the happiness of others, he is no better than an animal and perhaps worse. His superiority to the animal is seen only when we find him caring for his family. He is still more human, that is, much higher than the animal, when he extends his concept of the family to include his country or community as well. He climbs still higher in the scale when he comes to regard the human race as his family. A man is an animal or imperfect to the extent that he falls behind in his service to humanity. If I feel my wife's injury or that of my community, yet have no sympathy for anyone outside the circle, it is clear that I do not have any feeling for humanity as such; but I have, simply out of selfishness or a sense of discrimination, a certain feeling for my wife, my children or the community which I hold as my own.

That is to say, we have neither practised nor known ethical religion so long as we do not feel sympathy for every human being. Now we know that the higher morality must be comprehensive; it must embrace all men. Considering our relation to mankind, every man has a claim over us, as it is our duty always to serve him. We should act on the assumption that we have no claim on others. He is merely ignorant who would here argue that the man acting in this manner will be trampled in the world's scramble. For it is a universal experience that God always saves the man who wholeheartedly devotes himself to the service of others.

The Spirit of Service

The following is a letter written in Trichinolopy to the women of the Satyagraha Ashram Gandhi had founded in 1915.[8] It is dated September 19, 1927. "Bapu"—father—is the term of respect and affection by which Gandhi was known among his friends.

Sisters,

I get your notes regularly. I keep an eye on your work from here. One who works according to one's full capacity does all that can be expected of one. But in our work we should develop the *Gita* attitude which we want to have. That attitude is that, whatever we do, we do it selflessly in a spirit of service. The spirit of service means a spirit of dedication to God. One who does so, loses all idea of self. He has no hatred for anybody. On the contrary, he is generous to others. Even about the smallest piece of service you render, ask yourselves from time to time whether you have this same attitude. . . . My health continues to be good enough to let me do my work.

Blessings from
Bapu

Society's Seven Sins
Mohandas K. Gandhi

The following is a list of societal practices the Mahatma disdained, which in turn reveal the philosophy by which he strove to live.[9]

1. Wealth without work.

2. Pleasure without conscience.

3. Knowledge without character.

4. Commerce without morality.

5. Science without humanity.

6. Worship without sacrifice.

7. Politics without principle.

Amazing! Such Service All Belongs to God
V. V. Gokhale

According to the Rev. Pandurangshastri Athavale—the subject of the following article—"*Swadhyaya* means self-study, introspection, and the study of scriptures. Each one has to do one's utmost to elevate oneself morally and spiritually. It is only through spiritual awakening that man can stand on his own legs and face adversity. This self-respect and divine consciousness must be tapped. Each man must be made aware of his divine heritage, that the Lord is with and within him."

A miraculous silent spiritual revolution is underway in over 80,000 Indian villages under the leadership of a living saint, Sri Pandurangshastri Athavle, also known as "Sri Dada." His swadhyaya service movement started in 1958 with a few villages in Surashtra (Gujarat). It has spread to eighteen Indian states and parts of Africa, England, and the USA.

In November, 1993, the "unbelievable until you see it" transformation was celebrated in twenty-four tribal villages surrounding Gavhali, in Dhulia district near the boarder of Maharashtra and Gujarat. It was Sri Dada's seventy-fourth year, so his followers planted 7400 saplings that day amidst Vedic chanting in praise of trees; 500,000 people came to listen to his talks. Eighteen of the twenty-four villages around Gavhali have established *Yogeshwar Krushi*—"Krishna Farming"—a term used by Sri Dada for spiritual community farming. Rich and poor farmers and landless workers in divine friendship for annual bumper crops. The produce belongs to Yogeshwar (one of Krishna's names in the Gita) and is used for the village's poor. Yogeshwar Krushi has been established in over 4,000 Indian hamlets, with the state of Gujarat leading.

Urban swadhyayis began in the Gavhali area ten years ago with devotional friendship visits to these villages, then ridden with illicit liquor trade, crime and exploitation of the indigent illiterate tribals. They began by singing and chanting the glories of God and talking about God's grace with the villagers. Living in small huts, temples, and under trees during weekend visits, volunteers took their own food and did not ask the tribals for anything, not even tea, but only to be allowed to nurture their friendship.

Even when threatened by gangsters, they held firm faith in God, that He was present in everybody's heart. By devotional persistence they gradually made a few friends, then more and more. Within a few months, the tribals started looking forward to the weekly chanting and stories from the *Bhagavadgītā* and Sri Dada's work in other places. Slowly, inevitably, they stopped quarreling, stopped smuggling, and started helping each other from day to day. Some liquor-makers moved; some changed their ways. After ten years, the work culminated with 400 doctors vowing at Sri Dada's Jayanti in Gavhali to build "Patanjali Hospital" there to serve local people.

A deep thinker and analyst of religious and political philosophy both East and West, Sri Dada promotes a paradigm for social development that transcends both capitalist and communist models. He believes the educated middle class can wield a spiritual power. City engineers, merchants, tractor owners, carpenters, students and women, all swadhyayis, work with villagers, chanting and offering prayers. They build small cottages, clear land, engineer small roads and dams for water, and dig wells.

Swadhyayis do not accept monetary donations or government grants. The organization works like a family. There is no membership fee, no registered trust, no paid staff and no press conferences. I accompanied a lady from Pune who wanted to personally donate 100,000 rupees to Sri Dada. He was very sweet and loving but declined to accept the donation. He also does not accept or solicit donations in India or from nonresidents elsewhere. Dada feels that when the need arises, God fulfills it, through his working devotees.

From Veraval in North Saurashtra, to Goa in South Konkan, a large number of fishing villages on the western coast of India have been transformed by visiting devotees. Crime is down, while devotional and collective social activities are up. Twenty villages have constructed over twenty-four large fishing boats called Matsya-Ghandha, which belong to God. The ocean harvest is used for the common good.

Fruit and other trees are grown and looked after collectively, sometimes by a number of villages coming together. There is no building or idol-worship, but the trees are worshipped as God's manifestation. There are more than twenty such large sacred orchards, called Vriksha Mandir's Tree Temples. Among other things, Sri Dada is a religious ecologist. In July of 1993, he had asked his followers everywhere to plant tree saplings. Wife and husband were to jointly nurture their plants for one hundred days with daily chanting of Narayanopanishad verses. On October 19, 1993, it was announced that seven million saplings survived.

Bhakti yoga is at the core of Sri Dada's teachings and all swadyayis worship three times daily—a practice which is called *Trikala Sandhya.* Verses from the *Bhagavadgītā* and other spiritual books are sung during meals, at bedtime, and upon arising in the morning to invoke the feeling of nearness to God, the first stage of devotion.

Dada has also set up six colleges for farmers' sons who return after graduation. There are no fees, no degrees, no teachers' salaries. They receive a good education in agriculture, Vedic traditions, scripture, Sanskrit, community work and peaceful collective cultural revival, the students become effective swadhyayis. They develop friendship, not for pleasure or profit, but the highest form of friendship in devotion, based on the brotherhood of God.

Rev. Pandurangshastri Athavale says: "I pray to God to give you strength to do this spiritual work and solve man's family problems, his national and universal problems. But unless devotionalism becomes a social force, these problems can never be solved."

The Wisdom of Sri Dada: Excerpts from the teaching of Rev. Pandurangshastri Athavale

- Religion, or dharma, must teach us to have respect for others. A reverential attitude towards the world is a natural corollary to the acceptance of God who resides in one and all. Love of God within, implying reverence of our fellow-beings, is bound to be translated into altruistic actions. This attitude will not allow man to sit idle and remain indifferent. It is bound to result in what the *Bhagavadgītā* calls "selfless activism." Swadhyaya work has shown that people can rise above self-interest and self-love to do the divine work of human upliftment. The rural visits are known as *Bhakti-Feri*— Devotional Trips. They result in *Kriti-Bhakti*—Devotional Action—which transforms people for great collective action. The rich and poor, educated and tribals, young and old, have been working together, with a true spiritual attitude and orientation.

- Everyone talks about the urgency to eliminate poverty. The words *aid* and *help* have become fashionable. It is a doctrine of helping out of pity and sympathy. But unless God in man is awakened, there is no hope of solving this problem between the have's and the have-nots. Economic differences will always exist. The have's and the have-not's must all be made aware of God with and within us. Such a spiritually awakened man cannot do injustice to others. And who can do this work? The mature, educated middle class. It is their duty.

- The Lord works with me. Naturally there is His share in my income. His share must be kept aside and offered to the temples, and the temples must distribute this wealth in the form of divine gifts. There is also another kind of wealth that arises from collective effort. The wealth produced in our Yogeshwar Krushi farms is spiritual. The farms belong to God alone. The Swadhyayis collectively cultivate the divine farm and the wealth is used to solve the socioeconomic problems of the same village. This swadhyaya work attempts to transform humanity into the global family of Yogeshwar.

Swamini Saradapriyananda & the Chinmaya Mission Ashrams
Lavina Melwani

The author is a journalist for several publications in the US, India, and the Far East. Born in Sindh, she grew up in New Delhi, and has lived in Hong Kong and Africa. She currently resides in New York.

Why would anyone in this age of greed and need, of credit cards and wealth, choose to give up creature comforts and live in poverty? Why are many young people sacrificing material ease to live in Chinmayaranyam in kutir huts of mud and thatched roofs, just like the poorest of poor villagers? "Our aim is to prove to the poor strata of society that a decent and spiritual life does not depend upon money but on the way of living. You may call it an experiment in poverty," said Swamini Saradapriyananda, the force behind this novel delving into dearth's hidden dignity.

The Swamini, "Amma" to all who know her, is a senior monk of the Chinmaya Mission in Andhra Pradesh. In the various sequences of her life, each episode seems to have brought her closer to the spiritual. Born in 1927, in Masulipatum, her father was a teacher, and her mother established the first Mahila Seva Madali in Andhra Pradesh.

After studying law, Amma became an attorney and practiced for seven years. Having been weaned on service to others, she soon joined the Social Welfare Advisory Board and served for almost nine years in Hyderabad. Around this time, she started attending Swami Chinmayananda's discourses, and in 1965, she joined his ashram.

After several years of training, Swamini Saradapriyananda received *sannyasa diksha* from Swami Chinmayananda. All over India, she has conducted *Gnana Yagnas* (sacred knowledge gatherings) on the *Bhagavadgītā*, the *Upanishads*, and other spiritual texts for the past twenty years. She has written commentaries on the *Upanishads* and made the text easier to comprehend in her book, *Vedanta in Day to Day Life.* The *bhajans* and poems composed by her, the songs she sings, and the discourses she gives on the *Upanishads* all bring the listener a little closer to God.

Swamini Saradapriyananda has also ventured, with Swami Chinmayananda's blessings, into starting two ashrams, Chinmayaranyam Ellayapalle and Chinmayaranyam Trikoota. It was in Ellayapalle that a barren tract was turned into a flourishing, livable village in 1982. Earlier it was an arid land without water or electricity. With the aid of the Chinmaya Ashram, it now has wells and improved agriculture.

Swamini Saradapriyananda remembers the transformation of the drought-stricken village: "We drilled borewells to a depth of 200 to 450 feet during these thirteen years. We also helped the villagers in getting four government borewells. Becoming bold, the villagers came together to pool their resources and started drilling their own borewells. Now the land has been brought under cultivation."

The ashram residents live in clean, modest mud huts and also conduct classes in this sanctuary. At Trikoota, the Swamini and residents give *Dharma Veer*— heroic spirituality—training to guide the youth in righteous living. Clad in ochre robes, Swamini Saradapriyananda is dedicated to the life of the spirit, but part of her missionary work is to see to the needs of the less fortunate. Her day begins at four a.m., and by five a.m., the residents of the ashram gather for an hour-long morning *satsang.* Her days are filled with spiritual matters and those pertaining to the ashram. She observed: "Our dates and engagements are with Him who is a relentless taskmaster. The more you give, the greater are His demands."

Among these demands are several programs of social welfare handled by the Chinmaya Mission. There is Satyakama Mandir, an orphanage with forty-two children whom the Mission is committed to getting on their feet. Five girls have been married, and two boys were admitted to college. There are several schools including Harihar Vocational School where, besides training, poor village children get midday meals and evening dinner. The Mission has a library and a homeopathy clinic serving the neighborhood.

Both the frail elderly and our ravaged environment need nurturing, and the Chinmaya Mission tends to both: Hari Seva feeds and clothes one hundred twenty-five elderly, destitute villagers. The Mission also has the "Save a Tree, Save a Man" program addressing environmental concerns. "We have been given eighty-six acres of hillock land by the Government to create a forest," enthuses Swamini. "Now one hundred twenty trees are growing there and in the coming rainy season we plan to plant 300–400 more."

Asked if the Mission addresses India's myriad problems such as child labor, domestic violence, and abuse of women, the Swamini offered: "The social problems exist in one shape or other as long as society exists. We are philosophers enough to know that there will be no time when the society will be without any problems. That does not mean we do not do anything to help the situation, but we do not despair when the problems rise up in another shape."

We inquired about the source of these problems and she elaborated: "Wife abuse and child labor are both based on greed and the needs of men which are naturally in him. Hence, the Dharma Sastras and the scriptures give him the dos and don'ts. If a man follows these rules, then the greed and need will remain under control and the abuse will be lessened."

The Swamini has strong opinions on poverty which continues to mar the future of India's children: "There is enough in the world to serve the need of everyone but not enough to serve the greed of any. Human beings, until they realize their true nature of Self, continue to be ignorant and greedy. The past greed gives the present suffering as poverty. The greedy man of the present day is exacting his bleak future life of suffering by his own actions."

Swamini Saradapriyananda believes the most important principle to guide people through life can be summed up in four words: "Be true to yourselves."

Hindus to the Rescue
Sujata Anandan

On September 30, 1993, the Latur region of Maharashtra, India, sustained a massive pre-dawn earthquake which flattened or severely damaged one hundred seven villages, leaving 10,000 people dead in the rubble, and another 65,000 homeless. Because the quake occurred the day after the conclusion of a celebration of Ganesha Chaturthi, rumors were trafficked that somehow Lord Ganesha was responsible for the quake. But as in the pre-dawn, January 17th 6.6 earthquake that jolted Los Angeles, California—killing fifty-six, injuring 8000, and leaving 25,000 homeless—the disaster was natural geology, not supernatural eschatology. As here reported by *Hinduism Today,* in the wake of the earthquake, "historic and heroic rehabilitation efforts by Hindu organizations and individuals, casteism, and religious competition are blending into a complicated social curry." The author is from Bombay, India.

The green grapes are sweetening once more in the rich, black soil of Killari (the quake's epicenter) and will be ripe for the picking in a few weeks. It would be no surprise if these grapes went on to win the top prize at an international grape show as they did in London in 1991. It is difficult to believe so much has changed here. But the new temporary settlements of galvanized iron or stiff straw stand witness to a complete rupture in the village ethos. Ironically, most of the survivors are the very poor who couldn't afford to live in stone houses—rock bound together by mud, not cement, which could have prevented the huge death toll. The poor had to content themselves with straw houses, with—at best—asbestos sheets for a roof. The straw homes either withstood the quake or, if they caved in, caused little harm.

"Many believe their fate is some kind of divine punishment and a volcano will erupt from the earth," says Shrikumar Poddar, who toured the earthquake scene in mid-December, when tremors were still rumbling and steam was rising from the cracks in the earth. Poddar, who lives in Lansing Michigan, USA, and in Bombay, is a Vaishnava Hindu and founder of the International Service Society. He explained that a lot of money came in earmarked for relief measures but not for rehab projects. Aromar Revi, a disaster consultant, says the rehab effort is running into a serious problem of too much promised in the future, with too few people and little money at work now.

Among the cadres that are toiling in a sun-baked karma yoga are religious organizations—both Hindu and Christian—and secular groups like the Hindustan Petroleum Corp., Ltd., manned by corporate employees who are mainly Hindu. The Hindu relief teams rushed to the Latur region like cavalry out of the Old West. Swaminarayan Fellowship, Vishva Hindu Parishad, ISKCON Hare Krishna, Ananda Marg, and others saddled up to the rescue. Hare Krishna filed this press release report:

> The devotees staying in the six-storied brahmachari ashram in Bombay were getting ready for the Mangala Arati at 4 am. Suddenly, the whole building started shaking as the earthquake struck Latur. The temple devotees rallied around for a short meeting and decided to dispatch a relief team immediately. All available material from Food for Life (FFL) supplies was collected within the next four hours. Two temple FFL vans, a hired truck stuffed with food, and a jeep left at 10 pm. The FFL troop went every day to a very severely affected area: Ganjankhed. Often the roads were in bad shape and the adjoining fields were mushy due to incessant rains. One evening, the FFL team was forced to halt one kilometer from their destination. Leaving the driver, the others loaded baskets of prasadam and started walking. The local police ordered the lone driver to remove the vehicle. He pleaded with them, but they insisted. Fearing the devotees would miss the van in the darkness, the driver pleaded again with the police. Regarding this as defiance, the police started hitting him with a *lathi* (bamboo stick). Raghunath, the driver, shouted for fellow devotees. Hearing the shouts of "Haribol, Haribol," two of the devotees in the end of the racing party rushed back. The others joined them and, boarding the van, tried to move away. There was no space to turn and eventually, it ploughed into the field and got stuck in the mud. The FFL relief team had to walk to the village and stay that night. The next morning, the devotees rescued the van with the aid of a tractor. The FFL distributed halva, puri and sabji—a pleasant and much appreciated turn from the daily quota of dal, rice and sabji. The villagers expressed their appreciation for the help from the Hare Krishna devotees by touching their feet.

In the ruddy, smoke-laced twilight of another tiring day, dozens of orange-robed swamis from the Swaminarayan Temple Trust (STT) sit in chairs at an impromptu conference, hurry on important errands, or are leading a melodious bhajan before huddled male villagers. Bhajans and kathak storytelling were welcome spiritual salve provided by many Hindu groups. STT is part of the worldwide Swaminarayan Fellowship presence out here, the only organization to take on full-scale rehab work, something brand new to them. They are pros at relief work, but re-engineering a village from the dirt up is a daunting task.

Redefining Hindu Charity
Shrikumar Poddar

The author of the following letter to the editor is a devotee of Vishnu and the founder of the International Service Society. He visited the Latur region shortly after the September, 1993, earthquake. He divides his time between Lansing, Michigan, USA, and Bombay, India.

The earthquake struck on the night of September 30, 1993, just after a ten-day celebration of Ganesh Chaturthi. It measured 6.1 on the Richter scale and caused the loss of nearly 10,000 lives, most of which could have been saved had the government heeded the warning signs which came a year in advance in the form of two hundred to three hundred tremors. This was dismissed by the government scientists, and they assured the people that the Marathawada region was safe from a major earthquake. In countries with much bigger earthquakes, loss of life is much less because earthquake–resistant design features are required by government building codes and people are made aware of the precautions they must take before a disaster strikes.

The epicenter of the earthquake was near Killari village in the Latur district of Maharashtra, where more than half the population died. Here, virtually all the homes totally collapsed because they were built of stones haphazardly put together with mud as the binding material and earthen roofs two feet thick. Most of the dead were from the upper class families. They could afford to build the stone houses. The poor, who lived in simple huts, survived. The karma theory, which made some people rich supposedly because of the good deeds of their past, quickly took their lives because they believed the government scientists. Bad karma, indeed!

Thousands of volunteers from as far away as 1,000 miles poured into the area with relief supplies, forcing the police to seal off the area. Nevertheless, the massive response of the people of India showed the basic spiritual unity. Government machinery moved in and did an exemplary rescue operation to save the survivors and to provide temporary shelters to the nearly 300,000 people rendered homeless. The task before the people of India now is to first provide mental and emotional support to those who lost loved ones and to help put them back on their feet. This is where the real challenge to the Hindu concept of charity lies. Until now, Hindus have, by and large, neglected long-term development, social equality, and harmonizing of the higher and lower castes to knit them together as one family. This is why Islam, with its idea of brotherhood, and Christianity, with its promise of a casteless society, have made inroads into many parts of India while Hindus are content to give alms for charity and leave everyone to their fate because their karma had predetermined the outcome. But now, this earthquake gives an opportunity to provide economic rehabilitation, emotional counseling, and education about earthquakes, as well as to remove superstitions and provide training to rebuild homes with earthquake-resistant features. Nature has already equalized the rich and the poor. So today, we can all work harmoniously.

While offering a helping hand to the people, we must not make them dependent and helpless. In this process, we will not only be doing a favor to the victims of the disaster, but also will be setting an example to others on how to rebuild a society brick by brick—just as we rebuild the homes brick by brick—based on equality. According to our Shastras, each Hindu is supposed to contribute one-sixth of his income to the society. But how many of us actually do that? Here is an opportunity to pitch in together and stand united to help those in need, and that is truly the Vaishnava way!

A Spiritual Response to the Environment
Jagmohan

Jagmohan, member of the Indian Parliament in the Rajya Sabha, is the former Governor of Jammu and Kashmir, India, and Lieutenant Governor of Delhi.

In 1972, international leaders met at Stockholm and expressed grave concern over the deteriorating environment. Since then, thousands of conferences, seminars and symposia have been held all over the world, and millions of dollars spent. Hosts of "expert" bodies have cropped up. Non-governmental organizations have sprouted like mushrooms. But what has been the net outcome of all this? During the twenty-year period between Stockholm and Rio de Janeiro (1992), the world's environment has deteriorated further and ecological imbalance intensified.

This is happening because awareness of environmental problems is only skin-deep. Unfortunately, our thinking and actions are still being shaped by a mechanical view of nature. Unless concern for the environment acquires a spiritual base and becomes a part of contemporary man's psyche, declarations will not get converted into commitments and no real change in existing practices and no real improvement in existing conditions will take place. Could religious and cultural traditions help bring the desired change? Could ancient values be regenerated to evolve a new ethos which would enable the present-day man to perceive life as an organic entity and understand that sea, soil, forests, clouds, mountains and teeming millions spread over the earth are inseparable parts of the cosmic web? My answer to both questions is in the affirmative.

No religion, perhaps, lays as much emphasis on environmental ethics as Hinduism. The *Mahabharata, Ramayana, Vedas, Upanishads, Bhagavad Gita, Puranas* and *Smriti* contain the earliest messages for preservation of environment and ecological balance. Nature, or Earth, has never been considered a hostile element to be conquered or dominated. In fact, man is forbidden from exploiting nature. He is taught to live in harmony with nature and recognize that divinity prevails in all elements, including plants and animals. The *Mahabharata* hints that the basic elements of nature constitute the Cosmic Being—the mountains His bones, the earth His flesh, the sea His blood, the sky His abdomen, the air His breath and *agni* (fire) His energy. The whole emphasis of the ancient Hindu scriptures is that human beings cannot separate themselves from natural surroundings and Earth has the same relationship with man as the mother with her child.

Planting and preservation of trees are made sacred in religious functions. The *Varah Purāna* says, "One who plants one peepal, one neem, one bar, ten flowering plants or creepers, two pomegranates, two oranges and five mangos, does not go to hell." In the *Charak Sanhita,* destruction of forests is taken as destruction of the state, and reforestation an act of rebuilding the state and advancing its welfare. Protection of animals is considered a sacred duty. Our scriptures warn, "Oh wicked persons! If you roast a bird, then your bathing in sacred rivers, pilgrimage, worship and *yagnas* are useless." In our ancient mythology, birds and animals have always been identified with gods and goddesses.

The current deplorable condition demands a spiritual response. A fundamental reorientation of human consciousness, accompanied by action that is born out of inner commitment, is very much needed. One of the measures that could help a great deal to fulfill this need is to regenerate and rejuvenate basic values of Hindu culture and propagate them.

ENDNOTES

[1] Emphasis his.

[2] Vivekananda, *The Complete Works,* Vol. VI, p. 254.

[3] *Ibid.,* Vol. V, p. 15, 10, 215.

[4] Nikhilananda, *Hinduism: Its Meaning for the Liberation of the Spirit* (New York: Harper, 1958). Chapter 4, p. 57.

[5] Prabhavananda, "The Wisdom of the Upanishads," *Vedanta and the West* 3 (March–April 1940), pp. 6–7.

[6] "Interview with Swami Vivekananda," *Prabuddha Bharata* 3 (September 1898), p. 19. (Emphasis his.)

[7] Swami Prabhavananda, "Sri Ramakrishna, Modern Spirit and Religion," in *Vedanta for the Western World,* Christopher Isherwood, ed (Hollywood: Vedanta Press, 1945), p. 246.

[8] The name was later changed to Sabarmati Ashram.

[9] The list of society's seven sins as articulated by Gandhi is found in many sources. It first came to my attention in a study guide for Christians entitled *Private Choices; Public Consequences: A Discussion on Ethical Choices Using Gandhi's Seven Sins As Challenges and Guides* by Alanson B. Houghton, May B. Morris, & Kay K. Stricklin (Cincinnati, Ohio: Forward Movement, 1992).

Chapter Three

Buddhist Literature and Compassion

The sacred scriptures of Buddhism form a tremendous library of writings—a collection so vast that more than a half-million pages would be required to print all of it. Unlike the sacred writings of other religions, Buddhist scriptures are considered the result of human rather than divine effort; that is, they are not believed to be "revealed." While these writings are considered to be uniquely helpful in our human striving to solve life's dilemmas, Buddhists believe that ultimately, words—even of scripture—can get in the way of reaching enlightenment. The three broad divisions of Buddhism—Theravada, Mahāyanā, and Mantrāyanā (Tantra)—each have their own canon of scripture.

THERAVADA SCRIPTURES

In 3 CE, Buddhist scholars came together in Sri Lanka to sift through all writings and oral tradition said to be the teachings of Siddhartha Gautama, and to determine which were authoritative. The result was a library known as the Pali Canon, so called because of the ancient dialect of Sanskrit in which it is recorded. Because its thirty-two books are organized into three major divisions, Buddhists call it the Tipiṭaka (Tripiṭaka in Sanskrit)—that is, the Three Baskets: the Basket of Discipline, the Basket of Discourse, and the Basket of Scholasticism.

The Basket of Discipline

The *Vinaya-Piṭaka* is the division of the Pali Canon which contains instructions for monks and nuns, and case law to help adherents apply these instructions to life situations. The Mahavāstu, which means "great event" in Sanskrit, is a biography of Siddhartha Gautama, and is considered part of the Basket of Discipline. It consists of three subdivisions: Siddhartha's previous life as a bodhisattva; his incarnation; and the establishment of the Buddhist Order.

Monks, you have not a mother or a father who might tend you. If you do not tend one another, who is there who will tend you? Whoever, monks, would tend me, he should tend the sick. —*Vinaya-piṭaka I, 302*

They are Bodhisattvas who live on from life to life in the possession of manifold good qualities. They are Bodhisattvas who have won the mastery over karma, and made their deeds renowned through their accumulation of merit. They are resolute and valiant, intent on endurance, trustworthy, upright and sincere. They are generous, firm, gentle, tender, patient, whole and tranquil of heart, difficult to overcome and defeat, intent on what is real, charitable, and faithful to their promises. —*Mahavāstu*

Basket of Discourses

The second division of the Pali Canon, the *Sutta-Pitaka,* consists of sermons or lectures by the Buddha. Many of its subdivisions have been translated as separate volumes, a few of which are sampled here.

Dhammapada

The *Dhammapada* is probably the best known portion of the Second Basket. Meaning "words of truth," the *Dhammapada* is a collection of the Buddha's sayings collected by his followers who came together for this purpose soon after his death. Its 423 verses span forty-five years of oral teaching on practical matters of life. Because it has been translated into many languages, and because its teachings are in concert with writings considered canonical by other branches than Theravada, the *Dhammapada* makes an approachable, accessible introduction to Buddhism and its scriptures. In time, commentary to the *Dhammapada* was provided by the sage known as Buddhaghosa, who lived in the fifth century CE. He is considered to be the greatest interpreter of the Theravada tradition. His commentaries are included with the excerpts below.

Just as many garland strands
One could make from a mass of flowers,
So, much that is wholesome ought to be done
By a mortal born into this world. —*Dhammapada 53*

> *Commentary: One could make from a mass of flowers of many kinds many different kinds of garlands... By the living being called "the mortal one," because of the fact that one is liable to die, much wholesome work ought to be done. Here the mention of a "mass of flowers" is to indicate a large quantity of flowers. If the flowers are not many, and the garland-maker is a skilled craftsman, he would still not be able to make garlands with them. The one who is not a skilled craftsman does not of course succeed, whether the flowers be many or few. When the quantity of flowers is large, a skillful maker of garlands, clever and able, will turn out a large number of garlands. In the same way, if one's faith is meager and one's riches ample, one still is not able to do a great deal of wholesome deeds. When faith is meager and riches are also meager, it is indeed not possible to do much good; but one is capable of doing this when faith is ample and riches are also ample.*

Whose bad deed done
Is covered by what is wholesome
He this world illumines
Like the moon set free from a cloud. —*Dhammapada 173*

Commentary: Here "what is wholesome" is said with reference to the Path of Arhatship. The meaning of the rest is clear.

Let one tell the truth, let one not be angry.
Asked, let one give even when one has but little,
By these three factors,
One would go into the presence of the gods. —*Dhammapada 224*

Commentary: Let one glorify the truth, deal in truth, be established in truth— that is the meaning. Let one not bear anger toward another. "Those who beg" in this context are the virtuous ones who have gone forth into the monastic life. They stand at the doorstep of householders, without requesting "Give something!" but in effect they do indeed beg. So requested by the virtuous, let one give even a little thing, if what is available to be given is little. One may go to the heavenly world by means of any of one of these three factors. That is the meaning.

A bhikku dwelling in loving-kindness,
Who is pleased in the Buddha's instruction,
Would attain the state that is peace...

Let one be in the habit of friendly relations,
Of competent conduct let one be.
Being of Abundant joy thereby,
One shall make an end of suffering. —*Dhammapada 368, 376*

Commentary: Let one who is exerting oneself in loving-kindness [metta] be one who observes "friendly relations" by maintaining a personal conduct of which the constituent elements are a relationship of cordial sharing with regard to material things and a similar cordial relationship with regard to dhamma that one has understood. That is the meaning. What is referred to here as conduct is virtue as well as observance of due rites and practices. Be skillful therein, be one who is proficient therein. Being "of abundant joy" on account of your being born of the observance of mutual sharing and competence of conduct, you will put an end to the entire suffering of the world. That is the meaning.

Khuddaka Pāṭha

The *Khuddaka Pāṭha*—Minor Readings—constitute a short guidebook to the Buddha's teachings, including such well known formulas as the Three Jewels and the Ten Precepts. Its varied contents are subdivided into nine sections, the last of which is the Loving-kindness Discourse, the ending of which is given here. As he did for the *Dhammapada*, Bhadantācariya Buddhaghosa also wrote commentary on the *Khuddaka Pāṭha*. An excerpt of his interpretation of the Loving-kindness Discourse is included.

As a mother with her life
Might guard her son, her only child,
Would he maintain unboundedly
His thought for every living being.
His thought of love for all the world
He would maintain unboundedly,

Above, below, and all around,
Unchecked, no malice with or foe.
Standing or walking, seated too,
Or lying down the while undrowsing,
He would pursue this mindfulness:
This is Divine Abiding here, they say. —*Metta Sutta 7–9*

Commentary: Its meaning is this. As a mother might guard her son, the child of her breast born in herself, and that being also her only child, might guard it with her life by laying down her own life in order to ward off the coming of suffering, thus would he generate again and again, would he augment, his loving-kindness... By his inclination to welfare he acts as a lubricant and protects from harm's coming.

Vimānavatthu

Meaning "Stories of the Mansions," the *Vimānavatthu* is part of the *Khuddaka-nikāya.* The following stories come from the second and third divisions of the *Vimānavatthu.*

The Blessed One was dwelling at Sāvatthi. And at that time in Uttaramadhurā was a certain woman whose span of life had come to an end and who was due for rebirth in a state of woe. As the Blessed One, towards dawn, was emerging from an attainment of great compassion, and was surveying the world he saw that woman. Desiring to establish her in a good destination, he went alone to Madhurā and entered the outskirts of the town in search of alms. And at that time the woman had prepared food in her home, had set it aside, gone to the watering place with a pitcher, and bathed. She was returning home with the pitcher full when she saw the Blessed One, and said, "Perhaps the reverend sir has already received alms?" and when the Blessed One said, "We shall receive," she knew that he had not yet received alms. So she set down her pitcher, went up to the Blessed one, paid homage to him and said, "Reverend sir, I will make an almsgiving. Permit me." The Blessed One gave consent by keeping silent. She, knowing his consent, went on ahead, prepared a seat in a place sprinkled and swept and stood watching for his arrival. He went in and sat down. She gave him to eat, and sat down. When his meal was finished and his hand withdrawn from the bowl, the Blessed One gave thanks to her and went on his way. She heard his benediction and, experiencing great joy and happiness, not losing the joy caused by the Buddha, stood doing homage until he had passed out of view. After the passage of only a few days she died and was reborn in the realm of the Thirty-Three.
—*Cittalatā 10: Almsgiver's Mansion*

The Blessed One was dwelling at Rājagaha, in Bamboo Grove. At that time in Rājagaha in a household that ministered on the venerable Mahā-Moggallāna was a young girl who was intent on giving alms and loved giving. In that house the hard and soft food and so on was prepared before the main meal. Then the girl would give away half her own portion. Unless she had given alms she did not eat. Even when she saw no one worthy to receive a gift she put some food aside till she saw such a one. She gave to beggars as well. Now her mother was joyful and happy as she said to herself, "My daughter is intent on giving and loves to give," and she gave her a double portion. When the single portion she was given was shared, the mother gave her yet another. She even proceeded to share from that.

As time thus went by, her mother and father gave her, when of age, to the son of another family in the same city. But the family was of false views, unbelieving. Now the venerable Mahā-Moggallāna, while walking for alms from house to house, stopped at the door of the young girl's father-in-law. When she saw him, the young girl, having faith, said, "Enter, sir," ushered him in, greeted him with honor, and took a cake which had been set aside by her mother-in-law; not being able to see her to ask permission, she said to herself, "I will tell her about it later and make her rejoice in my good deed," and she gave it to the Elder. The Elder thanked her and went on his way. The young girl told her mother-in-law, "I gave the cake you had put aside to the Elder Mahā-Moggallāna." When she heard that, the mother-in-law cried, "What impertinence is this! You gave a monk something of mine without even asking!" and spluttering with rage, overcome with anger, without thinking of right and wrong, she took up a broken piece of a pestle and struck the girl on the shoulder. The girl, because she had been delicately reared and her life-span had come to an end, was overcome with severe pain and in only a few days died and was reborn among the Thirty-three. Although she had karma of other good deeds, that particular almsgiving to the Elder was the pre-eminent one. —*Pāricchattaka 1: Splendid Mansion*

Itivuttaka

The title of this collection of one hundred twelve suttas means, "As it was said," or "The Thus Spoken." It is a record of the Buddha's teachings to a school of monks, as related by the female disciple, Khujjuttarā. The suttas were set down originally in Pali, but it was from the Sanskrit version that the Chinese translation was made in 650 CE. Its four divisions are accompanied by ancient commentary; an example of this is included with the last entry below.

If beings knew, as I know, the ripening of sharing gifts, they would not enjoy their use without sharing them, nor would the taint of stinginess obsess the heart and stay there. Even if it were their last bit, their last morsel of food, they would not enjoy its use without sharing it, if there were anyone to receive it. But inasmuch as beings do not know, I as I know, the ripening of sharing gifts, therefore they enjoy their use without sharing them, and the taint of stinginess obsesses their heart and stays there. —*The Ones III, vi*

Monks, whatsoever grounds there be for good works undertaken with a view to rebirth, all of them are not worth one-sixteenth part of that goodwill which is the heart's release; goodwill alone, which is the heart's release, shines and burns and flashes forth in surpassing them. Just as, monks, the radiance of all the starry bodies is not worth one sixteenth part of the moon's radiance, but the moon's radiance shines and burns and flashes forth in surpassing them, even so, monks, goodwill flashes forth in surpassing good works undertaken with a view to rebirth.

Just as, monks, in the last month of the rains, in autumn time, when the sky is opened up and cleared of clouds, the sun, leaping up into the firmament, drives away all darkness from the heavens and shines and burns and flashes forth, — even so, monks, whatsoever grounds there be for good works, goodwill flashes forth in surpassing them.

Just as, monks, in the night at time of daybreak the star of healing shines and burns and flashes forth, even so, whatever grounds there be for good works undertaken with a view to rebirth, all of them are not worth one sixteenth part of that goodwill which is the heart's release, alone shines and burns and flashes forth in surpassing them. — *The Ones III, vii*

This was said by the Exalted One: Monks, there are these three persons found existing in the world. What three? The one who is like a drought, the one who rains locally, and the one who pours down everywhere.

And how, monks, is a person like a drought? Herein, monks, a certain person is not a giver to all alike, no giver of food and drink, clothing and vehicle, flowers, scents and unguents, bed, lodging and light to recluses and brāhmins or wretched and needy beggars. In this way, monks, a person is like a drought.

And how, monks, is a person like a local rainfall? In this case a person is a giver to some, but to others he gives not; be they recluses and brāhmins or wretched, needy beggars, he is no giver of food and drink, lodging and lights. In this way a person is like a local rainfall.

And how, monks, does a person rain down everywhere? In this case a certain person gives to all, be they recluses and brāhmins or wretched, needy beggars; he is a giver of food and drink, lodging and lights. In this way a person rains down everywhere.

This is the meaning . . .
Not to recluse and brāhmin, not to the poor and needy,
Does he distribute gains of food, drink, sustenance:
One of the baser sort, "like a drought" men call him.
To some he gives not, but with others share his goods,
Shrewd folk call such a man "like to a local shower."
The man who rains alms everywhere, and for all creatures
Compassion feels, doth scatter gladly everywhere.
"Give ye! Give ye!" he cries and, like a rain-cloud thundering
And rumbling, down he rains and fills uplands and slopes
With drench of water. Just like that is such an one,
Lawfully gathering wealth by effort won, with food
And drink rightly the needy beings he regales. —The Threes III, v

MAHĀYANĀ SCRIPTURES

Aṣṭasāhasrikā Prajñāpāramitā Sūtra

"The Perfection of Wisdom in Eight Thousand Lines" is also sometimes called the Shobon Hannya Sūtra, the Makahannya Haramitsu Sūtra, or the Smaller Wisdom Sūtra. *Prajñāpāramitā* means "the perfection of wisdom;" thus, these writings show how Siddhartha Gautama used the perfection of wisdom to attain Buddhahood. It is said that complete faith in this sūtra guarantees the attaining of Buddhahood. A *bodhisattva* is a person seeking the goal of enlightenment or whose apparent spiritual destination is Buddhahood. As with many Mahāyanā texts, this sūtra has come down to us in both poetic and prose forms. It was written in Sanskrit, and following the convention of Mahāyanā scripture, is a dialogue between the Buddha and two disciples.

The Bodhisattva should adopt the same attitude towards all beings, his mind should be even towards all beings, he should not handle others with an uneven mind, but with a mind which is friendly, well-disposed, helpful, free from aversion, avoiding harm and hurt, he should handle others as if they were his mother, father, son, or daughter. As a savior of all beings should a Bodhisattva behave towards all beings, should he train himself, if he wants to know the full and supreme enlightenment.

—*Aṣṭasāhasrikā Prajñāpāramitā Sūtra 16:5 (lines 321–22a)*

Avatamsaka Sūtra

The Flower Garland Sūtra is a collection of thirty-nine books of varying lengths is said to be a compendium of Siddhartha Gautama's teachings immediately after achieving enlightenment. It is a comprehensive presentation of the scope of Buddhist teaching. Having taken shape in India, it was translated from Sanskrit into Chinese several times during the first five centuries of its existence, and became the primary text of the Huayan form of Buddhism. It was then carried to Japan, where it became the basic text of that country's Kegon sect, and also exerted considerable influence on Zen.

Enlightening Beings cultivate practice in emulation of Buddhas of past, present, and future. Buddha-Children, great enlightening beings have ten kinds of practices, which are expounded by the Buddhas of past, present, and future. What are the ten? The practice of giving joy; beneficial practice; the practice of non-opposition; the practice of indomitability; the practice of non-confusion; the practice of non–manifestation; the practice of non-attachment; the practice of that which is difficult to attain; the practice of good teachings; the practice of truth.

What is the great enlightening being's practice of giving joy? Here the enlightening beings are magnanimous givers, bestowing whatever they have with an equanimous mind, without regret, without hoping for reward, without seeking honor, without coveting material benefits, but only to rescue and safeguard all living beings, to include all living beings in their care, and to emulate the original practice of all Buddhas, recall the original practice of all Buddhas, delight in the original practice of all Buddhas, purify the original practice of all Buddhas, further develop the original practices of all Buddhas, make manifest the original practice of all Buddhas, and expound the original practice of all Buddhas, to cause all sentient beings to be relieved of pain and suffering and attain comfort and happiness.

When great enlightening beings cultivate this practice, they cause all living beings joy and delight. In any place there is poverty and want, they go there by the power of will to be born noble and wealthy, so that even if every single moment countless beings come to the enlightening beings and say, "O benevolent one, we are poor and in need, without sustenance, hungry and weak, worn out and miserable, on the brink of death; please pity us and give us your flesh to eat so that we may live," the enlightening beings would immediately give it to them, to gladden and satisfy them. Even should countless hundreds of thousands of beings come begging this way, the enlightening beings would not shrink back, but would rather increase even more in kindness and compassion. Indeed, because sentient beings all come seeking, the enlightening beings, seeing them, would become more joyful, and think, "I have gained a fine boon; these beings are my field of blessings, they are my good friends and benefactors—without my asking them, they come to cause me to enter into the Buddha's teaching. I should now cultivate learning in this way, not controverting the wishes of sentient beings." They also form this thought:

> May all the good that I have done, do, and will do, cause me in the future, in all worlds, among all beings, to receive an immense body, so as to satisfy all starving beings with the flesh of this body, and may I not die so long as even a single tiny creature is still not filled, and may the flesh I cut off be inexhaustible. By this virtue may I attain unexcelled complete perfect enlightenment, and experience great nirvana; and may those who eat my flesh also attain perfect enlightenment, attain impartial knowledge, fulfill all Buddha teachings, extensively perform Buddha work until entering remainder. If the heart of even one sentient being is unfulfilled, I will not attain unexcelled perfect enlightenment.

Thus do enlightening beings benefit the living, yet without any concept of self or any concept of sentient beings, or any concept of existence, or any concept of life, without various concepts—no concept of personality, no concept of person, no concept of human being, no concept of doer or receiver—they only observe the infinity of the realm of reality and the realm of sentient beings, their emptiness, absence of existents, signlessness, insubstantiality, indeterminacy, non-dependence, and non-creation.

When they perform this contemplation, they do not see themselves, they do not see anything given, they do not see a receiver, they do not see a field of blessings, they do not see a deed, they do not see any reward, they do not see any result, they do not see a great result, they do not see a small result.

Then the enlightening beings observe that all the bodies taken on by living beings in the past, future, and present eventually perish; then they form this thought:

> How remarkable it is, how foolish and ignorant sentient beings are; within birth and death they receive countless bodies, which are perish-

able and transient, soon returning to decay and extinction: having already passed away, now passing away, and yet to pass away, they still cannot use the destructible body to seek the indestructible body. I should learn all that the Buddhas learn, to realize omniscience, know all truths, and explain to sentient beings the indestructible nature of reality, which is equal in past, present, and future, and which accords with utmost tranquility and serenity, to cause them to permanently attain peace and happiness.

This is called the great enlightening beings' first practice, of giving joy.
—*Avatamsaka Sūtra 21 (Ten Practices)*

What is the great enlightening beings' dedication to saving all sentient beings? Here the enlightening beings practice transcendent giving, purify transcendent discipline, cultivate transcendent forbearance, arouse transcendent energy, enter transcendent meditation, abide in transcendent wisdom, great compassion, great kindness, great joy, and great equanimity. Cultivating boundless roots of goodness such as these, they form this thought: "May these roots of goodness universally benefit all sentient beings, causing them to be purified, to reach the ultimate, and to forever leave the innumerable pains and afflictions of the realms of hells, ghosts, and animals, and so on." When the great enlightening beings plant these roots of goodness, they dedicate their won roots of goodness thus:

I should be a hostel for all sentient beings, to let them escape from painful things. I should be a protector for all sentient beings, to let them be liberated from all afflictions. I should be a refuge for all sentient beings, to free them from all fears. I should be a goal for all sentient beings, to cause them to reach universal knowledge. I should make a resting place for all sentient beings, to enable them to find a place of peace and security. I should be a light for all sentient beings, to enable them to attain the light of knowledge to annihilate the darkness of ignorance. I should be a torch for all sentient beings, to destroy all darkness of ignorance. I should be a lamp for all sentient beings, to cause them to abide in the realm of ultimate purity. I should be a guide for all sentient beings, to lead them into the truth. I should be a great leader for all sentient beings, to give them great knowledge.

They also form this thought:

I should accept all sufferings for the sake of sentient beings, and enable them to escape from the abyss of immeasurable woes of birth and death. I should accept all suffering for the sake of sentient beings in all worlds, in all states of misery, for ever and ever, and still always cultivate foundations of goodness for the sake of all beings. Why? I would rather take all this suffering on myself than to allow sentient beings to fall into hell. I should be a hostage to those perilous places—hells, animal realms, the nether world, etc.—as a ransom to rescue all sentient beings in states of woe and enable them to gain liberation.

They also form this thought:

I vow to protect all sentient beings and never abandon them. What I say is sincerely true, without falsehood. Why? Because I have set my mind

on enlightenment in order to liberate all sentient beings; I do not seek
the unexcelled Way for my own sake. . . —*Avatamsaka Sūtra 25 (Ten
Dedications)*

Bodhisattvacharyāvatāra

The *Bodhisattvacharyāvatāra* (A Guide to the Bodhisattva's Way of Life) consists of approximately 1000 stanzas which lay down the essentials of Mahāyanā practice. Acharya Śantideva, its compiler, was an 8th century master from the monastic university in Nalanda, India. The translation given here has received the blessing of the Dalai Lama.

"If I give this, what shall I enjoy?"—
Such selfish thinking is the way of the ghosts;
"If I enjoy this, what shall I give?"
Such selfless thinking is the quality of the gods.

If, for my own sake, I cause harm to others,
I shall be tormented in hellish realms;
But if for the sake of others I cause harm to myself,
I shall acquire all that is magnificent.

By holding myself in high esteem
I shall find myself in unpleasant realms, ugly and stupid;
But should this [attitude] be shifted to others
I shall acquire honors in a joyful realm.

If I employ others for my own purposes
I myself shall experience servitude,
But if I use myself for the sake of others
I shall experience only lordliness.
 — *Bodhisattvacharyāvatāra 8.125-28*

Sūtra of Forty-two Sections

This brief collection of the Buddha's teachings was first translated into Chinese in 69 CE. While it is addressed to monks, its message of ultimate liberation through renunciation is meant for people of all walks of life in all ages.

The Buddha said: "When you see someone practicing the Way of giving, aid him joyously, and you will obtain vast and great blessings." A shramana asked: "Is there an end to those blessings?" The Buddha said: "Consider the flame of a single lamp. Though a hundred thousand people come and light their own lamps from it so that they can cook their food and ward off the darkness, the first lamp remains the same as before. Blessings are like this, too." —*Sūtra of Forty-two Sections 10*

Śikshāsamuccaya

Sanskrit for "the Compendium of Training," *Śikshāsamuccaya* forms part of the anthology of Mahāyanā scripture compiled by Śantideva in the 8th century CE. The passage below uses several vocabulary words critical to Buddhism: *Samsāra* is the continuous cycle of birth, death, and rebirth; *Yama* means Death; and *Mara* is the personification of death.

A bodhisattva resolves: I take upon myself the burden of all suffering, I am resolved to do so, I will endure it. I do not turn or run away, do not tremble, am not terrified, nor afraid, do not turn back or despond.

And why? At all costs I must bear the burdens of all beings. In that, I do not follow my own inclinations. I have made the vow to save all beings. All beings I must set free. The whole world of living beings I must rescue from the terrors of birth, of old age, of sickness, of death and rebirth, of all kinds of moral offense, of all states of woe. My endeavors do not merely aim at my own deliverance. For with the help of the boat of the thought of all-knowledge, I must rescue all these beings from the stream of *Samsāra,* which is so difficult to cross, I must pull them back from the great precipice, I must free them from all calamities, I must ferry them across the stream of *Samsāra.* I myself must grapple with the whole mass of suffering of all beings. To the limit of my endurance I will experience in all states of woe, found in any world system, all the abodes of suffering. And I must not cheat all beings out of my store of merit. I am resolved to abide in each single state of woe for numberless eons; and so I will help all beings to freedom, in all states of woe that may be found in any world system whatsoever.

And why? Because it is surely better that I alone should be in pain than that all these beings should fall into the states of woe. There I must give myself away as a pawn through which the whole world is redeemed from the terrors of hells, of animal birth, of the world of Yama, and with this my own body I must experience, for the sake of all beings, the whole mass of all painful feelings. And on behalf of all beings I give surety for all beings, and in doing so I speak truthfully, am trustworthy, and do not go back on my word. I must not abandon all beings.

And why? There has arisen in me the will to win all-knowledge, with all beings for its object, that is to say, for the purpose of setting free the entire world of beings. And I have not set out for the supreme enlightenment from a desire for delights of the five sense-qualities, or because I wish to indulge in the pleasures of the senses. And I do not pursue the course of a Bodhisattva in order to achieve the array of delights that can be found in the various worlds of sense-desire.

And why? Truly no delights are all these delights of the world. All this indulging in the pleasures of the senses belongs to the sphere of *Mara.*
—*Sikshāsamuccaya 280-1, Vajradhvaja Sūtra*

Mantrāyanā Texts

Mantrāyanā, or Tantrāyanā, is the form of Buddhism which took root in Tibet. It purports to be an accelerated path to enlightenment, making it possible to attain this goal in only one lifetime. It is, however, a path which is rigorous, mysterious, and not to be practiced in isolation. The following is an excerpt from Saraha's *Treasury of Songs,* a poem of 112 stanzas and a coda.

The fair tree of thought that knows no duality,
Spreads through the triple world.
It bears the flower and fruit of compassion,
And its name is service of others.

The fair tree of the Void abounds with flowers,
Acts of compassion of many kinds.
And fruit for others appearing spontaneously,
For this joy has no actual thought of another. —*Dohākosha 107-08*

Chapter Four

Readings on Buddhism and Compassion

The Buddhist world view, as is that of Hinduism, is based on *samsāra*—the endless cycle of birth, death, and rebirth. The goal is enlightenment, which allows one to leave the cycle and enter the indescribable, incomprehensible existence known as Nirvana. Buddhist practice and ethics are based upon two formulas: *The Noble Eightfold Path:* right understanding, right thought, right speech, right action, right livelihood, right effort, right mindfulness, and right meditation; and *The Five Precepts:* no killing; no stealing; not being unchaste; no lying; no use of intoxicants.

So familiar are we with the quiet practices of Buddhism, especially its emphasis on meditation, that it is easy to overlook Buddhism's activist side. The readings in this chapter seek to illustrate the particularly Buddhist understanding of the concept of compassionate action.

Saintly Virtues
Antony Fernando with Leonard Swidler

Antony Fernando holds a doctorate in theology from the Gregorian University of Rome and a Ph.D. in Buddhist studies from the University of Sri Lanka. He specializes in teaching Buddhism to Christians and Christianity to Buddhists. He chairs the Department of Classical and Christian Cultures of the Kelaniya University of Sri Lanka. Leonard Swidler is Professor of Catholic Thought and Interreligious Dialogue at Temple University in Philadelphia, where he edits the Journal of Ecumenical Studies.

According to Gautama there were four basic qualities that were to characterize any Buddhist saint or liberated person. They are: *mettā*—friendliness or loving kindness; *karunā*—compassion; *muditā*—gentleness; and *upekkhā*—equanimity. These four qualities that he recommended to others were also qualities that he practiced himself. One little incident shows how seriously he practiced such virtues in his own life. As the order grew and established itself in distant places, he made it a point to visit groups of monks residing in different areas and assure himself of their welfare. One monastery he so visited had a monk who was very ill. The monk was suffering from an advanced skin disease. The eczema had spread so much that his entire body seemed one single sore. Blood and pus oozed out to the extent that his clothes were stuck to his body. His companions, because of the filthiness of his state, had kept aloof and abandoned him to endure his misfortune alone.

Gautama visited this monk in the company of his close associate, Ananda. Then, taking a basin of water and a towel, Gautama washed the patient himself and cleaned him. After doing whatever was possible to bring relief to him, he walked down to the little huts of the other monks. He inquired from them about the sick monk and why they neglected to look after him. Their reply was that, inasmuch as he was certain to die, he was of no benefit to the order. Then, with the intention of opening their eyes to the heartlessness of such behavior, Gautama said:

> Monks, you do not have a mother, you do not have a father here who can tend you; if you, monks, do not tend one another, who is there to tend you? Remember that whoever tends a sick person, as it were, tends me.[1]

Gautama thus showed himself to be a person who practiced the virtues he preached.

Compassion is a virtue that is very important to Buddhism. In Mahayana Buddhism it is considered the central virtue. As Rev. Piyadassi Thera says: "If you remove *karunā* (compassion) from the teachings of the Buddha you remove the heart of Buddhism; for, all virtues, all goodness and righteousness have *karunā* as their basis, as their matrix."[2]

Karunā
Winston L. King

Karunā, or compassion, is much the same in its root meaning as that same word in the New Testament when it is recorded that Jesus looked upon the multitudes and had compassion on them. It represents sympathy for the sufferings of others, be those sufferings mental or physical. And its peculiar Buddhist flavor is that of fellow feeling on the part of the compassionator toward all other sentient beings who, like himself, are caught in the toils of *samsāra, i.e.,* the endless birth–life–death cycle of individual existences that is under the iron rule of *karma.*

And what, then, is the order of the extension of compassion to others? Here the Buddhist method is to extend *karunā* first to *hostile* persons. The reasons for this are not so clearly outlined as in the case of extending *metta* first to oneself. Perhaps it is by the process of elimination that it is achieved, since equanimity begins most naturally with the neutral person, and sympathetic joy with a dear friend. Or it may be that in an enemy we most easily observe some specific failure, weakness, or misfortune; or that we can certainly reflect that even enemies also are caught in the same birth-death rounds as we ourselves. This is probably what Buddhaghosa means when he describes compassion-centered meditation as meditation upon the "helplessness in those overwhelmed by suffering," which includes all mankind.

And in a distinctly Buddhist emphasis he goes on to affirm that indeed the hostile person is to be compassionated *because* of his hostility. For hostility is more grievous than misfortune. It is indeed the basic cause of misfortune, since the hostile feeling or disposition of mind, and the unfriendly act, have their *primary* effects upon the actor and the feeler himself. They set in motion karmic forces that will later bear evil fruit within the life, or subsequent lives, of the hostile person.

In fact, each person in his present character and situation is completely and only the result of his own deeds, i.e., his karma; whatever he does, harms or benefits himself far more than the supposed recipients of his deeds.

By their deeds ye shall know them
Donald K. Swearer

"By their deeds ye shall know them." This terse saying from the West has much in common with the Buddhist understanding of *karma.* In its most general usage, *karma* simply refers to any action. In Buddhism and several other Indian religious traditions, action came to be invested with a causative power extending beyond an immediate, pragmatic effect. An act produces a visible result, e.g., teasing a friend makes him angry, but a less visible result is the effect it produces on us. Every action we perform has both external and internal consequences. The external consequences are often, though not necessarily, measurable or quantifiable. The internal consequences, that is, the effect of our actions on our character and our psychological and physiological well-being, are less evident. In both cases, however, our actions are not neutral. They produce an effect either for good or for ill. The Buddhist is particularly concerned about the internal effects of *karma.* One's *karma,* or character, affects one's total well-being in this life as well as in the next. To act for good is to produce good; to act for evil is to produce evil:

> Let any one who holds self dear,
> That self keep free from wickedness;
> For happiness can ne'er be found
> By any one of evil deeds.
> Assailed by death, in life's last throes,
> At quitting of this human state,
> What is it one can call his own?
> What with him take as he goes hence?
> What is it follows after him,
> And like a shadow ne'er departs?
>
> His good deeds and his wickedness,
> Whate'er a mortal does while here;
> 'Tis this that he can call his own,
> This with him take as he goes hence.
> This is what follows after him,

And like a shadow ne'er departs.

Let all, then, noble deeds perform,
A treasure-store for future weal;
For merit gained this life within,
Will yield a blessing in the next. (*Samyutta-Nikaya,* III. i. 4.)

Every act, good or bad, produces a corresponding good or bad effect. These effects *(vipaka)* have a causative force, calculable either *ad seriatim* or cumulatively depending on the interpreter, which conditions the individual's well-being in the present as well as in the future. In practice most contemporary Theravada Buddhists perceive the conditioning power of *karma* in terms of religiously meritorious good deeds such as giving donations to a temple, providing food for the monks on morning alms rounds, and so on, rather than ethically meritorious good deeds such as keeping the five precepts, or helping those in need. The latter is karmically wholesome, to be sure, but "doing merit" is calculated primarily in terms of action benefiting the Buddhist monkhood. It should be noted that in contemporary Buddhist practice in Southeast Asia a broadening of the range of religiously meritorious acts is taking place. Due largely to the impact of training programs in community and rural development, projects such as the building of new roads, sanitary wells, and classrooms under the encouragement of the Buddhist monastic order are perceived as religiously meritorious acts. Thus acts performed that are not of direct benefit to the order are now being interpreted as "doing merit."

Buddhism and Social Outreach
Thomas Berry

Even more important than the assistance that men render to each other is the heavenly assistance rendered by Buddha. The need of help from a higher source received increasing emphasis through the years. The reasons for this might be listed as follows:

(1) realization of the inherent limitations of the masses of mankind;
(2) conviction that the world had deteriorated considerably since the time of Buddha and that in this new age of depravity men generally could of themselves do very little for their salvation;
(3) awareness that Buddha had infinite compassion and infinite ability to aid others and that one of the greatest ways of honoring and glorifying the Buddha was by casting a person's self in total dependence on his aid.

Impelled by these forces, Buddhism at this time reached out to encompass the multitudes of mankind—the poor, the ignorant, the helpless, the suffering, the unwanted. This tide of compassion that reached forth to the people was something unique in the Asian world. While Hinduism did not have this sense of compassion for human suffering found in Buddhism, it did manifest a similar movement away from salvation for an elite through sophisticated ritual and intellectual processes toward a salvation bestowed from above in response to faith and devotion. The rise of Hindu devotionalism took place at the same time as these developments were taking place in Buddhism. It is difficult to know which influenced the other most. It is likely that both were responding to common primordial forces within India and also to influences toward devotional worship of personal deities that came to India from the Hellenic world after the invasion of India by Alexander in the late fourth century BC. Buddhism, which might easily have turned in the direction of an exclusive concern for a spiritually gifted elite, turned rather in the direction of a total concern for all mankind.

In one of the most beautiful presentations of heavenly compassion in the *Lotus Sūtra,* Buddha's saving grace is depicted as a raincloud that gathers massively above the earth: "That great raincloud, big with water, is wreathed with flashes of lightning and rouses with its thundering call all creatures. By warding off the sunbeams, it cools the region: and gradually lowering so as to come in reach of hands, it begins pouring down its water all around. And so, flashing on every side, it pours out an abundant mass of water equally, and refreshes this earth." In this manner Buddha pours down his salvation upon the earth, heals the entire world and brings all mankind to spiritual enlightenment. "I recreate the whole world like a cloud shedding its water without distinction: I have the same feelings for respectable people as for the low; for moral persons as for the immoral. I preach the law to the mentally inferior as well as to persons of superior understanding and exceptional faculties." By this deluge of heavenly grace the world is transformed, all beings are refreshed, especially "all those beings whose bodies are withered and who are bound to the phenomenal world." Bliss is brought to those wasting away in their toil. Then after the deluge the wisdom of the Buddha "shines like the sun and moon, leading all beings without partiality." (*Lotus Sūtra,* 5: 7–8, 18, 24, 26, 46.)

I am my brother...
Nancy Wilson Ross

Ross explains the Buddhist notion of *metta*—loving-kindness—by referring to the Hebrew Bible story of the murder of Abel by Cain, in which Cain asks God, "Am I my brother's keeper?" An interesting parallel to the Buddhist understanding of compassion and service given below can be found by turning in Chapter Eight to Robert Coles's discussion of Christian social activist Dorothy Day.

The *metta* meditation may well have its origin in the scripture known as *The Discourse on Universal Love,* in which the Buddha is quoted as saying:

> As a mother, even at risk of her own life, protects and loves her child, her only child, so let a man cultivate love without measure toward the whole world, above, below, and around, unstinted, unmixed with any feeling of differing or opposing interests. Let a man remain steadfastly in this state of mind all the while he is awake, whether he be standing, walking, sitting or lying down. This state of mind is the best in the world.

The Buddha himself is described in one of the old scriptures as personally undertaking the care of a sick and neglected monk, bathing and tending him as if he were his own child and chiding the neglectful brothers in words that have a curiously New Testament ring. "He who would wait on me, let him wait on the sick."

In an account of 19th century life in Burma, British civil servant Sir George Scott describes the daily existence of a warmhearted, generous, friendly people imbued with the spirit of Buddhist brotherliness which, to be sure, did not exclude the gathering of "merit" for brotherly deeds. If a Burman built a little bridge over a stream to keep the traveler from wetting his feet, if he placed pots of cool water on a shaded platform before his house to allay the thirst of any passerby, he could follow these meritorious small acts by a visit to the local pagoda, where he could strike a bronze bell and utter a significant invocation, "May all who hear this sound share in the merit my deed has earned. "

Helpfulness to others is, in Buddhism, significantly not equated with the idea, "I am my brother's keeper." Instead Buddhism teaches "I am my brother." This all-important key to Buddhist practice expresses that essential unity or oneness of all life taught by the historic Buddha.

In Zen monasteries, work is accepted as a basic and integral part of human existence. In the midst of such ordinary activities as sweeping and cleaning, cooking and washing, even in administrative work, the individual should be able to find total concentration. No labor is considered beneath anyone's dignity; in every monastery, tasks are rotated as a part of the fixed monastic routine. One who has been in a position of power and influence, as for example, a manager or a treasurer, can find himself assigned to menial labor. A most respected modern Zen master, the late Yasutani Roshi, even when he became a distinguished and famous abbot, continued doing self-assigned service in cleaning latrines.

The idea of service is central to the Zen way of life. Through disciplined meditation the interdependence of all beings and all things becomes clear, and from this understanding the ideal of service to others grows quite naturally.

November Third
Miyazawa Kenji

In the Mahāyanā tradition, a *bodhisattva* is one who, having achieved enlightenment and, thus, having succeeded in meriting access to nirvana, rejects it and throws him- or herself back into *samsāra*—the cycle of rebirth—in order help others to enlightenment. The following is a poetic description of this ideal, written while the author was seriously ill.

Bending neither to the rain
Nor to the wind
Nor to snow nor to summer heat,
Firm in body, yet
Without greed, without anger,
Always smiling serenely.
Eating his four cups of rough rice a day

With bean paste and a few vegetables,
Never taking himself into account
But seeing and hearing everything,
Understanding
And never forgetting.
In the shade of a pine grove
He lives in a tiny thatched hut:
If there is a sick child in the east
He goes and tends him:
If there is a tired mother in the west
He goes and shoulders her rice sheaves:
If there is a man dying in the south
He goes and soothes his fears:
If there are quarrels and litigation in the north
He tells them, "Stop your pettiness".
In drought he sheds tears,
In cold summer he walks through tears.
Everyone calls him a fool.
Neither praised
Nor taken to heart.
That man
Is what I wish to be.

Generosity
Thich Nhat Hanh

Thich Nhat Hanh, a Vietnamese Buddhist monk, has restated the Five Precepts in positive terms which clarify the relevance of this ancient code of behavior for the late twentieth century.

> *Aware of the suffering caused by exploitation, social injustice, stealing, and oppression, I vow to cultivate loving kindness and learn ways to work for the well-being of people, animals, plants, and minerals. I vow to practice generosity by sharing my time, energy, and material resources with those who are in real need. I am determined not to steal and not to possess anything that should belong to others. I will respect the property of others, but I will prevent others from profiting from human suffering or the suffering of other species on Earth.*

Exploitation, social injustice, and stealing come in many forms. Oppression is one form of stealing that causes much suffering both here and in the Third World. The moment we vow to cultivate loving kindness, loving kindness is born in us, and we make every effort to stop exploitation, social injustice, stealing, and oppression.

In the First Precept, we found the word "compassion." Here, we find the words "loving kindness." Compassion and loving kindness are the two aspects of love taught by the Buddha. Compassion, karunā in Sanskrit and Pali, is the intention and capacity to relieve the suffering of another person or living being. Loving kindness, *maitri* in Sanskrit, *metta* in Pali, is the intention and capacity to bring joy and happiness to another person or living being. It was predicted by Shakyamuni Buddha that the next Buddha will bear the name Maitreya, the Buddha of Love.

"Aware of the suffering caused by exploitation, social injustice, stealing, and oppression, I vow to cultivate loving kindness and learn ways to work for the well-being of people, animals, plants, and minerals." Even with *maitri* as a source of energy in ourselves, we still need to learn to look deeply in order to find ways to do it as a nation. To promote the well-being of people, animals, plants, and minerals, we have to come together as a community and examine our situation, exercising our intelligence and our ability to look deeply so that we can discover appropriate ways to express our maitri in the midst of real problems.

It requires time to practice generosity. We may want to help those who are hungry, but we are caught in the problems of our own daily lives. Sometimes, one pill or a little rice could save the life of a child, but we do not take the time to help, because we think we do not have the time. In Ho Chi Minh City, for example, there are street children who call themselves "the dust of life." They are homeless, and they wander the streets by day and sleep under trees at night. They scavenge in garbage heaps to find things like plastic bags they can sell for one or two cents per pound. The nuns and monks in Ho Chi Minh City have opened their temples to these children, and if the children agree to stay four hours in the morning— learning to read and write and playing with the monks and nuns—they are offered a vegetarian lunch. Then they can go to the Buddha hall for a nap.

Then, at two o'clock, there is more teaching and playing with the children, and children who stay for the afternoon receive dinner. The temple does not have a place for them to sleep overnight. In our community in France, we have been supporting these nuns and monks. It costs only twenty cents for a child to have both lunch and dinner, and it will keep him from being out on the streets, where he might steal cigarettes, smoke, use delinquent language, and learn the worst behavior. By encouraging the children to go to the temple, we help prevent them from becoming delinquent and entering prison later on. It takes time to help these children, not much money. There are so many simple things like this we can do to help people, but because we cannot free ourselves from our situation and our lifestyle, we do nothing at all. We need to come together as a community, and, looking deeply, find ways to free ourselves so we can practice the Second Precept.

"I vow to practice generosity by sharing my time, energy, and material resources with those who are in real need." This sentence is clear. The feeling of generosity and the capacity for being generous are not enough. We also need to express our generosity. We may feel that we don't have the time to make people happy—we say, "Time is money," but time is more than money. Life is for more than using time to make money. Time is for being alive, for sharing joy and happiness with others. The wealthy are often the least able to make others happy Only those with time can do so.

I know a man named Bac Siêu in Thua Thiên Province in Vietnam, who has been practicing generosity for fifty years; he is a living *bodhisattva*. With only a bicycle, he visits villages of thirteen provinces, bringing something for this family and something for that family. When I met him in 1965, I was a little too proud of our School of Youth for Social Service. We had begun to train three hundred workers, including monks and nuns, to go out to rural villages to help people rebuild homes and modernize local economies, healthcare systems, and education. Eventually, we had ten thousand workers throughout the country. As I was telling Bac Siêu about our projects, I was looking at his bicycle and thinking that with a bicycle he could help only a few people. But when the communists took over and closed our School, Bac Siêu continued, because his way of working was formless. Our orphanages, dispensaries, schools, and resettlement centers were all shut down or taken by the government. Thousands of our workers had to stop their work and hide. But Bac Siêu had nothing to take. He was truly a bodhisattva, working for the well-being of others. I feel more humble now concerning the ways of practicing generosity.

The war created many thousands of orphans. Instead of raising money to build orphanages, we sought people in the West to sponsor a child. We found families in the villages to each take care of one orphan, then we sent $6 every month to that family to feed the child and send him or her to school. Whenever possible, we tried to place the child in the family of an aunt, an uncle, or a grandparent. With just $6, the child was fed and sent to school, and the rest of the children in the family were also helped. Being in an orphanage can be like being in the army—children do not grow up naturally. If we look for and learn ways to practice generosity, we will improve all the time.

The Second Precept is not to steal. Instead of stealing, exploiting, or oppressing, we practice generosity. In Buddhism, we say there are three kinds of gifts. The first is the gift of material resources. The second is to help people rely on themselves, to offer them the technology and know-how to stand on their own feet. Helping people with the Dharma so they can transform their fear, anger, and depression belongs to the second kind of gift. The third is the gift of non-fear. We are afraid of many things. We feel insecure, afraid of being alone, afraid of sickness and dying. To help people not be destroyed by their fears, we practice the third kind of gift-giving.

Buddhism and the Thai Refugee Camps
Keno Visakha Kawasaki.

From 1975 until 1979, Cambodia was under the control of Pol Pot's brutal Marxist regime, the Khmer Rouge. By the time Vietnam seized control in 1979, approximately one quarter of Cambodia's population had been destroyed by Pol Pot's well-orchestrated genocide. Many Cambodians fled their devastated country. Thailand still provides a refuge for many such victims of Southeast Asia's political turmoil. Some definitions will help in reading this article. *Dana* is the Pali term for alms. An *Arahat (Arhat),* in the Theravada tradition, is a person who has achieved Nirvana in his or her present life. The *Sangha* is, for Theravada Buddhists, the community of monks.

This summer we visited several refugee camps on Thailand's borders. We wanted to offer *dana*—some things we had carried from Japan, some we had purchased in Thailand, and some from foreign monks in Bangkok. We also wanted to see for ourselves what the camps were like. Our previous firsthand knowledge was limited to Ban Vinai, Panat Nikom, and Bataan (Philippines), where we worked as ESL[3] specialists in U.S. government programs for America-bound refugees a few years ago. As we began our travels to the various camps, our main concern was to ascertain the circumstances and the needs of the various refugee Buddhist communities.

The first camp we visited was Khao I Dang near the Thai town of Aranya-pratet. We spent the entire morning in the temple, talking with the monks and laymen who gathered at the temple to serve the monks and to assist us. The past two years we had carried *dana* from the Sangha—the Buddhist monastic community—in Burma to offer to the Cambodian Sangha (through the good offices of UNHCR and UNDRO),[4] so we had been in correspondence with these people. We were delighted at last to have the chance to meet them. Last year we had included a small pagoda with *Arahat* relics from Burma. The monks immediately asked that the pagoda and its glass case be brought out so that we could pay our respects to it. It was indeed a joyous occasion.

This simple bamboo temple/monastery was neat and orderly. There were some very interesting paintings on the temple walls. In one, below a serenely beautiful face of the Buddha, a young family stood on skulls, with war scenes behind them. The people appeared half normal, in ordinary clothes, and half skeletons. It was a very effective depiction of the reality we spend so much time trying to beautify, ignore, and deny. The abbot of the temple is 87, and he survives only because he was in Thailand during the Pol Pot years when the Cambodian Sangha was almost totally eradicated.

After our brief tour of the buildings and grounds, we returned to find the monks gathered for their meal. They sat in silence while little temple boys, orphans living under their care, waited and served them mindfully and respect-fully. Afterwards, the boys carefully packed the leftovers and carried them away for their own lunch in the back.

When we left the temple on foot, we realized how far from the center of the camp it really was. It was at the very edge, separated from the residential area by a wide road. We tried to follow the map, but we got lost getting back to our meeting point at one of the agency offices.

At one voluntary agency school we spent a quiet interlude with an old man (actually not so old, but with grey hair), who worked as "day guard" there. He offered us glasses of bottled water to go with our peanut butter sandwiches, and we gave him bananas. As we talked in simple English, we learned that he had been there since 1979 when the Vietnamese invasion made it possible for tens of thousands of Khmers to escape their devastated country. In the camp he was reunited with two of his children who had also survived. His wife had accom-panied him, but she died in camp a week after arrival. All was said so quietly, so straightforwardly, we recalled the verse from the *Jataka:* "Uninvited he came, unexpected he left... what cause is there here for grief?"[5]

Ban Thad Camp is divided into Vietnamese and Khmer sections. When we were there, most of the Vietnamese had just been relocated to Panat Nikom for interviews. Actually, all the Vietnamese were expecting to be moved soon. The

Vietnamese temple had been built when the community was very large. It was an impressive and sturdy structure with a gracefully curved roof. In the garden stood a beautiful white image of Kuan Yin which had been made in four days by a Vietnamese who had been informed that he would soon be transferred. We offered our *dana,* including Dhamma books in Vietnamese printed by our Refugee friend Loi in Japan, and talked with the two monks and two nuns remaining there.

We arrived at Ban Na Pho, the Lowland Lao camp, the day before the full moon. The monks invited us to return early the next morning for the ceremony. At seven o'clock we found many believers already sitting quietly inside the temple. On full moon days the monks do not go out for alms. Instead their alms bowls are placed on tables outside the temple, and the people bring their food to offer. The bowls filled quickly, and more refugees entered the temple and sat down. It was an impressive sight—this lovely bamboo and thatch temple filled to overflowing with devotees in their finest clothes.

While white-robed lay-people keeping the Eight Precepts at the temple meditated or talked softly together, we had an interesting conversation with the monks, who were unanimous in the opinion that no matter how conditions in Laos might appear, the real truth was that it was impossible to practise Buddhism freely there. It was difficult for young men to ordain; monks were watched; they were forced to study (and teach) Marxism; and people were discouraged from supporting the temples liberally as they had in the past. The monks felt it was clearly not possible for Buddhism to thrive under communism.

The lowland Lao camp's library is obviously very popular, especially with the refugee youth. We were impressed by the excellent organization and good supply of books, but there were virtually none on Buddhism or meditation in English, Lao, or Thai. As always, we were glad to be able to donate basic Dhamma books but wished we had more. As we left, the librarians themselves were browsing through those we had bought before stamping them and putting them on the shelves.

Prior to going to the far north of Thailand to the Lao Hilltribes' camp, we had contacted everyone suggested as likely to know about Buddhist literature in Hmong (a major hilltribe language). No one had any suggestions. There are no Dhamma books whatsoever printed in hilltribe languages. In contrast, there is an over abundance of Christian literature available. The Thai Government policy, as explained to us, is that the hilltribes should learn Thai, and that, therefore, all literature should use the national language. Unfortunately, not all groups seem to observe this policy.

In the camp at Phayao, we were immediately struck by the crowding and by the sheer numbers of children, many apparently sickly. There also seemed to be a paucity of services, compared to other camps we had seen. We saw a great need for more basic education, for children and for women, including better libraries, with basic Dhamma books in Hmong. Perhaps we felt so much enthusiasm for sharing the Dhamma with the hilltribes, because we are Buddhists by persuasion rather than upbringing. That makes us particularly conscious that the Buddha's Dhamma applies equally to all people and cultures, and that it isn't a special preserve of any group or tradition.

Although not officially classified as refugees, thousands of Burmese students are staying in rough camps where they have sought refuge from their government's oppression and persecution. There are about twenty-five of these camps scattered along the borders. There are some women among them, but most are young men, from junior high school age through college. Some of the refugees were journalists, teachers, or university professors before the repression started in 1988. Most of them are, of course, Buddhist. They showed great devotion to the monks we were travelling with. Several young men knelt immediately in the mud to show their respect. That was wonderful to us, but simply natural to them. At the first camp, the students offered their *best* food—eggs, vegetables and rice—to the monks before noon. They themselves ate later, without any eggs.

Our last opportunity to visit a refugee camp was in Pusan, South Korea on our return to Japan. The camp is a temporary site amid warehouses at the port and holds about 300 Vietnamese boat people in tents. Some have been there for as long as five years; others had arrived only two weeks earlier. It required a great deal of convincing talk and patience before we were allowed to enter the camp commander's office and speak to a representative of the Buddhist community. The camp was officially "closed" while the newcomers were being interrogated. We learned that we were the first Buddhists to visit in a year, but Christian ministers and workers came frequently for services. When we asked what was needed, the young Vietnamese laymen asked for candles and for incense. Every day about sixty refugees gather at the temple for chanting.

One presupposition we encountered when talking with Westerners often leads to a misunderstanding for western, religious organizations operating in Buddhist countries. That is the concept of charity. Christians seem to feel it is most important to serve the neediest, that is, the lower and most helpless. It is to these that Christians offer the most charity.

Buddhists, on the other hand, think first of giving to the Sangha. It is by offering *dana* to monks that believers can make the most merit. These members of the community, the most highly respected by Asian people themselves, are often entirely ignored by agencies. While being the most highly respected, it is also true that members of the Sangha are, in material terms, the very poorest, since they are, by the rules of Vinaya, totally dependent upon the people for their daily food, robes, medicine and shelter.

Western voluntary agencies may operate in camps with little accountability. Recipients of aid usually have little protection since they are not represented in interagency meetings. In some cases, abuses are a matter of organization policy. In others, they arise from individual ignorance or prejudice. In one hilltribe refugee camp, for example, evangelical medical volunteers routinely forced refugee workers to attend worship services. These same missionaries berated refugee patients for seeking help from their traditional shamans, sometimes cutting the strings tied on patients wrists in earlier healing ceremonies. If a Buddhist doctor treats an unwell monk, it would be with proper respect, but a non-Buddhist physician might not be so well disposed.

Looking beyond the refugee camp situation, such an agency would also be useful in undertaking relief and development work in those countries from which these Southeast Asian refugees have recently come. Buddhism in Cambodia, Laos, Vietnam, and Burma, faces many critical problems. Actively persecuted under Communism the Lao, Cambodian and Vietnamese Sanghas need active and vocal *international* protection. Everywhere—including Sri Lanka, India, Tibet, and Bangladesh—the Buddha Sasana requires tremendous financial and moral support to hold its own and to struggle to recover from the terrible damage done over the past violent, poverty-stricken years.

When the Buddhist countries of Southeast Asia become more democratic and open to foreign assistance, international agencies will probably suffer from myopia we observed in the camps. In Burma, for example, international donors may attempt to work through feeble, mainly Rangoon-based Christian organizations. They may not be able to locate, or may not feel comfortable operating with, the efficient associations that currently exist within the Buddhist community, under the auspices of the Buddhist Sangha.

In order to succeed, we believe, an international Buddhist organization would best be conservative in order to work well on behalf of traditional Buddhist communities. A Western-dominated, nontraditional Buddhist agency would most likely create misunderstandings and friction. Certainly, the Theravada Sangha should not be asked to perform functions prohibited by Vinaya. Theravada monks are not supposed to act as social workers, as administrators handling money, or as counsellors to lay-people as Christian ministers and priests do. The organization, wholly administered by lay-people, would cooperate with local lay organizations to support the Sangha. There would be close cooperation with local lay organizations to support the Sangha. There would be close consultation with the monks, temple committee members, and nuns, to ensure that the concerns of the Buddhist communities were fully represented.

Please Call Me by My True Names
Thich Nhat Hanh

I have a poem for you. This poem is about three of us. The first is a twelve-year-old girl, one of the boat people crossing the Gulf of Siam. She was raped by a sea pirate, and after that she threw herself into the sea. The second person is the sea pirate, who was born in a remote village in Thailand. And the third person is me. I was not on the boat; I was tens of thousands of miles away, but because I was mindful, I knew what was going on in the Gulf. I was very angry, of course. But I could not take sides against the sea pirate. If I could have, it would have been easier, but I couldn't. I realized that if I had been born in his village and had lived a similar life—economic, educational, and so on—it is likely that I would now be that sea pirate. So it is not easy to take sides. Out of suffering, I wrote this poem. It is called, "Please Call Me by My True Names," because I have many names, and when you call me by any of them, I have to say, "Yes."

Do not say that I'll depart tomorrow
because even today I still arrive.

Look deeply: I arrive in every second
to be a bud on a spring branch,
to be a tiny bird, whose wings are still fragile,
learning to sing in my new nest,
to be a caterpillar in the heart of a flower,
to be a jewel hiding itself in a stone.

I still arrive, in order to laugh and to cry,
in order to fear and to hope,
the rhythm of my heart is the birth and death
of all that are alive.

I am the mayfly
metamorphosing on the surface of the river,
and I am the bird which, when spring comes,
arrives in time to eat the mayfly.

I am the frog swimming happily
in the clear water of a pond,
and I am also the grass-snake who,
approaching in silence, feeds itself on the frog.

I am the child in Uganda, all skin and bones,
my legs as thin as bamboo sticks.
and I am the arms merchant,
selling deadly weapons to Uganda.

I am the 12-year-old girl, refugee on a small boat,
who throws herself into the ocean
after being raped by a sea pirate,
and I am the pirate,
my heart not yet capable of seeing and loving.

I am a member of the politburo,
with plenty of power in my hands.
and I am the man
who has to pay his "debt of blood" to my people,
dying slowly in a forced labor camp.

My joy is like Spring, so warm it makes flowers bloom.
My pain is like a river of tears,
so full it fills up the four oceans.

Please call me by my true names,
so I can hear all my cries and my laughs at once,
so I can see that my joy and pain are but one.

Please call me by my true names,
so I can wake up,
and so the door of my heart can be left open,
the door of compassion.

I still have the theme of this poem in mind. "Where is our enemy?" I ask myself this all the time. Our earth, our green, beautiful earth, is in danger and all of us know it. We are not facing a pirate, but we are facing the destruction of the earth where our small boat has been. It will sink if we are not careful. We think that the enemy is the other, and that is why we can never see him. Everyone needs an enemy in order to survive. The Soviet Union needs an enemy. The United States needs an enemy, China needs an enemy. Vietnam needs an enemy. Everyone needs an enemy. Without an enemy we cannot survive. In order to rally people, governments need enemies. They want us to be afraid, to hate, so we will rally behind them. And if they do not have a real enemy, they will invent one in order to mobilize us. Yet there are people in the United States who have gone to the Soviet Union and discovered that the Russian people are very nice, and there are Soviet citizens who visit here, and when they return home, report that the American people are fine.

One friend in the peace movement told me, "Every time I see the President on television, I cannot bear it. I have to turn the TV off, or I become livid." I think I understand him. He believes that the situation of the world is in the hands of the government, and if only the President would change his policies we would have peace. I told him that that is not entirely correct. The President is in each of us. We always deserve our government. In Buddhism, we speak of interdependent origination. "This is, because that is. This is not, because that is not." Do our daily lives have nothing to do with our government? I invite you to meditate on this question. We seem to believe that our daily lives have nothing to do with the situation of the world. But if we do not change our daily lives, we cannot change the world.

In Japan, in the past, people took three hours to drink one cup of tea. You might think this is a waste of time, because time is money. But two people spending three hours drinking tea, being with each other, has to do with peace. The two men or two women did not speak a lot. They exchanged only a word or two, but they were really there, enjoying the time and the tea. They really knew the tea and the presence of each other.

Nowadays, we allow only a few minutes for tea, or coffee. We go into a cafe and order a cup of tea or coffee and listen to music and other loud noises, thinking about the business we will transact afterwards. In that situation, the tea does not exist. We are violent to the tea. We do not recognize it as a living reality, and that it is related to why our situation is as it is. When we pick up a Sunday newspaper, we should know that in order to print that edition, which sometimes weighs ten or twelve pounds, they had to cut down a whole forest. We are destroying our earth without knowing it.

Drinking a cup of tea, picking up a newspaper, using toilet paper, all of these things have to do with peace. Nonviolence can be called "awareness." We must be aware of what we are, of who we are, and of what we are doing. When I became a novice in a Buddhist monastery, I was taught to be aware of every act during the day. Since then, I have been practicing mindfulness and awareness. I used to think that practicing like that was only important for beginners, that advanced people did other important things, but now I know that practicing awareness is for everyone, including the Abbot. The purpose of Buddhist meditation is to see into your own nature and to become a Buddha. That can be done only through awareness. If you are not aware of what is going on in yourself and in the world, how can you see into your own nature and become a Buddha?

The word "Buddha" comes from the root, *buddh,* which means "awake." A Buddha is one who is awake. Are we really awake in our daily lives? That is a question I invite you to think about. Are we awake when we drink tea? Are we awake when we pick up the newspaper? Are we awake when we eat ice cream?

Society makes it difficult to be awake. We know that 40,000 children in the Third World die every day of hunger, but we keep forgetting. The kind of society we live in makes us forgetful. That is why we need exercises for mindfulness. For example, a number of Buddhists I know refrain from eating a few times a week in order to remember the situation in the Third World.

One day I asked a Vietnamese refugee boy who was eating a bowl of rice, whether children in his country eat such high quality rice. He said, "No," because he knows the situation. He experienced hunger in Vietnam—he ate only dry potatoes and he longed for a bowl of rice. In France, he has been eating rice for a year, and sometimes he begins to forget. But when I ask him, he remembers. I cannot ask the same question of a French or American child, because they have not had that kind of experience. They cannot understand. I realize how difficult it is for the people who live in Western countries to know what the situation in the Third World really is. It seems to have nothing to do with the situation here. I told the Vietnamese boy that his rice comes from Thailand, and that most Thai children do not have this rice to eat. They eat rice of poor quality, because the best rice is for export. Their government needs foreign currency, and they reserve the best rice for Westerners and not them. Some of us practice this exercise of mindfulness: We sponsor a child in the Third World in order to get news from him or her, thus keeping in touch with the reality outside. We try many ways to be awake, but society keeps us forgetful. It is so difficult to practice awareness in this society.

A French economist named François Peroux, who is the head of the Institute of Applied Mathematics and Economics in Paris, said that if Western countries would reduce the consumption of meat and alcohol by 50%, that would be enough to change the fate of the Third World. How can we do it when we do not remember to be aware? We are intelligent people, but we keep forgetting. Meditation is to remember.

The boat people said that every time their small boats were caught in storms, they knew their lives were in danger. But if one person on the boat could keep calm and not panic, that was a great help for everyone. People would listen to him or her and keep serene, and there was a chance for the boat to survive the danger. Our Earth is like a small boat. Compared with the rest of the cosmos, it is a very small boat, and it is in danger of sinking. We need such a person to inspire us with calm confidence, to tell us what to do. Who is that person? The Mahayana Buddhist sutras tell us that you are that person. If you are yourself, if you are your best, then you are that person. Only with such a person—calm, lucid, aware—will our situation improve. I wish you good luck. Please be yourself. Please be that person.

In our tradition, we are taught to look at things very deeply. For instance, if we look at a table, we can see a cloud, or a forest, or the sun in it, because without the cloud there would be no water for the tree which became the table. We also see the logger and the wheat which made the bread for the logger to eat. In the same way, if we look more deeply, we can see that our daily life has very much to do with the situation of the world. The President of the United States is in your daily life, not just in the White House. Nonviolence is not a question of belief. It is a way of life. It is awareness in order to have an accurate vision of reality, and having an accurate vision of reality in order to be in the most lucid state possible. From that basis, you can act.

It is very difficult to say that someone is nonviolent or violent. We can only say that a person is more or less nonviolent at a particular time. When I drink tea, I know that it is not entirely nonviolent because in the cup there are many tiny living beings. It is a question of direction. If you think that violence is sometimes needed, then I think you need more awareness and more love. Then I am sure you will go in the other direction. You cannot just separate people and say some are violent and some are not. That is why people with love, compassion, and nonviolence should be everywhere, even in the Pentagon, in order to encourage nonviolent attitudes within those we think are our enemies. That is why we have to love the President of the United States. Otherwise we cannot influence him, we cannot encourage him to move in the direction of nonviolence.

I would like to suggest that in each house we have a small room for breathing. We have rooms for sleeping, eating, and cooking, why not have one room for breathing? Breathing is very important. I know of families where children go into a room like that after breakfast, sit down and breathe ten times, in-out-one, in-out-two, in-out-three, and so on, before they go to school. This is a beautiful practice. Beginning the day with being a Buddha is a very nice way to start the day. If we are a Buddha in the morning and we try to nourish the Buddha throughout the day, we may be able to come home at the end of a day with a smile—the Buddha is still there. It is really beautiful to begin the day by being a Buddha. Each time we feel ourselves about to leave our Buddha, we can sit and breathe until we return to our true self. Doing these kinds of things can change our civilization.

ENDNOTES

1   *Mahavagga* of the *Vinaya Piṭaka,* p. 302, Chapter viii, section 26:3 in the Pali text.

2   Piyadassi Thera, *Buddhism's Ancient Path.* London: Rider, 1964, p. 120.

3   English as a Second Language.

4   UNHCR stands for United Nations High Commission for Refugees; UNDRO is United Nations Office of Disaster Relief.

5   The *Jataka* is the collection of birth and childhood stories of the Buddha.

Chapter Five

Judaism and Torah
The Moral Imperative for Service

The Torah—God's instruction to humanity—is the sacred scripture of Judaism. The basis of the written Torah is the Five Books of Moses—the Pentateuch—believed to have been revealed by God to Moses on Mt. Sinai. To this was added two more subdivisions, the collections of scrolls known as the Prophets and the Writings. Thus, the written Torah is sometimes represented by the acronym, TANAKH, standing for *Torah, Nevi'im,* and *Kethuvim:* Instruction, Prophets, and Writings. Thus, Torah can refer simply to the first section of the TANAKH, or can be used to mean all of scripture—all of God's instruction. Ancient rabbinic commentary—Midrash—is available on every book of the written Torah. Jewish sacred literature also includes vast numbers of volumes of rabbinic teachings and interpretations. This is the Talmud—the oral Torah, now committed to written form. Although not revealed scripture, these writings are indeed considered authoritative. The regular study of scripture is one of the primary activities of Judaism. It is expected of the faithful, and is always done in conjunction with the study of commentaries on the particular passage.

TANAKH

The selections are arranged according to the order in which they are found in the TANAKH; however, the books from which they come are identified by their common English—rather than Hebrew—titles.

If you lend money to My people, to the poor among you, do not act toward them as a creditor: exact no interest from them. If you take your neighbor's garment in pledge, you must return it to him before the sun sets; it is his only clothing, the sole covering for his skin. In what else shall he sleep? Therefore, if he cries out to Me, I will pay heed, for I am compassionate.[1] —*Exodus 22:24-26*

You shall not subvert the rights of your needy in their disputes. —*Exodus 23:6*

Six years you shall sow your land and gather in its yield; but in the seventh you shall let it rest and lie fallow. Let the needy among your people eat of it, and what they leave let the wild beasts eat. You shall do the same with your vineyards and your olive groves. —*Exodus 23:10-11*

You shall love your neighbor as yourself. —*Leviticus 19:18b*

When you reap the harvest of your land, you shall not reap all the way to the edges of your field, or gather the gleanings of your harvest. You shall not pick your vineyard bare, or gather the fallen fruit of your vineyard; you shall leave them for the poor and the stranger: I the LORD am your God. —*Leviticus 19:9-10*

When a stranger resides with you in your land, you shall not wrong him. The stranger who resides with you shall be to you as one of your citizens; you shall love him as yourself, for you were strangers in the land of Egypt: I the LORD am your God. [2] —*Leviticus 19:33-34*

And when you reap the harvest of your land, you shall not reap all the way to the edges of your field, or gather the gleanings of your harvest; you shall leave them for the poor and the stranger: I the LORD am your God. —*Leviticus 23:22*

If however, there is a needy person among you, one of your kinsmen in any of your settlements in the land that the LORD your God is giving you, do not harden your heart and shut your hand against your needy kinsman. Rather, you must open your hand and lend him sufficient for whatever he needs. Beware lest you harbor the base thought, "The seventh year, the year of remission, is approaching," so that you are mean to your needy kinsman and give nothing. He will cry out to the LORD against you, and you will incur guilt. Give to him readily and have no regrets when you do so, for in return the LORD your God will bless you in all your efforts and in all your undertakings. For there will never cease to be needy ones in your land, which is why I command you: open your hand to the poor and needy kinsman in your land. [3] —*Deuteronomy 15:7-11*

When you make your neighbor a loan of any kind, you shall not enter the house to take a pledge. You shall wait outside, while the person to whom you are making the loan brings the pledge out to you. If the person is poor, you shall not sleep in the garment given you as the pledge. You shall give the pledge back by sunset, so that your neighbor may sleep in the cloak; and it will be to your credit before the LORD your God. You shall not withhold the wages of poor and needy laborers, whether other Israelites or aliens who reside in your land in one of your towns. You shall pay them their wages daily before sunset, because they are poor and their livelihood depends on them; otherwise they might cry to the LORD against you, and you would incur guilt. —*Deuteronomy 24:10-15*

Indeed the LORD will vindicate his people,
    have compassion on his servants,
when he sees that their power is gone,
    neither bond nor free remaining. —*Deuteronomy 32:36*

The LORD makes poor and makes rich;
He casts down, He also lifts high.
He raises the poor from the dust,

Lifts up the needy from the dunghill,
Setting them with nobles,
Granting them seats of honor.
For the pillars of the earth are the LORD's;
He has set the world upon them. —*I Samuel 2:7-8*

The LORD will bring this charge
Against the elders and officers of His people:
"It is you who have ravaged the vineyard;
That which was robbed from the poor is in your houses.
How dare you crush My people
And grind the faces of the poor?"
    —says my Lord GOD of Hosts. —*Isaiah 3:14-15*

Ha!
Those who write out evil writs
And compose iniquitous documents,
To subvert the cause of the poor,
To rob of their rights the needy of My people;
That widows may be their spoil,
And fatherless children their booty!
What will you do on the day of punishment,
When calamity comes from afar?
To whom will you flee for help,
And how will you save your carcasses
From collapsing under fellow prisoners,
From falling beneath the slain?
    Yet his anger has not turned back,
    And his arm is outstretched still. —*Isaiah 10:1-4*

He shall not judge by what his eyes behold,
Nor decide by what his ears perceive.
Thus he shall judge the poor with equity
And decide with justice for the lowly of the land.
He shall strike down a land with the rod of his mouth
And slay the wicked with the breath of his lips. —*Isaiah 11:3b-4*

And what will he answer the messengers of any nation?
That Zion has been established by the LORD;
In it, the needy of His people shall find shelter. —*Isaiah 14:32*

O LORD, you are my God;
    I will exalt you, I will praise your name;
for you have done wonderful things,
    plans formed of old, faithful and sure...
For you have been a refuge to the poor,
    a refuge to the needy in their distress,
    a shelter from the rainstorm and a shade from the heat.
—*Isaiah 25:1, 4a*

The poor and needy
seek water, and there is none;
Their tongue is parched with thirst.
I the LORD will respond to them.
I, the God of Israel, will not forsake them. —*Isaiah 41:17*

For the LORD will not
     reject forever.
Sing for joy, O heavens, and exult, O earth;
     break forth, O mountains, into singing!
For the LORD has comforted his people;
     and will have compassion on his suffering ones. —*Isaiah 49:13*

For a little while I forsook you,
But with vast love I will bring you back.
In slight anger, for a moment,
I hid My face from you;
But with kindness everlasting
I will take you back in love
     —said the LORD your Redeemer.
For this to Me is like the waters of Noah:
As I swore that the waters of Noah
Nevermore would flood the earth,
So I swear that I will not
Be angry with you or rebuke you.
For the mountains may move
And the hills be shaken,
But my loyalty shall never move from you,
Nor My covenant of friendship be shaken
     —said the LORD, who takes you back in love. —*Isaiah 54:7-10*

Is such the fast I desire,
A day for men to starve their bodies?
Is it bowing the head like a bulrush
And lying in sackcloth and ashes?
Do you call that a fast,
A day when the LORD is favorable?
No, this is the fast I desire:
To unlock the fetters of wickedness,
And untie the cords of the yoke
To let the oppressed go free;
To break off every yoke.
It is to share your bread with the hungry,
And to take the wretched poor into your home;
When you see the naked, to clothe him,
And not to ignore your own kin.
Then shall your light burst through like the dawn,
And your healing spring up quickly;

Your Vindicator shall march before you,
The Presence of the LORD shall be your rear guard.
Then, when you call, the LORD will answer;
When you cry, He will say: Here I am. —*Isaiah 58:5-9a*

They pass beyond the bounds of wickedness;
And they prosper.
They will not judge the case of the orphan,
Nor give a hearing to the plea of the needy.
Shall I not punish such deeds—says the Lord—
Shall I not bring retribution
On a nation such as this? —*Jeremiah 5:28-29*

Only this was the sin of your sister Sodom: arrogance! She and her daughters had plenty of bread and untroubled tranquility; yet she did not support the poor and the needy. —*Ezekiel 16:49*

If a man is righteous and does what is just and right: If he has not eaten on the mountains or raised his eyes to the fetishes of the House of Israel; if he has not defiled another man's wife or approached a menstruous woman; if he has not wronged anyone; if he has returned the debtor's pledge to him and has taken nothing by robbery; if he has given bread to the hungry and clothed the naked; if he has not lent at advance interest or exacted accrued interest; if he has abstained from wrongdoing and executed true justice between man and man; if he has followed My laws and kept My rules and acted honestly—he is righteous. Such a man shall live—declares the Lord GOD.

Suppose, now that he has begotten a son who is a ruffian, a shedder of blood, who does any of these, whereas he himself did none of these things. That is, [the son] has eaten on the mountains, has defiled another man's wife, has wronged the poor and the needy, has taken by robbery, has not returned a pledge, has raised his eyes to the fetishes, has committed abomination, has lent at advance interest, or exacted accrued interest—shall he live? He shall not live! If he has committed any of these abominations, he shall die; he has forfeited his life.

Now suppose that he, in turn, has begotten a son who has seen all the sins that his father committed, but has taken heed and has not imitated them: He has not eaten on the mountains or raised his eyes to the fetishes of the House of Israel; he has not defiled another man's wife; he has not wronged anyone; he has not seized a pledge to him or taken anything by robbery; he has given his bread to the hungry and clothed the naked; he has refrained from oppressing the poor; he has not exacted advance or accrued interest; he has obeyed My rules and followed My laws—he shall not die for the iniquity of his father, but shall live. To be sure, his father, because he practiced fraud, robbed his brother, and acted wickedly among his kin, did die for his iniquity; and now you ask, "Why has not the son shared the burden of his father's guilt?" But the son has done what is right and just, and has carefully kept all My laws: he shall live![4] —*Ezekiel 18:5-19*

Thus said the LORD:
For three transgressions of Israel,

For four, I will not revoke the punishment:
Because they have sold for silver [taken bribes for] those whose cause is just,
And the needy for a pair of sandals. —*Amos 2:6*

Assuredly,
Because you impose a tax on the poor
And exact from him a levy of grain,
You have built houses hewn of stone,
But you shall not live in them;
You have planted delightful vineyards,
But shall not drink their wine.
For I have noted how many are your crimes,
And how countless your sins—
You enemies of the righteous,
You takers of bribes,
You who subvert in the gate
The cause of the needy! —*Amos 5:11-12*

Listen to this, you who devour the needy, annihilating the poor of the land, saying,
"If only the new moon were over, so that we could sell grain; the sabbath, so that
we could offer wheat for sale, using an *ephah* that is too small, and a shekel that
is too big, tilting a dishonest scale, and selling grain refuse as grain! We will buy
the poor for silver, the needy for a pair of sandals." The LORD swears by the Pride
of Jacob: "I will never forget any of their doings."[5] —*Amos 8:4-7*

And the word of the LORD to Zechariah continued: Thus said the LORD of Hosts:
Execute true justice; deal loyally and compassionately with one another. Do not
defraud the widow, the orphan, the stranger, and the poor; and do not plot evil
against one another. —*Zechariah 7:8-10*

In arrogance the wicked persecute the poor—
    let the wicked be caught in the schemes they have devised. —*Psalms 10:2*

"Because of the groans of the plundered poor and needy,
    I will now act," says the LORD.
"I will give help," He affirms to him. —*Psalms 12:6*

The poor shall eat and be satisfied;
    those who seek him shall praise the LORD.
May your hearts live forever! —*Psalms 22:26*

Here was a lowly man[6] who called,
    and the LORD listened,
    and delivered him from all his troubles. —*Psalms 34:7*

Then shall I exult the LORD,
    rejoice in His deliverance.
All my bones shall say,
    "LORD, who is like You?
You save the poor from one stronger than he,
    the poor and needy from his despoiler." —*Psalms 35:9-10*

The wicked draw the sword and bend their bows
    to bring down the poor and needy,
    to kill those who walk uprightly; —*Psalms 37:14*

But I am poor and needy;
    may the Lord devise deliverance for me.
    You are my help and my rescuer;
    my God, do not delay. —*Psalms 40:18*

Happy are those who consider the poor;
    the LORD delivers them in the day of trouble.
The LORD protects them and keeps them alive;
    they are called happy in the land. —*Psalms 41:1-2a*

Exult in His presence—
    the father of orphans, the champion of widows,
    God, in His holy habitation.
God restores the lonely to their homes,
    sets free the imprisoned, safe and sound,
    while the rebellious must live in a parched land. —*Psalms 68:5b-6*

O God, endow the king with Your judgments,
    the king's son with Your righteousness;
    that he may judge Your people rightly,
    Your lowly ones, justly.
Let the mountains produce well-being for the people,
    the hills, the reward of justice.
Let him champion the lowly among the people,
    deliver the needy folk,
    and crush those who wrong them. . .
Let him rule from sea to sea,
    from the river to the ends of the earth. . .
For he saves the needy who cry out,
    the lowly who have no helper.
He cares about the poor and the needy;
    He brings the needy deliverance.
He redeems them from fraud and lawlessness;
    the shedding of their blood weighs heavily upon him.
    —*Psalms 72:1-4, 8, 12-14*

Do not hold our former iniquities against us;
    let Your compassion come swiftly toward us,
    for we have sunk very low. —*Psalms 79:8*

God stands in the divine assembly;
    among the divine beings He pronounces judgment.
How long will you judge perversely,
    showing favor to the wicked?
Judge the wretched and the orphan,
    vindicate the lowly and the poor,

rescue the wretched and the needy;
save them from the hand of the wicked. —*Psalms 82:1-4*

Turn, O LORD!
How long?
Show mercy to Your servants.
Satisfy us at daybreak with Your steadfast love
that we may sing for joy all our days. —*Psalms 90:13-14*

My days are like a lengthening shadow;
I wither like grass.
But You, O LORD, are enthroned forever;
Your fame endures throughout the ages.
You will surely arise and take pity on Zion,
for it is time to be gracious to her;
the appointed time has come. —*Psalms 102:12-14*

As a father has compassion for his children,
so the LORD has compassion for those who fear Him.
For He knows how we are formed;
He is mindful that we are dust. —*Psalms 103:13-14*

It is well with those who deal generously and lend,
who conduct their affairs with justice.
For the righteous will never be moved;
they will be remembered forever. —*Psalms 112:5-6*

Who is like the LORD our God,
who, enthroned on high,
sees what is below,
in heaven and on earth?
He raises the poor from the dust,
lifts up the needy from the refuse heap
to set them with the great,
with the great men of His people. —*Psalms 113:5-8*

The LORD is gracious and compassionate,
slow to anger and abounding in kindness.
The LORD is good to all,
and His mercy is upon all His works. —*Psalms 145:8-9*

Praise the Lord!
Praise the Lord, O my soul!
I will praise the Lord as long as I live;
I will sing praises to my God all my life long.

Do not put your trust in princes,
in mortals, in whom there is no help.
When their breath departs, they return to the earth;
on that very day their plans perish.

Happy are those whose help is in the God of Jacob,
    whose hope is in the Lord their God,
who made heaven and earth,
    the sea, and all that is in them;
who keeps faith forever;
    who executes justice for the oppressed;
    who gives food to the hungry.

The Lord sets the prisoners free;
    the Lord opens the eyes of the blind.
The Lord lifts up those who are bowed down;
    the Lord loves the righteous.
The Lord watches over the strangers;
    he upholds the orphan and the widow,
    but the way of the wicked he brings to ruin.

The Lord will reign forever,
    your God, O Zion, for all generations.
Praise the Lord! —*Psalms 146*

Those who despise their neighbors are sinners,
    but happy are those who are kind to the poor. —*Proverbs 14:21*

Those who oppress the poor insult their Maker,
    but those who are kind to the needy honor him. —*Proverbs 14:31*

Better to be humble and among the lowly
Than to share in the spoils with the proud. —*Proverbs 16:19*

Better a poor man who lives blamelessly
Than one who speaks perversely and is a dullard. —*Proverbs 19:1*

Whoever is kind to the poor lends to the LORD,
    and will be repaid in full. —*Proverbs 19:17*

If you close your ear to the cry of the poor,
    you will cry out and not be heard. —*Proverbs 21:13*

The rich and the poor have this in common:
    the LORD is the maker of them all. —*Proverbs 22:2*

Those who are generous are blessed,
    for they share their bread with the poor. —*Proverbs 22:9*

To profit by withholding what is due to the poor
Is like making gifts to the rich—pure loss. —*Proverbs 22:16*

Do not rob the poor because they are poor,
    or crush the afflicted at the gate;

For the LORD pleads their cause
    and despoils of life those who despoil them. —*Proverbs 22:22-3*

A ruler who oppresses the poor
  is a beating rain that leaves no food. —*Proverbs 28:3*

Better to be poor and walk in integrity
  than to be crooked in one's ways even though rich. —*Proverbs 28:6*

He who increases his wealth by loans at discount or interest
masses it for one who is generous to the poor. —*Proverbs 28:8*

Whoever gives to the poor will lack nothing,
  but one who turns a blind eye will get many a curse. —*Proverbs 28:27*

The righteous know the rights of the poor;
  the wicked have no such understanding. —*Proverbs 29:7*

If a king judges the poor with equity,
  his throne will be established forever. —*Proverbs 29:14*

Speak up, judge righteously,
Champion the poor and the needy. —*Proverbs 31:9*

What a rare find is a capable wife! . . .
She gives generously to the poor;
Her hands are stretched out to the needy. —*Proverbs 31:10a, 20*

Although he causes grief, he will have compassion
  according to the abundance of his steadfast love;
for he does not willingly afflict
  or grieve anyone. —*Lamentations 3:31–33*

Mordecai recorded these events. And he sent dispatches to all the Jews throughout the provinces of King Ahasuerus, near and far, charging them to observe the
fourteenth and fifteenth days of Adar, every year—the same days on which the
Jews enjoyed relief from their foes and the same month which had been
transformed for them from one of grief and mourning to one of festive joy. They
were to observe them as days of feasting and merrymaking, and as an occasion
for sending gifts to one another and presents to the poor. The Jews accordingly
assumed as an obligation that which they had begun to practice and which
Mordecai prescribed for them. —*Esther 9:20–23*

"Do not be like your ancestors and your kindred, who were faithless to the LORD
God of their ancestors, so that he made them a desolation as you see. Do not now
be stiff-necked as your ancestors were, but yield yourselves to the LORD and
come into his sanctuary, which he has sanctified forever, and serve the LORD your
God, so that his fierce anger may turn away from you. For as you return to the
LORD, your kindred and your children will find compassion with their captors,
and return to this land. For the LORD your God is gracious and merciful, and will
not turn away his face from you, if you return to him."
—*II Chronicles 30:7–9*[7]

The LORD, the God of their ancestors, sent persistently to them by his messengers, because he had compassion on his people and on his dwelling place.
—*II Chronicles 36:15*

Midrash

From the Hebrew word meaning "to study" or "to investigate," Midrash seeks to bring clarity to the laws and lessons of the Torah. It takes two distinct literary forms: *Halakhah,* which focuses on legal issues; and *Haggadah,* which clarifies a biblical phrase or provides a motive for a biblical incident through such means as folktales, sermons, proverbs, anecdotes, metaphors, allegories, and puns. Once these teachings were committed to written form, the material was arranged in Torah order. Thus, *Sifré Deuteronomy* contains Midrash—both halakhic and haggadic in style—on the fifth book of the TANAKH. Below, whenever a Midrash quotes a portion of the TANAKH it is seeking to clarify, that phrase appears in italics.

Commentary on Deuteronomy 24:10: *When thou dost lend thy neighbor.* I conclude that this refers only to a loan; what about the wages of a hired man or store debts? The verse goes on to say, *Any manner of loan, thou shalt not go into his house.* One might think that the creditor may not seize the pledge from within but may seize it from without; therefore the verse goes on to say, *to fetch his pledge without* (24:10). One might think that he may not seize his pledge from without, but may seize it from within; therefore the Scripture goes on to say, *Thou shalt stand without* (24:11). When Scripture says, *And the man . . . (shall bring forth the pledge)* (24:11), it includes the messenger of the court.
—*Sifré Deuteronomy 276*

Commentary on Deuteronomy 24:12-13. *And if he be a poor man (24:12).* I conclude that this applies only to a poor man; what about a rich man? The verse states, *And if he be a man.* If so, why does it say poor? Because I requite the cause of a poor man more quickly than that of a rich man.[8]

Thou shalt not sleep with his pledge (24:12): Would you possibly think of actually sleeping (wrapped) in his pledge? The meaning is rather that you should not sleep overnight with his pledge in your possession.

Thou shalt surely restore to him the pledge (24:13): This shows that one must restore a daytime garment to him in the daytime and a nighttime garment in the nighttime, a blanket at night and a plow during the day, but not the blanket during the day and the plow at night.

That he may sleep in his garment, and bless thee (24:13): Hence we learn that the pledger is commanded to bless you. Lest one should think that if he blesses you, you are blessed, but if he fails to bless you, you are not blessed, the verse goes on to say, and it shall be righteousness unto thee (24:13)—you create your righteousness by your action. And it shall be righteousness unto thee—hence you learn that righteousness ascends before the throne of glory, as it is said, *Righteousness shall go before Him, and shall make His footsteps a way* (Ps. 85:14). —*Sifré Deuteronomy 277*

Commentary on Deuteronomy 24:19: *And hast thou forgot a sheaf in the field... Thou shalt not go back to fetch it.* Hence R. Ismael said: If an ear of corn is left over after the harvest, and its head touches the standing corn, the rule is as follows: if it can be cut together with the standing corn, it belongs to the owner; if not, it belongs to the poor. If the owner wishes to take it from the poor, he must show cause,[9] for he who wishes to take something from another person must show cause. Whence do we learn that doubtful gleanings are gleanings, doubtful forgotten sheaf is forgotten sheaf, and doubtful corner crop is corner crop? From the verse, It shall be for the stranger, for the fatherless, and for the widow (24:19). —*Sifré Deuteronomy 283*

Commentary on Psalm 37: *Fret not thyself because of evil-doers, neither be thou envious against the workers of iniquity* (Ps. 37:1). These words are to be considered in the light of the verse *Let not thy heart envy sinners* (Prov. 23:17). Of whom should you be envious? Only of those who have the *fear of the Lord all the day (ibid.).* Therefore, in saying *Be not the rival of sinners* (Prov. 23:17a), the Holy One, blessed be He, meant: "Be My rival!" If it were not for such rivalry, the world could not endure, for no man would take a woman to wife, nor build a house. If Abraham had not sought to rival God, he would not have become possessor of heaven and earth. When did Abraham seek to rival God? When he asked Melchizedek: "On account of what righteous act didst thou and thy kin come forth alive from the ark?" and Melchizedek answered: "Because of the alms which we gave in the ark." Abraham asked: "What occasion did you have for giving alms in the ark? Were there poor people there? Were not only Noah and his sons there? To whom did you give alms?" Melchizedek replied: "We gave alms to the cattle, to the beasts, and to the birds. We did not sleep because all night we were setting food before this one and before that one." Thereupon Abraham reflected: "Had they not given alms to the cattle, to the beasts, and to the birds, Noah and his sons would not have come forth alive from the ark; it was only because they gave alms that they came forth from it alive! Therefore, if I give alms to the sons of men, how much greater the deed!" At once Abraham planted an *'sl* [tamarisk tree] in Beersheba, that is, he gave food, drink, and escort to all the sons of men. —*Sifré on Psalms* [10]

Commentary on Psalm 118: *Open to me the gates of righteousness* (Ps. 118:19). When a man is asked in the world-to-come: "What was thy work?" and he answers: "I fed the hungry," it will be said to him: *"This is the gate of the Lord* (Ps. 118:20). Enter into it, O thou that didst feed the hungry."When a man answers: "I gave drink to the thirsty," it will be said to him: *"This is the gate of the Lord.* Enter into it, O thou that didst give drink to the thirsty."When a man answers: "I clothed the naked," it will be said to him: *"This is the gate of the Lord.* Enter into it, O thou that didst clothe the naked."This will be said also to him that brought up the fatherless, and to them that gave alms or performed deeds of loving-kindness. And David said: I have done all these things. Therefore let all the gates be opened to me. Hence it is said *Open to me the gates of righteousness; I will enter into them, I will give thanks unto the Lord* (Ps. 118:19). —*Sifré on Psalms*

Talmud

In approximately 210 CE, Rabbi Judah ha Nasi committed to writing this body of rabbinical oral teachings produced by the same rabbis who had contributed to the Midrash. As they had for the TANAKH, the rabbis generated as well extensive commentary for the Mishnah— Gemara—which clarifies and expands upon the oral Torah much as the Midrash does for the written Torah. The Gemara preserves the record of the lengthy discussion and debate by the rabbis—whose names are usually cited—as they wrestled with a particular verse from the Torah or an entry in the Mishnah, as well as other related matters. When published together, the Mishnah and the Gemara became the Talmud, which evolved in two forms: the Jerusalem—or Palestinian—and the Babylonian Talmuds. Those passages taken from the Jerusalem Talmud are indicated as such.

The Mishnah has six main sections called *Sedarim*—or Orders—within each of which are found a number of subsections variously called divisions, books, or tractates. These writings often expand upon or clarify specific verses of the written torah, but usually do not cite the written torah directly; nor is the material of the Mishnah arranged in written torah order. In fact, some of the Mishnaic material covers topics not raised in the written torah at all. Within the First Order, *Zera'im* (Seeds)—which contains instruction regarding agriculture—the second tractate is the book of *Pe'ah* (Edge, or Corners, of the Field, i.e.., that portion of the field to be left unharvested for the benefit of the poor). Within it are many detailed guides to interpreting and heeding the mandate of Leviticus 19:9–10 which grants gleaning rights to the poor.

Abot is Hebrew for "Fathers;" *Pirké Abot* means "sayings (or chapters) of the Fathers," that is, the collected wisdom of the sixty ancient rabbis who are credited within the text, and whose lives spanned the era from 300 BCE to 200 CE. It is usually placed at the end of the Fourth Order (*Nezikin:* Damages—case law, both civil and criminal). The Talmud contains no Gemara on *Pirké Abot.*

Sometime during the period 100–200 CE, a tractate known as *Pirké Abot Rabbi Nathan* took form. Its forty-one chapters are entirely haggadic in style, and serve to comment and expand upon *Pirké Abot.* It is often included in Order *Nezikin,* following *Pirké Abot.*

As was true for the Midrash examples above, whenever the Mishnah or Gemara quotes a portion of the TANAKH in order to clarify a passage, that phrase appears in italics in the examples included below.

Mishnah: These are things that are not subject to a specific measure: the quantity of produce set aside as *pe'ah,* the quantity of produce designated as first fruits and brought to the Temple on Pentecost (see Deuteronomy 26:1–11), the value of the appearance-offering, brought to Jerusalem on each of the three pilgrimage festivals (see Deut. 16:16–17), the quantity of righteous deeds performed, and time spent in study of Torah. These are things the benefits of which a person enjoys in this world, while the principal remains for him in the world-to-come: deeds done in honor of father and mother, performance of righteous deeds, and acts that bring about peace between one person and another. But the study of Torah is equal to all of them together. —*Pe'ah 1:1 [Jerusalem Talmud]*

Gemara: *Acts of loving-kindness*—This refers to physical acts of loving-kindness, such as visiting the sick, which should be performed without limit, as specified by *M. Pe'ah 1:1.* But as regards acts of loving-kindness of a monetary nature, such as charity—these acts are subject to a limit. And this statement, that monetary acts of loving-kindness are subject to a limit, accords with that which R. Simeon b. Laqish said in the name of R. Judah b. Hanina, "At Usha they voted that a person may separate up to one-fifth of his possessions in order to have enough money to perform any particular religious duty, including acts of loving-kindness." [By setting this limit on the amount one may spend on a religious duty in general, the sages in fact limit the amount to be spent on monetary acts of loving-kindness. The remainder of this unit explains the notion that one may set aside only one-fifth of one's estate for the performance of a religious duty.]

God will keep your feet from being caught (Proverbs 3:26b) —R. Dosa said, "God will keep you from being caught in erroneous judgments." And the rabbis say, "God will keep you from being caught in transgression." R. Levy says, "God will keep you from demons." Said R. Abba, "Proverbs 3:26 should be interpreted this way: 'The Lord will be your trust: If you give charity out of your pocket, God will keep you from general taxes, the poll tax, and the crop tax.'" . . .

R. Yohanan bar Maria in the name of R. Yohanan: "We cannot say which is more important, giving charity or performing acts of loving-kindness. But since Scripture states, 'But the Lord's steadfast love [i.e., acts of loving-kindness] is for all eternity toward those who fear him, and his charitable-beneficence is for the children's children' *(Ps. 103:17)*, this proves that acts of loving-kindness are more important than giving charity."

And acts of loving-kindness (M. Peah 1:1) —How may we determine on the basis of Scripture that acts of loving-kindness earn rewards both in this world and in the world-to-come? As it is written in Scripture, "He who strives to do good and kind deeds attains life, success, and honor" *(Prov. 21:21)*. That is, by performing acts of loving-kindness, one attains honor in this world, and life in the world to come.

R. Samuel bar Rav Isaac used to take a branch and dance in front of bridal parties, as an act of loving-kindness, wishing the couple fertility and joy. R. Zeira saw him and hid from him and said, "Look at this old man—how he embarrasses us!" When Samuel died, for three hours thunder and lightning shook the world. A heavenly voice cried out and said, "R. Samuel bar Rav Isaac, who always performed acts of loving-kindness, has died!" When people came out to perform the final act of loving-kindness by burying him, a fire went forth from Heaven in the shape of a burning branch and interposed itself between his bier and the public. And people said, "Come and see this old man—how his branch vindicates him!" The branch had indicated that, because of his acts of loving-kindness, Samuel had earned life in the world-to-come.

—Yerushalmi Pe'ah 1:1 (excerpts).

Mishnah: They may designate as *pe'ah* no less than one-sixtieth of a field's produce. And even though they said, "*Pe'ah* has no specified measure, the quantity designated should always accord with: the size of the field, the number of poor people, and the extent of the yield. *—Pe'ah 1:2*

Gemara: *They must designate as pe'ah no less than one-sixtieth of a field's produce.* —It was taught on Tannaitic [rabbinic] authority: In a case in which there are but a few poor people near the field to collect poor-offerings, householders are not obligated to say to a poor person,

"Bring camels and gather all of the peah I set aside from this field."
Rather, the householder allows the poor to take what they can carry and
thereafter may retain that which they did not gather.

The previous rule speaks about a case in which one designates more
than the requisite measure of one-sixtieth of the yield. Since the extra
grain is merely a voluntary gift to the poor, the farmer need not allow an
individual poor person to gather so much that he would have to cart off
grain on his camel's back.

But in a case in which the householder designates only the requisite
measure of one-sixtieth of the field's produce, and in which very few poor
people are around to gather the poor-offerings, people must say, "Bring
camels to carry your share of the grain." Since all of this produce, by law,
belongs to the poor, the householder must encourage them to take all of
it. This is the case even if this means an individual poor person will gather
so much grain that he will have to cart it off on his camel's back."

But in the case in which the householder designates only the
requisite measure of one-sixtieth of the field's produce, and in which
very few poor people are around to gather the poor-offerings, people
must say, "Bring camels to carry your share of the grain." Since all of this
produce, by law, belongs to the poor, the householder must encourage
them to take all of it. This is the case even if this means an individual poor
person will gather so much grain that he will have to cart it off on his
camel's back."

If the field's yield is abundant, but poor people are few—the
householder sets aside the larger amount, namely, that dictated by the
field's abundance. Similarly, if the field's yield is limited, but poor people
are many—the householder sets aside the larger amount, namely, that
dictated by the number of poor people.

Rabbi Simeon, by contrast, expounded these two cases to the benefit
of the householder, as follows: If the field's yield is abundant, but poor
people are few—the householder sets aside the smaller amount, namely,
that dictated by the number of poor people. Likewise, if the field's yield
is limited, but poor people are many—the householder sets aside the
smaller amount, namely, that dictated by the field's yield.

Nonetheless, the present Mishnah-passage does not rule in agreement with R. Simeon, but rather states, "The quantity designated should
always accord with the size of the field, the number of poor people in the
vicinity, and the extent of the yield." — *Yerushalmi Pe'ah 1:2 (excerpts).*

Mishnah: As regards *pe'ah*—they may not harvest it with sickles, nor may they
uproot it with spades, so that poor people will not clobber each other with garden
tools. — *Pe'ah 4:4*

Mishnah: Three times in each day the poor may enter the field in order to collect
pe'ah: in the morning, at noon, and in the late afternoon. Rabban Gamaliel says,
"They said this only so that householders would not decrease the number of
times the poor would have to go out to the field to collect *pe'ah*, thus depriving
them of what is rightfully theirs." R. Aqiba says, "They said this only so that
householders would not increase the number of times the poor would have to

go out to the field to collect *pe'ah,* such that the poor have to wait all day by the edge of the fields in order to collect *pe'ah* when the householder gives them permission." In contrast to the ruling, the inhabitants of Bet Namer permitted the poor to collect gleanings from each row of the fields, as they were harvested, and designated *pe'ah* from each and every furrow. — *Pe'ah 4:5*

> Gemara: *In the morning*—for the benefit of nursing mothers, who need to eat early in the day. *At noon*—for the benefit of infants, who are not yet awake in the early morning. *And in the afternoon*—for the benefit of the old folks, who arrive at the fields only late in the day.
>
> Rabban Gamaliel says, "They stated this rule only so that householders would not increase the number of times in each day when the poor were permitted to collect peah." Nonetheless, if the householder wished to decrease the number of daily searches, he was not allowed to do so. —*Yerushalmi Pe'ah 4:3 (Mishnah Pe'ah 4:5) (excerpts).*

Mishnah: What produce is subject to the law of gleanings? That which falls to the ground during the harvest. If one was harvesting and harvested an armful of produce, or plucked a handful of produce, and a thorn pricked him so that the produce he was holding fell to the ground before he had fully grasped it—lo, this produce belongs to the householder, for only produce which falls to the ground while in the possession of the harvester is subject to the law of gleanings. Produce which falls from within the harvester's hand, or from within the sickle, produce of which the harvester had taken possession, belongs to the poor. Produce which falls from the back of the harvester's hand, or from the back of the sickle, belongs to the householder. Produce which falls from the tip of the harvester's hand, or from the tip of the sickle, such that it is unclear whether or not the harvester had taken possession,—R. Ishmael says, "Such produce belongs to the poor." R. Aqiba says, "It belongs to the householder." — *Pe'ah 4:10*

> Gemara: What produce is in the status of gleanings (see Lev. 19:9)? That which falls to the ground during the harvest. If a householder was harvesting his field, and harvested an armful, or plucked a handful, and a thorn pricked him so that the produce fell from his hand to the ground— this produce belongs to the householder. Produce that falls from within the householder's hand, or from within his sickle [i.e., that which he already has taken into his possession], belongs to the poor. Produce that falls from the back of the householder's hand, or from the back of his sickle [i.e., the produce fell before the householder took possession of it.], belongs to the householder. As regards produce that falls from the tip of the householder's hand, or from the tip of his sickle—R. Ishmael says, "Such produce belongs to the poor." R. Aqiba says, "It belongs to the householder." It has been taught on Tannaitic authority, "Scripture states, 'You shall not. . . gather the gleanings of your harvest' *(Lev. 19:10),* but it does not explicitly state that the law of gleanings applies to 'all that you pluck with your hands'. Similarly, with regard to the law of separated grapes, Scripture states, 'You shall not. . . gather the fallen fruit of your vineyard' *(Lev. 19:10),* but it does not explicitly state that the law of separated grapes applies to 'all fruit that you separate from the vine with

your hands.'" [In both cases, Scripture's wording may be interpreted to exclude from the law produce picked by hand, as if for a random snack (See *Sifré Qed. 2:5*).]

Rav Kahana and Rav Tahlifah had the following dispute. One cited Mishnah 4:10 as: *"Produce that falls from within the householder's hand or from within his sickle, i.e., that which he already has taken into his possession, belongs to the poor."* [This version reflects the premise as found in the Mishnah.] But the other cited the same premise as: *"Produce that falls from within the householder's hand or even produce that falls from the back of his sickle belongs to the poor."* [This version reflects the understanding that merely by his act of harvesting with a sickle, the householder takes possession of any grain he touches. Hence any produce that falls from the back of the farmer's sickle in fact already has entered his possession, and so, upon its falling to the earth, takes on the status of gleanings.] — *Y. Pe'ah 4:7 (M. Pe'ah 10)* [11]

Simeon the Righteous was one of the last survivors of the great assembly. He would say: "On three things does the world stand: on the Torah, and on the Temple service, and on deeds of loving kindness." —*Abot 1:2*

Hillel would say, "If I am not for myself, who is for me? And when I am only for myself, what am I? And if not now, when?[12] —*Abot 1:14*

A saying of Hillel: Do not separate yourself from the community, and do not believe only in yourself to the day of your death and do not judge your fellow human being until you reach his place.[13] —*Abot 2:5*

Rabbi Yohanan ben Zakkai said, "Go forth and see which is the good way to which a man should cleave." Rabbi Eliezar said, "A good eye"; Rabbi Joshua said, "A good friend"; Rabbi Jose said, "A good neighbor"; Rabbi Simeon said, "One who foresees the fruit of an action"; Rabbi Elazar said, "A good heart." Thereupon he said to them, "I approve the words of Elazar ben Arach, rather than your words, for in his words yours are included."[14] —*Abot 2:13*

Rabbi Tarfon would say, "It's not your job to finish the work, but you're are not free to walk away from it." —*Abot 2:21*

Who is honored? He who honors everybody, as it is said, For those who honor me I shall honor, and they who despise me will be treated as of no account. *(I Samuel 2:30)* —*Abot 4:1*

There are four sorts of people.
He who says, "What's mine is mine and what's yours is yours"—this is the average sort. (And some say, 'This is the sort of Sodom.')

He who says, "What's mine is yours and what's yours is mine"—this is a boor.
He who says, "What's mine is yours and what's yours is yours"—this is a truly pious man.
"What's mine is mine and what's yours is mine"—this is a truly wicked man. —*Abot 5:10.*

There was once a saint who was habitually charitable. One time he set out in a boat; a wind rose and sank his boat in the sea. Rabbi ʿAkiba witnessed this and came before the court to testify that his wife might remarry. Before he could take the stand, the man came back and stood before him.

"Art thou not he who went down in the sea?" Rabbi ʿAkiba said to him.

"Yes," he replied.

"And who raised thee up out of the sea?"

"The charity which I practiced," he answered, "it raised me out of the sea."

"How dost thou know this?" Rabbi ʿAkiba inquired.

He said to him: "When I sank to the depths of the sea, I heard the sound of a great noise of the waves of the sea, one wave saying to the other and the other to another 'Hurry! and let us raise this man out of the sea, for he practiced charity all his days.'"

Then Rabbi ʿAkiba spoke up and declared the words of the Torah and the words of the Sages, for the words of the Torah and the words of the Sages are established forever and unto all eternity. For it is said, *Cast thy bread upon the waters, for thou shalt find it after many days* (Eccles. 2:1); moreover it is written, *Charity delivereth from death"* (Prov. 10:2). — *Pirké Nathan 3*

The following occurred to Benjamin the Righteous, who was in charge of the community charity chest. A woman came before him and said: "Master, take care of me."

"By the Temple service!" he said to her, "there is nothing in the charity chest."

"Master," she said to him, "if thou dost not take care of me, thou wilt be the death of a widow and her seven sons." He thereupon gave her money from his own funds.

Some time after, Benjamin the Righteous fell sick and lay in bed in pain. Said the ministering angels to the Holy One, blessed be He: "Master of the Universe, Thou hast said 'One who saves a single soul in Israel is as though he had saved a whole world.' How much more so Benjamin the Righteous who saved a widow and her seven sons! Yet he is sorely sick upon his bed."

Forthwith they beseeched mercy for him, and his death sentence was torn up. And twenty-two years were added to his life. — *Pirké Nathan 3*

Commentary on a passage from Pirké Abot—*Joseph ben Johanan of Jerusalem says: Let thy house be opened wide, and let the poor be members of thy household: Let thy house be opened wide:* how so? This teaches that a man's house should have a spacious entrance on the north, south, east, and west, like Job's, who made four doors to his house. And why did Job make four doors to his house? So that the poor would not be troubled to go all around the house: one coming from the north could enter in his stride, one coming from the south could enter in his stride, and so in all directions. For that reason Job made four doors to his house.

And let the poor be members of thy household. Not actually members of thy household. But let the poor talk about what they had to eat and drink in thy house the way the poor used to talk about what they had to eat and drink in Job's house. When they met, one would say to the other:

"Where art thou coming from?"

"From Job's house. And where art *thou* going?"

"To Job's house."

Now when that great calamity came upon Job, he said unto the Holy One, blessed be He: "Master of the Universe, did I not feed the hungry and give the thirsty to drink; as it is said, *Or have I eaten my morsel myself alone and the fatherless hath not eaten thereof* (Job 31:17)? And did I not clothe the naked, as it is said, *And if he were not warmed with the fleece of my sheep"* (Job 31:20)?

Nevertheless the Holy One, blessed be He, said to Job: "Job, thou hast not yet reached half the measure of Abraham. Thou sittest and tarriest within thy house and the wayfarers come in to thee. To him who is accustomed to eat wheat bread, thou givest wheat bread to eat; to him who is accustomed to eat meat, thou givest meat to eat; to him who is accustomed to drink wine, thou givest wine to drink. But Abraham did not act in this way. Instead he would go forth and make the rounds everywhere, and when he found wayfarers he brought them in to his house. To him who was accustomed to eat bread, he gave bread to eat; to him who was accustomed to eat meat, he gave meat to eat; to him who was accustomed to drink wine, he gave wine to drink. Moreover he arose and built stately mansions on the highways and left there food and drink, and every passerby ate and drank and blessed Heaven. That is why delight of spirit was vouchsafed to him. And whatever one might ask for was to be found in Abraham's house, as it is said, *And Abraham planted a tamarisk tree in Beer-Sheba"* (Gen. 21:33).[15]—*Pirké Nathan 7*

Commentary on *Seven kinds of calamity come upon the world for seven classes of transgressions:* Rabbi Josiah says. . . *Pestilence comes upon the world* for neglect of the harvest gleanings, the forgotten sheaf, the corner of the field, and poor man's tithe.

There was once a poor woman who dwelt in the neighborhood of a landowner. Her two sons went out to gather gleanings, but the landowner did not let them take any. Their mother kept saying: "When will my sons come back from the field; perhaps I shall find that they have brought something to eat." And they kept saying: "When shall we go back to our mother; perhaps we shall discover that she has found something to eat." She found that they had nothing and they found that she had nothing to eat. So they laid their heads on their mother's lap and the three of them died in one day. Said the Holy One, blessed be He: "Their very existence you take away from them! By your life! I shall make you, too, pay for it with your very existence!" —*Pirké Nathan 38*

Three things were said of men: one gives charity, may blessing come upon him; superior to him is one who lends his funds; superior to all is one who forms a partnership with the poor on terms of half the profits for each, or on terms of sharing what remains. —*Pirké Nathan 40*

Tosefta

The Tosefta is four times the length of the Mishnah, and is organized according to the same divisions. The Jerusalem Talmud sometimes quotes the Tosefta extensively. Two such passages are given below.

It has been repeated in the name of R. Simeon, "For the following five reasons, a person must set aside produce as *peah* only while harvesting the rear of his field: "On account of robbery from the poor, the idleness of the poor, deceivers, appearance's sake, and because the Torah has dictated, 'You shall not reap to the very corner of your field' *(Lev. 19:9)*.

"Robbery from the poor—how so? This assures that the time will never come when there is no poor person there in the field to collect *peah*, such that the farmer may say to a poor relative, 'Come and collect all of this *peah* for yourself.' [If the farmer was allowed to designate all of the *peah* for his own family, the other poor people in the town would not have fair access to the produce, thus robbing them of what rightfully is theirs *(cf. M. Peah 8:6)*.]

"The idleness of the poor—how so? This assures that poor people will not be sitting around and watching the farmer all day saying, 'Now he is designating *peah!* Now he is designating *peah!*' Rather, since the farmer designates produce as *peah* while harvesting the rear of his field, the poor person may go about his business, and may return to collect the *peah* at the end of the harvest.

"Appearance's sake—how so? This assures that passersby will not say, 'Behold how So-and-so harvested his field and did not designate any produce as *peah!* For so it is written in Torah, 'You shall not reap all the way to the edges of your field' *(Lev. 19:9)*. That is, since the produce actually designated as *peah* will have been collected before the farmer finishes harvesting his field, when he does finish it will appear that he never designated any produce.

"Deceivers—how so? This assures that a deceiver does not retain the highest quality produce for himself, and designate *peah* from the lowest quality. Instead, he must designate produce while harvesting the rear of his field, regardless of its quality, high or low.

"And because the Torah has dictated, 'You shall not reap all the way to the edges of your field'" *(Lev. 19:9) (Tosefta Peah 1:6)*
—*Yerushalmi Peah 4:3 (excerpts)*.

Monobases the king of Abianbene went and gave away to the poor all of his possessions during years of famine. His relatives sent the following message to him: "Your ancestors increased the wealth left for them by their ancestors. But you went and gave away both your own and those of your ancestors!"

He replied to them, "All the more reason for my actions! While my ancestors stored up for this lower world, I, through giving charity, have stored up treasures for the heavenly world above, as it is stated in Scripture, 'Hail the charitably-just man, for he shall fare well; he shall eat the fruit of his works' *(Isa. 3:10)*. My ancestors stored up treasures in places where a thief's hand can reach, but I stored up treasures for the non-material world, where no thief's hand can reach, as it is stated in Scripture, 'Charitable–righteousness and justice are the base of your throne; steadfast love and faithfulness stand before you' *(Ps. 89:15)*. My ancestors stored up treasures of money, but I have stored up treasures of souls, as it is stated in Scripture, 'The fruit of the charitably-righteous is a tree of life; and a wise man saves people's souls' *(Prov. 11:30)*. My ancestors stored up treasures that eventually, after their deaths, would benefit only others, but I have stored up treasures that will benefit myself both in life and in death, as it is stated in Scripture, 'It will be to your charitable-merit before the Lord your God' *(Deut. 24:13)*. My ancestors stored up treasures in this world, but I have stored up treasures for myself in the world-to-come, as it is stated in Scripture, 'Charitable-righteousness saves from death' *(Prov. 10:2)*— now the term 'death' here means only that one who gives charity will not die an eternal death."

Charity and acts of loving-kindness outweigh all other religious duties in the Torah. Nevertheless, charity can be given only to the living, but acts of loving-kindness can be performed for the living and the dead. Charity is given only to poor people, but acts of loving-kindness are done for both poor and rich people. Charity is given as aid for a poor person's finances, but acts of loving-kindness aid both a poor person's finances and his physical needs *(T. Peah 4:18-19)*.

Zohar

The Zohar means "The Way of Splendor." It was compiled by Moses de Leon, who claimed its contents to be the work of a mystic from the second century whose teachings had been transmitted orally and secretly until his time. *The Zohar* is considered the most important writing of the *Kabbalah*, the Jewish mystical tradition of the 11th–13th centuries.

Rabbi Shim'on opened and said, "Anyone who rejoices on the festivals and does not give the Blessed Holy One His portion, that stingy one with the evil eye, Satan, Archenemy, appears and accuses him, removes him from the world. Oh, how much trouble and suffering he brings upon him!

What is the portion of the Blessed Holy One? To gladden the poor as best as one can. For on these days the Blessed Holy One comes to observe His broken vessels. He enters from above and if He sees that they have nothing to celebrate He cries over them. Then he ascends to destroy the world!

The members of the Academy of Heaven appear before Him and declare: "Master of the world! You are called Compassionate and Gracious. May Your Compassion be aroused for Your children!" He answers them: "Does not everyone know that I based the world solely on love? 'I have said, "The world is built by love"' *(Psalms 89:3)* It is love that sustains the world!"

The angels on high then declare: "Master of the world! Look at so-and-so who is eating and drinking his fill. He could share something with the poor but he gives them nothing at all!" Then the Accuser steps forward, claims authority and sets out in pursuit of that human being.

Who in the world was greater than Abraham? He was kindhearted to all creatures. One day he prepared a feast, as it is written: "The child grew up and was weaned, and Abraham held a great feast on the day that Isaac was weaned" *(Genesis 21:8)*. To this feast Abraham invited all the great people of his time.

Now we have learned that the Accuser comes to every joyous meal to see if the host has already provided for the poor or invited the poor into his home. If so, the Accuser departs and does not enter. If not, he enters and witnesses this chaos of joy without the poor, without gifts for the poor. Then he rises above and accuses the host.

When Abraham welcomed all those great people the Accuser descended and stood at the door disguised as a poor man. But no one noticed him. Abraham was serving the kings and celebrities. Sarah was nursing all their children, because no one believed that she had given birth: they said, "It is a foundling from off the street!" So Sarah took their children who had come along and nursed them in front of everyone, as it is written: "Who would have said to Abraham that Sarah would suckle children?" *(Genesis 21:7)*, "Children," in the plural!

Meanwhile, the Accuser was still at the door. Sarah said, "God has made me a laughingstock!" *(Genesis 21:6)*. At once, the Accuser rose to face the Blessed Holy One. He said, "Master of the world! You call Abraham "My friend"? *(Isaiah 41:8)*. He held a feast and gave nothing to me and nothing to the poor; not even a single dove did he present to You! Furthermore, Sarah says that You made fun of her!" The Blessed Holy One responded "Who in the world is like Abraham?"

But he held his ground until he ruined the whole celebration and the Blessed Holy One commanded that Isaac be brought as an offering and it was decreed that Sarah would die in anguish over her son's ordeal.

All that suffering Abraham brought about because he gave nothing to the poor!" *—Commentary on Genesis 22:1-10*

ENDNOTES

1   The implication is that there is to be no usury among Israelites, but that interest could be collected from a non-Israelite. However, by concluding the passage with a strong declaration of the compassion of God, the implication is that Israelites are meant to be compassionate as well.

2   The implication is that we are to behave as God behaves. While in the context of verse 18, loving one's neighbor as one loves oneself is restricted to Israelites, verses 33-34 extend that mandate to include resident aliens.

3   The NRSV uses "neighbor" in place of the TANAKH's "kinsman." In this context, a neighbor is defined as a member of the covenant community of the Israelites.

4   The moral of the story: neither the righteousness nor the transgressions of a previous generation are transferable to the next.

5   An ephah is a dry measure, approximately 10-20 liters.

6   THE NRSV translates this as "poor soul".

7   An excerpt from a letter from King Hezekiah to the people of Israel and Judah.

8   Hebrew places the adjective after the noun. Thus, if one pauses after the word "man", the meaning could be obscured and the phrase could be taken to mean anyone—rich as well as poor. The point here is that God considers the situation of the poor to be the more urgent.

9   i.e., legal evidence.

10 In Hebrew, the words for *tamarisk* and *ask* are formed by the same three consonants. Commentaries explain that these three letters form an acrostic for the Hebrew words for food, drink, and escort—the ingredients of hospitality.

11 The bracketed comments are by the translator.

12 The message is that we have no choice but to act, to respond to need.

13 In other words, we are not to judge others until we have stood in their shoes.

14 J. Hertz, ed., *Sayings of the Fathers* (New York: Behrman House, 1945).

15 See note 10 above.

Chapter Six

Readings on Judaism and Social Justice

Jewish scripture and tradition are replete with mandates to work for social justice. To meet the needs of others is a *mitzvah* —a good deed in obedience to God's instructions to humanity. Jewish philanthropy is well known. For example, Jews played a significant role in the civil rights movement of the mid-twentieth century. The following articles explain the Jewish theoretical basis for action on behalf of others, and provide illustrations as well of theory put to practice.

Toward a Just and Compassionate Society: A Jewish View
Byron L. Sherwin

The author is the Vice-President for Academic Affairs at the Spertus Institute of Jewish Studies in Chicago. This article was presented in the summer of 1995 in Warsaw, Poland, at the annual meeting of the International Council of Christians and Jews.

The Talmud tells that a certain Rabbi Joseph once became ill and he slipped into a coma. His father, Rabbi Joshua ben Levi, remained by his bedside, praying. Fortunately, Rabbi Joseph recovered. When he awoke from his coma, his father asked him: "What did you see as you hovered between this world and the next world?" Said Rabbi Joseph, "I saw a world turned upside down. I saw a topsy-turvy world." Rabbi Joshua listened, thought for a while, and said, "You saw a clear vision of how things really are. You saw the world as it is" (*Pesahim* 50a). As we move toward the third millennium, there is a sense of ending, but not a sense of a new beginning. There are many predictions of imminent catastrophe— ecological, military, nuclear, political, social, and economic—but few expectations of an oncoming renaissance. We are searching for our balance while living through an earthquake. In the words of the poet Matthew Arnold, we are "wandering between two worlds, one dead and the other powerless to be born."

The topsy-turvy world seen by Rabbi Joseph is our world. Many of the cultural, social, political, and economic conditions that we assumed to be lasting have been jarred off their moorings. Many of the values, ideologies, and institutions that seemed firmly in place not so long ago, have been shaken to their core. Foci of meaning and purpose, which served as the foundation for our individual and national identities, have been cast adrift. Rather than remaining clear and reliable, they have become vague and amorphous. The challenge before us is to apply our tradition, our inherited wisdom to our contemporary problem.

Justice and mercy are attributes of God. Without justice, evil would have license to run rampant; with mercy retribution for misdeeds would destroy the world. When divine justice is left unchecked, the problem of theodicy becomes inevitable. God's prayer,

> May it be My will that My mercy may suppress My anger, and that My mercy shall prevail over My other attributes, so that I may deal with My children in the attribute of mercy, and, on their behalf, restrain My attribute of strict justice (*Berakhot* 7a),

demonstrates that God is aware of the danger to creatures should divine justice remain unrestrained. God's attribute of mercy must always remain somewhat dominant over that of justice.

In the rabbinic and kabbalistic view, human deeds are the necessary catalyst in stimulating the divine flow of justice and compassion in the world.[1] For example, a verse in Deuteronomy (13:18) states, "God will show you mercy and will have compassion on you." The Talmud interprets this verse to mean that God is compassionate to those who are compassionate to others; to those who are not compassionate to others, compassion is not shown (*Sabbath* 151b). Furthermore, a verse in Isaiah (5:16) states that "The Lord of Hosts is exalted through justice." A midrash interprets this to mean that God is exalted through our doing justice. The text reads, "Because you exalt me through justice, I will act with righteousness and cause My holiness to dwell among you. And if you practice justice and righteousness, I will redeem you with a complete redemption" (*Deut. Rabbah* 5:7).

In the human realm, there also must be a polarity of justice and mercy, law and love. Each person, each society, must try to have the wisdom to know when to keep them in balance, as well as when one should take precedence over the other. For example, parents or teachers who show only compassion toward their children or students will leave them undisciplined, bereft of intellectual and moral guidance. One who is too compassionate toward the wicked will give them license to pursue their evil deeds. A judge who is too compassionate can no longer offer impartial justice. Though cruelty is considered among the worst moral vices (e.g., Jer. 6:23), there are nonetheless times when even cruelty—the opposite of compassion—is necessary. As a midrash puts it, "A person who is merciful when cruelty is needed will end up becoming cruel when mercy is needed" (*Eccles. Rabbah* 7:15, 1).

In Greek thought, justice is largely viewed as being retributive and distributive, as giving people their due. In Jewish thought, justice is largely viewed as being substantive. Justice is not only something one should *do,* but something one should *be.* A person should strive to *be* just. The just person is the foundation for the just society. But the goal of justice is not only that all should get what is coming to them. The more important goal is the formation of a just society, the enhancement of social life. However, society is always in formation. The completely just society or the completely compassionate society are not features of historical times, but only of messianic times. Indeed, there is a tradition that in messianic times, the distinction between justice and mercy will be eliminated. In historical times, justice and mercy both conflict and coexist. But in messianic times, they will become identical.

A society without justice leads to moral anarchy and destruction. A society where justice is perverted is endangered. Justice tends to follow the rule of law, the rule of reason. Compassion tends to follow the rule of the heart. One needs to know not only when to temper law and justice with compassion, but also when to go beyond the limits of the law, beyond the strict dictates of justice, to do what is right. This is the role of righteousness which is wedged between justice and compassion. As Nahmanides said, "It is possible to be a moral scoundrel within the strict limits of the law."

According to the Hebrew prophets and the talmudic rabbis, when righteousness is not part of the social fabric, a society's very stability is endangered.[2] But complete righteousness is impossible to attain. Until messianic redemption, there is no righteous person, and no society that can claim to be completely righteous, compassionate, and just. But while complete justice, compassion, and righteousness elude our grasp, we must nonetheless strive to be just, compassionate, and righteous. The way toward a just, righteous, and compassionate society must include three kinds of action: fighting against wickedness and injustice that already exist; trying to prevent additional wickedness and injustice from occurring (as with health care, preventive measures can allay the later need to deal with pathological phenomena); trying to improve the moral and spiritual quality of society by infusing the world with appropriate measures of justice, righteousness, and compassion. It is not a question of a just and compassionate society or one that is its opposite; rather, social and moral life exists on a spectrum. On one end is absolute wickedness—the completely corrupt society; on the other, is the messianic world. Our task is to try to prevent society from moving toward the pole of wickedness, and to enable it to move closer toward the pole of messianic redemption.

What can people of religious faith do to move toward a just, righteous, and compassionate society?

1. They can try to act justly, righteously, and with compassion. The starting point for building such a society is with the self. People of faith must set the standard for moral behavior. But this has not always been a feature of religious life in our century. Instead of interfaith fraternity, our century has witnessed and continues to witness ecumenical genocide. The Holocaust, the war in Viet Nam, the continuing slaughter in Bosnia, are examples.

Religions cannot expect to be credible in the opposition to strife unless they first eliminate triumphalism, strife, and injustice within and among themselves. Either we are *all* children of God or none of us are. As Malachi said (2:10): "Have

we not all one Father? Has not one God created us? Why then are we faithless
to one another, profaning the covenant of our ancestors?"

Commenting on the description of human beings as children of God,
Matthew Arnold wrote, "Children of God—it is an immense pretension—and
how are we to justify it? By the works we do and by the words we speak." Or
as Rabbi Aaron of Karlin put it, "What is the greatest sin a person can commit?:
To forget that he is a prince—a child of God, the King."

Job reminds us (31:15), "Did not God who made me in the womb make him?
Did not One God fashion us in the womb?" The Hebrew word for womb, *rehem,*
is etymologically linked to the word for compassion—*rahamin.* Compassion is
our link to one another and our link to God, whom the talmudic rabbis called
Rahmana—the Compassionate One.

2. Rather than combat one another, people of faith should join together to
fight common enemies, while following the advice of the talmudic rabbis to
despise and destroy the sin and not the sinner *(Berakhot 10a).* Our greatest
threats come from ideologies that deny human dignity and integrity, that teach
cynicism and nihilism.

3. Despite adversity, people of faith must be optimists—even against their
better judgment. This means affirming that there is meaning despite absurdity,
that there is redemption awaiting us at the twilight of history. But this optimism
must be neither utopian nor naïve. As Reinhold Niebuhr said, "If democratic
nations fail, their failure must be partly attributed to the faulty strategy of
idealists who have too many illusions when they face realists who have too little
conscience."

People of faith must learn how to employ love *and* law, justice *and* mercy,
compassion and sometimes *even* cruelty. In the battle against evil, love and
compassion are not adequate weapons. Although the messianic age will be an age
of justice, righteousness, compassion, and peace, meanwhile, there is war
injustice, and corruption. As long as our world remains unredeemed there are no
facile solutions to complex social problems; we must accept the fact that no social
order is completely perfectible, that the best we do can never be enough.

4. While human beings can work to make the world worthy of redemption,
they cannot redeem the world. They can accelerate redemption; they can
increase justice and compassion, but they cannot initiate a Messianic Age. As
Abraham Heschel wrote, "In messianic times evil will be conquered by the God
who is one, but in historical times, evils must be conquered one by one."[3] The
human task is not to bring the Messiah, but to bring about the realization of
holiness in history. We are to work in partnership with God in the fight against
evil, separating the evil from the good, moving society from injustice toward
justice, from cruelty to compassion, from corruption to holiness. The human goal
is to correlate our reality with the statement God made when the world was
created: "And God saw that it was good."

5. For people of faith, social action must be grounded in authentic theological
foundations. Theological scholars must find ways of relating the wisdom of the
past to the perplexities of the present. Religious ethics is a form of applied
theology. Theologians, scholars, and clergy cannot remain cloistered in acad-

emies, churches, and synagogues insulated from the problems that afflict our society. They must not only think actively but act actively as well. As a midrash puts it, "If a person in need comes to a scholar to help obtain justice, and he responds: I am occupied with my studies, I have no time. Whereupon God proclaims to such a scholar: I consider you responsible for the chaos of society" (*Exod. Rabbah* 30:10). Prerogatives for social action cannot be surrendered to politicians. According to Rabbi Mendel of Kotsk, the challenge to people of faith is to be mixed up with the sometimes dirty business of the world and yet to be able to have clean hands.

6. Soon we shall enter a new century, a new millennium. As André Malraux said, "The third millennium must be a spiritual millennium or there will be no third millennium."

In a world in search of spiritual moorings, our religious traditions can offer a wealth of wisdom, experience, and moral direction. People of faith are the custodians of those values which are the basis of all social justice and order. Ultimately, human dignity, human integrity, and the intrinsic sanctity of human life are theological axioms that rest upon the assumptions that there is a God and that we are created in the image of God. People of faith are the custodians of those ideas and values that are the ingredients for a life of moral and spiritual integrity. Their task is to keep those ideas and values alive, to cherish and to practice them, to convey them to a world whose very survival depends upon them. Finally, people of faith must realize that their judgments are partial, their achievements are limited, their grasp of truth remains flawed, their access to God's will is imperfect. The best one can do, in the words of Abraham Lincoln, is to act "with malice toward none, with charity for all, and with firmness in the right as God gives us to see the right, let us strive to finish the work we are in. . . ."

The Obligation of Tzedakah
Harold Kushner

Harold Kushner has been a rabbi for over thirty years, and has written several bestselling books.

Two major Jewish institutions serve as "calisthenics" to teach us to control our acquisitiveness without asking us to become so otherworldly that we forgo all the goods of this world in a kind of economic celibacy. One is the Sabbath, not only a day of rest from arduous physical labor, but a truce in the economic competition between us and the people around us. The second is the obligation of *tzedakah*, which is usually translated as "charity" but really means something closer to "doing the right thing." (Another example of the difficulty of trying to understand a culture while studying it in translation.) *Charity* implies that I give to the poor because I am a generous person. *Tzedakah* means that I give to the poor, even if I don't feel like giving, because Judaism tells me I should. It tells me that God has chosen to make me His intermediary in passing something on to the poor, so that I will be included in the good deed, but I have no right to keep that portion of my wealth for myself any more than the postman has the right to keep for himself a check addressed to me.

If you saw the play or movie *Fiddler on the Roof,* you may remember an exchange early in the play in which a man gives a beggar a coin. The beggar tells him, "Last week, you gave me more." The man answers. "I had a bad week," to which the beggar responds, "Just because *you* had a bad week, why should I suffer?" The exchange accurately captures the Jewish view that *tzedakah* is an obligation, not an act of charity.

I hesitate to make too much of this, but we may have a philosophical difference between Judaism and Christianity here. Is the purpose of charity to inculcate generosity in us or to provide sustenance for the poor? Both, obviously, but I think Christianity would emphasize the former a shade more, and Judaism the latter. In that famous passage in the Gospels *(Matthew 26:6-13)* in which a woman pours expensive oil on Jesus' head and the disciples scold her, saying she could have sold the oil and given the money to the poor, Jesus supports the woman, saying, "You will always have the poor with you"—that is, what you don't do for the poor today, you will be able to do for them tomorrow or next week— "but you will not always have me." The words 'the poor you will always have with you" come from the Torah, in the Book of Deuteronomy, *but there they have the exact opposite meaning.*[4] "For the poor shall never cease out of the land; therefore I command you to open your hand to your poor and needy brother." In other words, because there will always be poor people, society has to find a way of sustaining them without making them depend on your having some money left over after your shopping and vacation.

Whatever our philosophical position on the subject of good deeds with or without generous feelings, it remains an important teaching of Judaism that our money is not really ours, no matter how hard we may have worked for it. It is a gift from God, and God has instructed us to share a portion of it with the less fortunate.

In three generations, we American Jews, through education and hard work, have become a remarkably successful community, carving out a place for ourselves in the middle and upper-middle class of American society (though there is no shortage of poor Jews, many of them elderly). But we are a remarkably charitable community as well. We give generously to Israel and to Jewish causes and institutions in this country, and we give just as generously to the Red Cross, United Way, and medical research, to museums and symphonies. I know of several predominantly Jewish country clubs where one of the requirements of membership is that you document your having given a certain percentage of your annual income to charity. Prospective members may not enjoy that requirement at first, but they learn to like it.

Those Who Give: The Link Between Charity and Religion
CQ Researcher

Americans who give to charity hail from all walks of life, but none are counted on more readily than members of organized religion. "Religious groups give more in grants than corporations and foundations combined," says Robert O. Bothwell, executive director of the National Committee for Responsive Philanthropy, a Washington-based watchdog group. "It's partly that the golden rule of religion is do unto others. . . but there's also an assumption that if life in the hereafter is important, it may be important to give away things now."

A clear correlation betwen generous giving and regular attendance at worship was reflected in a 1992 Gallup Poll conducted for Independent Sector. "Respondents who attended religious services weekly gave 2.7 percent of their average household income in 1987, 3.8 percent in 1989, and 3.2 percent in 1991," it noted. "Those who did not attend services in the past year or never attended gave 1.1 percent of their household income in 1987, 0.8 percent in 1989, and 0.6 percent in 1991."

The link between charity and religion is particularly strong among the Jews. "You have to go into Jewish history and law to understand how deeply felt it is, and how very basic," a Jewish philanthropist and fundraiser has said. "The Talmud, which is the written law, makes one feel very strongly about tzedakah. The literal translation of it is righteousness, but in common usage, it's come to mean charity. . . The fact that this is a guiding principle of our religion means that every Jewish child understands. They start out in their first Jewish educational experiences giving for some Jewish purpose. The reason that it's for Jewish purposes and why the Jewish Community is so highly organized is because throughout our history, we have always lived a little bit outside of the general society; it has been the feeling of both Jews and the general community that Jews must take care of their own needs."

The Jewish emphasis on helping one's own, notes a spokesman for the United Jewish Appeal, does not mean that Jewish charities do not benefit non-Jews. "Jewish-supported hospitals, for example, often have as many non-Jews as patients as Jews," he says. "It means taking care of our neighbors so they don't have to apply for welfare or beg on the streets."

Ladder of Charity
Maimonides

Moses ben Maimon(1135–1204) well deserves to be called one of the most brilliant minds of all time, one who made outstanding contributions to the fields of talmudic scholarship, philosophy, medicine, astronomy, and mathematics. His *Mishneh Torah* parallels the Mishnah in organization. His classic statement on the proper approach to benevolent action comes from the division called *Pe'ah* (Seeds). Note that the Hebrew word *tzedakah* can be translated both as charity and as righteousness.

We are obligated to be more scrupulous in fulfilling the commandment of charity
[tzedakah] than any other positive commandment because charity is the sign of
the righteous man, the seed of Abraham our Father, as it is said, "For I know him,
that he will command his children. . . and do righteousness *[tzedakah]* (Gen.
18:19). The throne of Israel is established and the religion of truth is upheld only
through charity, as it is said, "In righteousness shall you be established" (Is.
54:14). Israel is redeemed only through charity, as it is written, "Zion shall be
redeemed with judgment and they that return of her with righteousness" (Is.
1:27).

No man has ever become impoverished by giving charity and no evil or
damage has ever resulted from charity, as it is said, "and the work of righteousness is peace" (Is. 32:17).

There are eight degrees of charity, one higher than the other. The highest
degree, exceeded by none, is that of the person who assists a poor Jew by
providing him with a gift or a loan or by accepting him into a business
partnership or by helping him find employment—in a word, by putting him
where he can dispense with other people's aid. With reference to such aid, it is
said, "You shall strengthen him, be he a stranger or a settler, he shall live with
you" (Lev. 25:35), which means strengthen him in such manner that his falling
into want is prevented.

A step below this stands the one who gives alms to the needy in such manner
that the giver knows not to whom he gives and the recipient knows not from
whom it is that he takes. Such exemplifies performing the meritorious act for its
own sake. An illustration would be the Hall of Secrecy in the ancient sanctuary
where the righteous would place their gift clandestinely and where poor people
of high lineage would come and secretly help themselves to succor.

The rank next to this is of him who drops money in the charity box. One
should not drop money in the charity box unless one is sure that the person in
charge is trustworthy, wise, and competent to handle the funds properly, as was
Rabbi Hananya ben Teradyon [a man renown for his scrupulousness].

One step lower is that in which the giver knows to whom he gives but the
poor person knows not from whom he receives. Examples of this were the great
sages who would go forth and throw coins covertly into poor peoples' doorways.
This method becomes fitting and exalted, should it happen that those in charge
of the charity fund do not conduct its affairs properly.

A step lower is that in which the poor person knows from whom he is taking
but the giver knows not to whom he is giving. Examples of this were the great
sages who would tie their coins in their scarves which they would fling over their
shoulders so that the poor might help themselves without suffering shame.

The next degree lower is that of him who, with his own hand, bestows a gift
before the poor person asks.

The next degree lower is that of him who gives less than is fitting, but gives
with a gracious mien.

The next degree lower is that of him who gives morosely. —*Mishneh Torah:*
Pe'ah 10:1-2a, 7-14

The Twofold Charity of the Benevolent Physician
Hyman Hurwitz

Hurwitz, a 19th century rabbi, enjoyed imparting his own personal flavor to the stories he translated. This one comes from the Talmud.

Abba Umana, a Jewish physician, was as much celebrated for his piety and humanity, as for his medical skill. He made no distinction between rich and poor, and was particularly attentive to learned men, from whom he never would accept the least reward for his professional services; considering them as a sort of fellow-laborers, whose functions were still more important than his own; since they were destined to cure the diseases of the mind. Unwilling to deter people from profiting by his medical knowledge, yet not wishing to put anyone to the blush for the smallness of the fee they might be able to give, he had a box fixed in his antechamber, into which the patients threw such sums as they thought proper.

His fame spread far and wide. Abaye, who was then the chief of the Academy, heard of it; and wishing to know whether everything reported of that benevolent man was true, sent to him two of his disciples, who were slightly indisposed. The physician received them kindly, gave them some medicine, and requested them to stay in his house over night. The offer was readily accepted. They remained till the next morning, when they departed, taking with them a piece of tapestry, which had served as a covering to the couch on which they had slept. This they carried to the marketplace; and waiting till their kind host had arrived, pretended to offer it for sale, and asked him how much he thought it was worth. Abba Umana mentioned a certain sum.

"Dost thou not think it worth more?" asked the men.

"No," answered the physician; "this is the very sum I gave for one much like it."

"Why, good man." rejoined the disciples, "this is thine own: we took it from thy house. Now tell us truly, we beseech thee, after missing it, hadst thou not a very bad opinion of us?"

"Certainly not," replied the pious man; "ye know that a son of Israel must not impute evil intentions to anyone, nor judge ill of a neighbor by a single action; and since I was satisfied in my mind that no ill use would be made of it, let it be so. Sell it, and distribute the money among the poor." The disciples complied with his wishes, left him with admiration and thanks, and increased, by their report, his well-earned fame.

But the most noble trait in this good man's character was, that he never accepted any remuneration from the poor, and even provided them with everything that could, during their illness, contribute to their comfort; and when he had, by his skill and assiduity, restored them to health, he would give them money, and say, "Now, my children, go and purchase bread and meat; these are the best and only medicines you require." —*Ta'anit 21b*

Judaism and Community Service
Shamai Kanter

Shamai Kanter is rabbi of Temple Beth El in Rochester. He teaches Judaic Studies at St. John Fisher College and at the State University College at Brockport. In this article, Kanter delineates how the Jewish sense of community translates into service to each other.

To be part of "Israel" means to share the telling of a story: the description of the creation of the people. Central to the story is the narrative from the Exodus out of Egypt through the revelatory event at Sinai. The tribes assembled there claim to be part of one family: they are the children of Israel. Their sense of community will derive from their being addressed by God. But God's people is not a spiritual elite: neither a hereditary priesthood (though one will be later appointed) nor a group of seventy elder-prophets (later to be selected) but an entire people in the totality of its human being.

This is why every aspect of the life of Israelite society falls under the Covenant and its commandments. Not only belief, sacrifice, or ethics, but also diet, clothing, sexuality, etc. The relationship with God is diffuse, rather than specific; it includes every aspect of behavioral and emotional life. And the relationship is affective, rather than neutral. A passionate God establishes a highly emotional people, concerned with what happens to each other.

Also, though Israel cherishes many cosmic values, it is highly particularistic, regularly retelling the stories of family squabbles as if they were of eternal importance (convincing a goodly portion of the world that this is indeed so); and it is embarrassingly assertive (considering its minor political, economic, and artistic status) of its central significance for humankind.

As in a family, being "Israel" is an ascribed rather than achieved status. Even when Israel gives birth to the concept of conversion, conversion itself is viewed as the birth of the individual retroactively (!) to Abraham and Sarah. And rabbinic tradition will proclaim that even the individual's climactic achievement of an afterlife, the World to Come, derives from being part of "all Israel" who share in it.

The group experience imposed upon Israel through Exodus–Sinai is not an expression of primitive tribal psychological fusion. It is addressed to people who were very much individuals (which helps explain the frustrating orneriness presented by the Israelites to their leaders, whether prophet, judge, priest, or king). The value for us is this: Israel may turn out to be what biblical narrative assumes that it is intended to be: a paradigm for human community.

Rabbinic Judaism is the continuator of the role of Israel as both community of faith and community of fate. We can accept the observation of Thomas Sowell that a little bit of oppression is helpful to create community feeling and creative incentive. But it should be recalled that another requirement is some kind of positive cultural content.

Ben Zoma uses the example of fresh bread in the morning to teach the idea of community (b. Ber. 58a): Adam had to plow, sow, harvest, thresh, grind the flour, knead, and bake before he could eat. But I get up and find it all prepared for me! Eleazar ben Azariah uses the parable of people in a boat (Lev. R. 4.6):

One of them drills a hole in the hull. His fellow passengers try to stop him. He asks, "Why should it bother you? I'm only drilling beneath my own seat!"

But what fleshes out community in rabbinic tradition is a network of voluntary small groups that bridge the gap between the individual and the People of Israel. All of the terms describing such groups that I list below are derived from either liturgy or the legal tradition and were adopted by people drawn to a particular kind of activity through personal interest and responsibility:

Malbish Arumim (clothing the naked)—clothing for the poor. (A contemporary variation would be a "library" of wedding gowns, currently operating in Brooklyn and in Jerusalem.)

Ozer Dalim (helping the poor)—charity fund

Bet Yetomim—orphanages

Talmud Toraic—scholarships for religious education

Hevra Mishnayot/Hevra Shas—small circles for the study of rabbinic law, either Mishnah or Talmud. (Other groups might specialize in the Five Books of Moses or the recitation of Psalms.)

Bikur Holim (visiting the sick)—providing medicine for the poor visitation for the sick

Haknassat Orhim (welcoming travelers)—temporary shelter

Haknassat Kallah (welcoming the bride)— funds for wedding celebrations and personal involvement in such celebrations

Moshav Zekenim (residence of the aged)

Hevra ra Kadisha (holy fellowship)—preparing bodies for burial. (The catalogue of the exhibit from the Prague Jewish Museum, entitled "Precious Legacy," includes a remarkable series of the eighteenth century paintings chronicling the activities of such a group.)

Gemilut Hesed (deeds of covenantal love)—providing interest-free loans

Maot Hitim (wheat funds)—providing for Passover celebrations for the poor

Pidyon Shevuim (redemption of captives)— ransom for people taken hostage

Within Judaism it is the force of the idea of being commanded that creates the primary experience of community. This is the source on the level of folk religion of otherwise puzzling behavior, still observable today. Jews are especially successful in certain kinds of charitable endeavors, those which concern the safety or welfare of overseas Jewish communities. When the representatives of such charitable enterprises approach a prospective donor, they do so with total absence of reticence and with remarkable vigor. Within the community value system, they are doing him the favor, not the reverse: It is his responsibility to help. They are doing something for him by providing the possibility for him to fulfill an obligation. The otherwise embarrassing experience of asking someone for money has been transformed because, in rabbinic terms, "All Israel are responsible for each other." In effect, the recognition of being part of "Israel" carries with it the consciousness of common fate and responsibility.

The Wisdom of Heschel
Ruth Marcus Goodhill

When Rabbi Abraham Joshua Heschel died on December 23, 1972, the world mourned the loss both of a great scholar and a far-reaching social activist. Understanding his heritage and his life story helps us better understand the impact he had on matters of religion and society.

Heschel came from a family boasting seven generations of Hasidic rabbis, spiritual leaders in a form of Polish Jewish mysticism they had helped to establish. His early years were spent in Poland, but he earned his Ph.D. from the University of Berlin, receiving that degree in 1933. In 1934, he graduated again—this time from the Hochschule für die Wissenschaft des Judentums, also in Berlin. Three major books published in the next three successive years established his reputation as a major Jewish scholar. However, the Nazi presence forced him to return to Poland in 1938. That country likewise quickly became unsafe for Jews; in 1940, Heschel fled to London, and in a matter of months, emigrated to the United States, where he would teach at the Hebrew Union College of Cincinnati, Ohio, until 1945.

From 1945–1960, Heschel joined the faculty of the Jewish Theological Seminary of America, New York City, and became much in demand as a lecturer all over the country. In the 1960s, he served as a visiting professor at several major universities. Most significantly, his highly successful year as a visiting professor at Union Theological Seminary, New York City—a school for the training of Protestant clergy—was the first time a Jew had ever held a position on the faculty there. He received national acclaim for facilitating dialogue and understanding between Christians and Jews, proclaimed all the more in 1964, when he journeyed to the Vatican for a meeting with Pope Paul VI. While this upset many Jews at the time, the ultimate outcome was the Vatican II statement that the Jews would no longer be held guilty for the Crucifixion by the Roman Catholic Church, which would now allow a far more liberal attitude toward non-Christians than before. This effort on Heschel's part is merely one of many examples of his fostering of interfaith dialogue.

As a social activist, Heschel was in the forefront of religious leaders speaking out against the Vietnam War through his position as co-chair of an organization called Clergy Concerned About Vietnam, and his willingness to confront President Johnson and the political establishment. He also strove against racism, and was a leader in the American civil rights movement, marching with Martin Luther King to Selma, Alabama, an experiences during which he is widely quoted to have said that he felt as if his legs were praying!

Heschel is an example of a man who, in many significant ways, put his faith into action for the betterment of society. Writing on March 24, 1975, Heschel's friend, Ruth Marcus Goodhill, offers her reflections on his life, which are followed by a few of the excerpts she collected from his voluminous writings.

Goodhill on Heschel

Rabbi Heschel was a devout Jew whose compassion embraced all mankind. "My major concern is the human situation," he once said. "I maintain that the agony of contemporary man is the agony of the spiritually stunted man." In the same spirit he held that "the main theme of Jewish law is the person rather than an institution," and that "the highest peak of spiritual living is not necessarily reached in rare moments of ecstasy; the highest peak lies wherever we are and may be ascended in a common deed. Religion is not made for extraordinary occasions." He epitomized his interpretation of law in this definition: "An act of injustice is condemned, not because the law is broken, but because a person has been hurt."

Heschel was in the forefront of every human concern. In the spring of 1965, he marched with Martin Luther King, Jr., at Selma, Alabama; he was a leader in the protests against American policy in Vietnam; he participated in many civil-rights marches and peace rallies. Following the Six-Day War in 1967, he responded to the historic moment with his book *Israel: An Echo of Eternity.* He was one of the first to urge world Jewry to come to aid of Soviet Jews. He was a strong ecumenist, urging Christian–Jewish dialogue. He was frequently invited to the Vatican and was asked to speak on prayer on Italian radio and television. Although he suffered a near-fatal heart attack in 1969, he continued his strenuous activities in behalf of human rights.

All humanity was his concern. "To be human," he said, "is to be involved, to act and to react, to wonder and to respond. For man to be is to play a part in a cosmic drama, knowingly or unknowingly." As he saw it, "Living involves responsible understanding of one's role in relation to all other beings." He also wrote: "God in the universe is a spirit of concern for life . . . We often fail in trying to understand Him, not because we do not know how to extend our concepts far enough, but because we do not know how to begin close enough. To think of God is not to find Him as an object in our minds, but to find ourselves in Him."

Following his sudden death, tribute was paid to him the world over. In this country, the Jesuit publication *America* devoted an entire issue (March 10, 1973) to Heschel's memory. [5] The editor stated: "Each of you, our readers, will have his own lesson to learn from Abraham Joshua Heschel as he speaks to you of the living tradition of Judaism, in all its energy, holiness and compassion. May the God whom Jews, Christians and Muslims worship bring us to live together in peace and understanding and mutual appreciation ."

From Heschel's Writings

There are three ways in which we may relate ourselves to the world—we may exploit it, we may enjoy it, we may accept it in awe.

I see the sick and the despised, the defeated and the bitter, the rejected and the lonely. I see them clustered together and alone, clinging to a hope for somebody's affection that does not come to pass. I hear them pray for release that comes with death. I see them deprived and forgotten, masters yesterday, outcasts today.

What we owe the old is reverence, but all they ask for is consideration, attention, not to be discarded and forgotten. What they deserve is prefer-ence, yet we do not even grant them equality. One father finds it possible to sustain a dozen children, yet a dozen children find it impossible to sustain one father.

Care for the old is regarded as an act of charity rather than as a supreme privilege. In the never-dying utterance of the Ten Commandments, the God of Israel did not proclaim: Honor me, revere me. He proclaimed instead: Revere your father and your mother. There is no reverence for God without reverence for father and mother.

The test of a people is how it behaves toward the old. It is easy to love children. Even tyrants and dictators make a point of being fond of children. But affection and care for the old, the incurable, the helpless, are the true gold mines of a culture.

Righteousness goes beyond justice. Justice is strict and exact, giving each person his due. Righteousness implies benevolence, kindness, generosity.

Justice may be legal; righteousness is associated with a burning compassion for the oppressed.

In a sense, the calling of the prophet may be described as that of an advocate or champion, speaking for those who are too weak to plead their own cause. Indeed, the major activity of the prophets was *interference,* remonstrating about wrongs inflicted on other people, meddling in affairs which were seemingly neither their concern nor their responsibility.

Justice is an interpersonal relationship, implying both a claim and a responsibility. Justice bespeaks a situation that transcends the individual, demanding from everyone a certain abnegation of self, defiance of self-interest, disregard of self-respect. The necessity of submitting to a law is derived from the necessity of identifying oneself with what concerns other individuals or the whole community of men.

The prophets proclaimed that justice is omnipotent, that right and wrong are dimensions of world history, not merely modes of conduct. The existence of the world is contingent upon right and wrong. The validity of justice and the motivation for its exercise lie in the blessings it brings to man. Justice exists in relation to a person. An act of injustice is condemned, not because the law is broken, but because a person has been hurt.

Affirmative Actions
Alyson Gold

Jews have been in the forefront of the American civil rights movement since its inception. Countless Jews marched arm-in-arm with Blacks during the demonstrations of the 1960s. Two Jewish young men—Andrew Goodman and Michael Schwerner—along with their African-American friend James Chaney, were murdered when they arrived in Mississippi to aid in the registration of Black voters. Yet the 1990s have witnessed a strain between these two groups. Alyson Gold, a staff writer for the B'nai B'rith *International Jewish Monthly,* documents several attempts at restoring a supportive relationship.

Lately it's been as clear as black and white: on campuses, in cities, across the nation, the black-Jewish relationship is in crisis. A Jewish-run store in Harlem is firebombed by a black assailant. At the University of Maryland, the Jewish student newspaper publishes a cartoon portraying a black campus leader as Hitler. Jews are vile and inhuman, and largely to blame for the slave trade, writes a black student in the Columbia University *Spectator.*

Crown Heights. The Million Man March. Segregated neighborhoods. The fears, misconceptions and causes for strife would seem overwhelming. But those who believe in the possibility of black-Jewish unity point out that the two groups share much in common: a profound experience of injustice, a mutual commitment to the civil rights movement, and similar voting patterns that should make them formidable political allies.

Seventeen-year-old Taneesha Guy is dedicated to such a partnership. An African-American female, Guy attended the Million Man March in Washington, DC this fall and stood arm-in-arm with her recently-acquired friends—Jewish student Melissa Pollack.

Guy and Pollack met earlier this year through Project Interchange's youth program, a long-term black-Jewish dialogue group based in Washington, DC. Along with dozens of other high-school and college students participating in the project and two other similar groups—Operation Understanding Philadelphia and Operation Understanding DC—Guy and Pollack are determined to make this partnership a reality.

But is it possible that such programs can break down barriers, hash out differences and promote understanding—something some African-American and Jewish leaders have been unable or unwilling to do? And can these groups overcome their own serious obstacles: a sore lack of funding and support from segments of the community that place greater emphasis on other priorities? In fact, Project Interchange has canceled its youth program for next year, and though its leaders hope to start up again in 1998, they say they may have to postpone the program indefinitely.

Despite the groups difficulties, participants insist that they have a dramatic impact. "The experience was life-altering," says one student. "I'd like to tell you about it," he adds. "Do you have twenty-four hours?" Moreover, these three groups have an advantage many others lack: while most other student dialogue efforts offer only short-term programs—a trip to black and Jewish museums, a lecture series, an interfaith Seder—these groups sponsor ongoing, intensive projects that combine education, travel, follow-up work and community outreach.

Operation Understanding Philadelphia, the oldest of the three groups, has been bringing together black and Jewish high-school juniors for more than a decade. Each year, twelve participants are selected from scores of applicants based on their leadership abilities, interpersonal skills, and dedication to social change. Those selected embark on a year-and-a-half-long journey through six orientation sessions, a month in Israel and Africa, and a stint as peer educators in their communities.

Like the Philadelphia group, to which it is connected by name only, Operation Understanding DC relies on a rigorous application process to select some eighteen high-schoolers. Created last year by community activist Karen Kalish, the fifteen-month-long program consists of study, travel to black and Jewish sites in the United States, and speaking engagements upon return.

Project Interchange, which is run by an American Jewish Committee institute that also takes members of Congress to Israel, brings together African-American and Jewish campus leaders from Washington, DC's Howard and George Washington Universities for a semester-long seminar, a two-week study tour to South Africa and Israel, and on-campus follow-up sessions.

So what happens when you bring together an impressive group of young people from different cultures and backgrounds? Ostensibly, true feelings and race can be aired and examined; political views can be shouted and shifted; confessions of prejudice can be whispered; stereotypes can be shattered; and tears of empathy can be cried.

But is that, in fact, what happens? Well, not at first. At the beginning, during the orientation phase, politeness reigns. Operation Understanding Philadelphia participant Nicole Williams recalls that at the group's first meeting participants were all nervous, but cordial. "We were friendly, but tiptoed around each other at first, voicing little of our true viewpoints," adds Terry Bruner, a Howard University student who participated in Project Interchange. "It's easy to be friends," he notes, chuckling, "when you think you're in accord."

But meaningful encounters are not the goal of orientation, say leaders of all three groups. Instead, the early meeting are designed to provide participants with the tools they will need for later phases of the programs. These early sessions last between six and twelve weeks and include information about the places students will visit, an overview of contemporary black-Jewish relations, and lectures on African-American and Jewish history and culture from such notables as civil rights leaders Julian Bond and Hyman Bookbinder. "We want them to learn about their separate and shared pasts from people who were there," explains Operation Understanding DC Executive Director Karen Kalish.

Although the orientations may not be intensely emotional, students say they do have an effect. Before his orientation with Operation Understanding DC, Atiba de Souza says he thought of Jews as "just more whites," but, he explains, the program provided eye-opening information about Jewish history and culture. Prepared with the relevant historical and cultural contexts to help students "form the right questions," Sharon Kershbaum of Operation Understanding Philadelphia says participants are ready to travel.

For veterans of all three groups, the travel portion of the program is not simply a journey to Africa and Israel or to sites in the United States. It is, they say, a journey of self-discovery. As Operation Understanding DC participant Kim Barrett puts it: "The seventeen teenagers who left Union Station in Washington, DC on July 23, 1995, are not the same people who returned three short weeks later."

The trips are designed to encourage such transformations; itineraries don't simply include visits to historical sites but also provide glimpses into the struggles of real people, past and present. So, while Operation Understanding DC visited Ellis Island when in New York, they also met with blacks and Jews in Crown Heights and Harlem. And participants in Project Interchange not only climbed Masada, they also spoke with Israeli experts on Arab-Jewish relations and brought dolls and toys to needy children at an orphanage in an impoverished section of South Africa.

How do such visits affect participants? Students note that their insights came on different levels. Many say the trip helped them understand the other group much better than before. Others offer that they gained a greater understanding of their own culture and background.

Nicole Williams admits that before her journey with Operation Understanding Philadelphia she held a number of misconceptions about Jews, even though her private school is predominantly Jewish. She says that while much of the trip helped educate and enlighten her, one stop on the itinerary taught her more about Jewish history and Jewish-black relations than any other. That place was Yad Vashem—Jerusalem's Holocaust museum. "Throughout the whole trip I hadn't been moved," recounts the African-American teen. "But when I visited Yad Vashem, I was moved to tears. It was very, very painful. I knew before going that we, African-Americans and Jews, are all connected, but being there reminded me. I wasn't thinking, 'These Jews and I'm black; it didn't happen to my people.' I was thinking that we are all members of the human race."

Other students, like Terry Bruner of Howard University, say they learned almost as much about their own cultures as they did about the other group's. As a child, Bruner's father would tell him about the suffering blacks endured in South Africa and about freedom fighters who devoted their lives to raising up black people. So when Bruner had the opportunity to meet with and talk to Archbishop Desmond Tutu in Cape Town, South Africa, it was a watershed moment in his life. "The day I met Archbishop Tutu will weigh heavily on me forever," Bruner says, his voice brimming with emotion. "To meet a legend, a freedom fighter, it was incredible. And he was so kind and personable. Like a long-lost grandfather."

Similarly, Jewish student Emily Levin embraced her religion for the first time during the program. "I realized it is our job as Jews to show our African-American friends what Judaism is all about, and I began to feel proud," she notes.

While the visits inspire strong reactions, the experience of simply traveling together can itself open doors. Leaders and participants all note that the group dynamic changes significantly once the travel phase begins. Students spend nearly every hour together and as they become more familiar and comfortable with one another, former inhibitions melt away.

Back at hotel rooms after days full of touring, students sometimes found themselves having discussions that would stretch late into the night about such hot-button topics as stereotypes, interracial dating, and affirmative action. Often, participants in Operation Understanding Philadelphia say, humor was the best way to deal with stereotypes. One night after a long day of touring in Senegal, the group got together and talked about the stereotypes they had heard about each other's cultures. What they realized was that some of the stereotypes were the same for both groups. "It was really funny," laughs Nicole Williams.

"African-Americans and Jews are both famous for being loud, having strong grandmothers, and eating a lot at family functions."

It was during one late-night conversation on the Project Interchange trip that Matthew Schwartz says he finally was able to comprehend why some blacks prefer the term "African-American." "The term is emotionally resonant," Schwartz explains, "because it connects African-Americans to a culture they were ripped away from. As a Jew I can understand the importance of connecting to your history." Atiba de Souza says he too was affected by such discussions. "You build a special relationship," he says. "You know how you argue with your mom, your little brother, but then the next day you love them again and you're friends? That's how it is with us now." In fact, many participants say they learned that getting to the heart of matters does not always mean getting along. In South Africa, the Project Interchange crew got into a "knockdown, drag-out, verbal brawl" over affirmative action, recounts Terry Bruner. Responses fell along fairly typical lines, with some Jews objecting to racial preferences as unfair and unnecessary. Things were said that inflamed a lot of people, recalls Bruner. "We unleashed a lot of stereotypes that night. But in the end, some points were conceded and people came to an understanding," he says. "Not necessarily agreement, but an understanding."

Clearly, students are affected by their travels. But when the trip is over and the moments of confrontation and realization, jubilance and frustration, personal revelation and hope are over, what becomes of them? They are transformed into action, say the students, who then set out to become ambassadors to their communities. Upon their return, members of Operation Understanding Philadelphia become part of a peer education team. Averaging about sixty-five engagements per year, the youths share their message in a variety of forums, and often start multicultural clubs or exchanges at their schools. Project Interchange graduates also address community groups and meet informally once a month to continue their dialogue. Operation Understanding DC students take their stories on the road in a number of ways, including performing vignettes that depict some of what they've learned. "The only way to make real change is to talk," says Melinda Pollack. "I try to explain to my Jewish friends at George Washington University what I experienced, and I introduce them to the black friends I made through Project Interchange."

Those who hear the students' stories are often deeply affected by them. An audience in Washington was moved by a student's description of a plantation tour that omitted any discussion of slavery. "The tour guide discussed the architecture and the furnishings in the house extensively," Simone Evans explained. "The trees were mentioned many times. But the people who built the plantation, the people who lived there, some of whom died there . . . these people were never mentioned." As Executive Director Karen Kalish attests, "There wasn't a dry eye in the house."

While the participants, and by extension the communities with whom they share their experiences, clearly benefit from these programs, organizers are the first to admit that they are not without their problems. Since the creation of Operation Understanding Philadelphia in 1985, countless groups across the country have tried to create similar programs. But many had trouble getting off the ground because of funding problems. "Funding is a huge issue," says Sharon Kershbaum of Operation Understanding Philadelphia. Run in cooperation with the American Jewish Committee and Urban League of Philadelphia, Operation Understanding Philadelphia receives grants from area corporations, individuals, and foundations. But with a $70,000 price tag for the travel portion of the program alone, the organization can afford only one full-time professional, relying heavily on parents and community leaders to volunteer time.

Operation Understanding DC President Karen Kalish's original design was to take the students to Israel and Africa. But when the funds she needed didn't come in, she created a US trip. She now concedes that with no track record and a Washington, DC government in crisis she had "unrealistic expectations for the first year." But Kalish, who is also a public relations executive, has managed to garner enough support to continue the program. Operation Understanding DC's backers is Steven Spielberg's Righteous Persons Foundation, which recently donated $50,000 to the group.

Besides funding woes, organizers, who are mostly Jewish, may have difficulty getting support from black communities with more pressing items on their agendas than black-Jewish relations. "The Jewish community buys into these programs one hundred percent but the African-American community has other priorities which are clearly more important, like putting food on the table and dealing with crime," says Kershbaum.

Dr. Russell Adams, chair of Afro-American Studies at Howard University and faculty advisor to the Project Interchange program, agrees that these programs are Jewish-initiated "more often than not" and notes that reasons other than priorities may also cause reticence among African-American organizations. "There's a shyness that you'll be rebuffed," says Adams. "Some blacks fear they will raise their hand and no one will touch it."

Still, Adams, who has been working for interracial harmony for more than 30 years, thinks blacks and Jews are better off as friends than foes and believes groups like Project Interchange, Operation Understanding DC, and Operation Understanding Philadelphia will help achieve that goal. "We need each other," says Adams. "Alone we are both small, but together we can be more powerful."

Perhaps most importantly, the students believe in their ability to create black-Jewish unity. They say unequivocally that their experiences have changed them, and have made them determined to bring about change. "We are very committed to this now," says Emily Levin, "And," she adds, "next year, there will be a whole new group of us." But African-American student Terry Bruner is more cautiously optimistic. "In five years, maybe," he says, "blacks and Jews will have reached new plateaus of understanding."

A Yom Kippur Plea
Ari Goldman

Ari Goldman, who now teaches at the Columbia University School of Journalism, served for many years on the religion desk of the *New York Times,* the source of the following article.

One week from today is Yom Kippur, the Day of Atonement, on which Jews traditionally undertake a voluntary fast by refraining for twenty-five hours from all food and drink. As in past years, a national organization, Mazon, is trying to harness this sacrifice for a good cause. The organization is asking that American Jews "help to end the involuntary fast of millions" by contributing to Mazon the amount of money they would have spent on food had they not fasted on Yom Kippur. In the past, contributions have ranged from $10 from people accustomed to eating at college cafeterias to more than $100 from regular patrons of Lutece.

Mazon (the Hebrew word is roughly translated as sustenance) raises money from American Jews and makes grants to both Jewish and non-Jewish relief organizations, both in the United States and abroad. Among the recipients are the Coalition on Ethiopian Jewry and the Gleaning Network of Central Point, Oregon, which collects one million pounds of unharvested fruits and vegetables each year for distribution to the poor.

Leonard Fein, the founder of Mazon, said the inspiration for the Yom Kippur program came from Isaiah 58:5 in which God says to the prophet: "Is this the fast I choose, a day to humble oneself? Is it to bow down the head like a bulrush and to live in sackcloth and ashes?" Isaiah concludes in verse 7: "Is it not to share your bread with the hungry and to bring the homeless poor into your house?" Since it was founded in 1985, Mazon has allocated $2.5 million to charitable programs.

Rolling Up Sleeves to Help Soviet Emigrés
New York Times

Founded in 1886, Yeshiva University is the oldest and largest Jewish University in the United States. The relevance curriculum affirms belief in the intrinsic relevance of the Judaism to the understanding of western civilization: all students take courses in Jewish studies and Hebrew. The University has grown into a vast complex of six undergraduate and seven graduate and professional schools plus auxiliary institutions. The events in the story below take place on and near Yeshiva College, the undergraduate campus for men located on West 185th Street in New York City's Washington Heights neighborhood.

Purim is a late winter holiday which celebrates the successful efforts of Esther—a Jewish member of the harem of the King of Persia—and her uncle, Mordecai, to save their fellow Jews from destruction through the devices of the wicked Haman.

How would the Yeshiva University students move the hulking bed up two flights of stairs? Besides being narrow and steep, the stairway was poorly lighted. The movers made it, however, and so did the bed, donated by Selma Gulack, a third-year law student at Yeshiva who lives nearby in Kew Gardens Hills, Queens. "We really need the bed for the baby," said Michael Aminov, fourteen years old, from Samarkand in the Soviet Republic of Uzbekistan. "The baby slept with mother. Now she can sleep on a bed." The delivery was part of a furniture distribution for Soviet immigrants to the New York metropolitan region.

The students are immigrants are celebrating Purim a week early today at 4 P.M. in the Morgenstern Residence Hall. Some Soviet Jews had been afraid to celebrate the festival, and others had not even known about it. Participants in the event, sponsored by the Philanthropy Society, will eat *hamantaschen*, the traditional holiday pastry, and watch a movie with Russian subtitles.

Next month the campus chapter of the Student Struggle for Soviet Jewry will collect clothing for the immigrants. "Now that they are out, our jobs are just not done," said Moshe Karash, a senior psychology major and a student intern at the Max Stern division of communal services. "We have marched and protested for them, and we still want to help them."

Miss Gulak donated nine pieces of furniture including a reclining armchair and a dining table. "I felt it almost an honor bestowed on me by being able to give the furniture to someone who needs it," she said. The Aminovs, who arrived here nine months ago, were delighted. Speaking from the hallway of the two-bedroom apartment he shares with his mother and four sisters, Michael, the only family member who speaks English, said, "I like America, but it has been hard." His father abandoned the family after their arrival, and a nearby Jewish day school did not have room for Michael. "The children [at his junior high school] are not so nice," he added. The Aminovs and similar families face daunting tasks of adjustment. Few understand English. Fewer know how to deal with aspects of American life like the variety of foods in supermarkets.

More than fifty Yeshiva students under the banner of the Philanthropy Society, which donates time and money to worthy causes, have volunteered to help the immigrants. "The Russian immigrant problem is critical, and the potential for helping is unlimited," said Daniel Wolff, president of the society and a senior English major from Brookline, Massachusetts.

To Stay Young: Walk, Feed Birds, Help Old People
Douglas Martin

Margaret Grossman, more than 87 years into this odd adventure called living, knows many things. "I will die with a smile on my face," is one of them. At 10 am, right after the Joan Rivers television show, Margaret begins her walk of more than two miles to her volunteer position at the Parker Jewish Geriatric Institute in New Hyde Park, Queens. Walking briskly through a cold drizzle, she looks like a tiny bird inside her huge down coat. After spending the day helping elderly people—many of them rather sad cases, many younger than she—she will walk home. She does this four times a week.

Margaret is a determined, ambitious and, yes, stubborn woman. "I tell everyone to move," she says in her Viennese accent. "Move! It's so important. If I didn't walk, I'd be finished."

In 1986, Congress gave Margaret an award for her voluntary service. Her daughter, Susan, with whom she lives in a house just across the Long Island line but in a separate apartment, had minutes earlier tried to show off this and other plaques. Margaret's sweet response? "You get on my nerves so much! You make me sick!"

Susan only laughed. She is used to this fiercely independent spirit. Used to the fact that her mother cooks for herself, saying she can't stand her daughter's cooking. So used to Margaret's turning down rides that she no longer even slows down, just waves as she drives past.

A few blocks from her home, the old woman's face brightens. "See, they're waiting for me," she chirps, pointing to ducks, geese, and gulls. She hurries to throw out pieces of the bread she collects from the geriatric home's dirty plates. A companion points out a sign saying not to feed the birds. Margaret peers at him as if he were crazy. "Don't you see they are hungry?"

Step by step, the picture emerges of a hugely generous woman. She spends most of her spare time knitting shawls for the homeless. She also knits hats for Israeli soldiers. She gives most of her pension to a wide range of charities. She loathes the idea of spending a dime in a restaurant. "People are hungry and I should stuff myself?" Margaret demands. "No!"

The details of her history are not easily forthcoming. "Please, I don't want to remember the past," she says. The past includes growing up in Vienna, then fleeing Hitler to France with her husband and two young children. Living there in a cellar with rats for two years. Eating grass because there was nothing else. A French woman, a Christian, who took her children for two years while she and her husband were in hiding. "I ask myself if I would have done what this woman did for us? This woman and her whole family were in such danger."

Other stops included Montreal, where she worked as business equipment supervisor for a paper company, and Israel, where she began to volunteer in hospitals. Dates and details seem to have long ago fallen by the roadside. "I don't count any more years," Margaret says flatly.

Indeed, the time has come when past and present sometimes seem equally real. Each night, just before falling asleep, she conjures up the faces of sixty-five or seventy deceased loved ones, clear as life. It is a pleasant few moments. Perhaps consequently, the effects of the Alzheimer's disease she sees so much of aren't terrifying. "You come to a point where perhaps it's better you don't know anymore what's going on," Margaret says.

The volunteer arrives exactly an hour after she left home—not a second late despite stopping to pick up two bags of hard candy at a drugstore. She brings some residents water, gives others candy and fruit, spoons food into the mouths of still others. "Sometimes I run out of steam," says Rosemarie Martin, a resident of the home who is 62. Her face sparkles when Margaret enters her room. "She always seems to be in the right place at the right time to give me a push."

Much of what Margaret sees is very sad. Some residents stare at the walls for hours. Some sit and sob. Many lack a leg or two. Not a few complain bitterly, since life in its final meanness has given them little else to do. "I pray to God not to end up here," she says quietly. Then she smiles, holding up a candy. "This goes to my boyfriend."

"Hi, sweetheart!" Margaret says. Only too late does she remember that the man, a diabetic amputee, can't eat candy. He continues to stare out a window, mumbling. "Such a nice person," Margaret says. "My heart bleeds." But she refuses to slow down, though she took a bad fall walking to work in a December snowstorm. "My whole life I've searched for peace," she says firmly. "Now I have it."

ENDNOTES

1 Kabbalistic: having to do with the Jewish mystical tradition.

2 Generally speaking, Sherwin identifies "justice" with the Hebrew words *"mishpat"* and *"din"; "hesed"* with "mercy"; *"rahmanut"* with "compassion"; *"zedek"* with "righteousness." See the article on "Righteousness" in *Encyclopedia Judaica* for sources and discussion. A poignant example of righteousness as doing right despite the strict interpretation of the law is in the talmudic story of the wine porters in *Baba Metzia* 83a. For the idea that the absence or perversion of justice leads to the destruction of society, see *Exodus Rabbah* 30:19. For the idea that too strict and literal an interpretation of law leads to destruction, see *Gittin* 56a.

3 Heschel, *God in Search of Man,* p. 377.

4 Emphasis Kushner's.

5 The Jesuits are a Roman Catholic order of priests.

Chapter Seven

Christianity, the Bible, and Selfless Service

C hristianity accepts as sacred text all of the Jewish written Torah; therefore, all passages from the TANAKH cited in Chapter Five are relevant here as well. To the TANAKH, Christians added a New Testament of twenty–seven more books: four Gospels, one history of the early church, twenty–one Epistles, and one apocalypse—a discourse on the end times, written in colorful, coded language. The result of this merger of Hebrew and Greek writings is the Bible. Christians believe its contents were written down by a variety of individuals from many different times and places, each while under divine inspiration. While some interpret this to mean that the Bible contains the *words* of God verbatim, most Christians believe that it is the *word* of God: God's message to humanity, but of human— albeit inspired—authorship. Ultimately, Christianity believes that Jesus himself is, as the Gospel of John puts it, "the Word made flesh."[1] It has been argued that if one were to cut out every passage in the Bible which has something to say about justice, compassion, and selfless service, nothing would remain. This chapter—along with its companion, Chapter Five—seek to isolate some of the most vivid and obvious portions.

Gospels

While they are not biographies in the modern sense, the Gospels are records of the life and teachings of Jesus written from within the Christian community of faith. The Bible includes four of the many which circulated during the early years of the Church. The first three (Matthew, Mark, and Luke) are said to be "synoptic"—of the same vision—because they recount events in a similar order and include much material in common. Excerpts from all four gospels are included here.

When Jesus saw the crowds, he went up the mountain; and after he sat down, his disciples came to him. Then he began to speak, and taught them, saying:

> Blessed are the poor in spirit, for theirs is the kingdom of heaven.
> Blessed are those who mourn, for they will be comforted.

Blessed are the meek, for they will inherit the earth.
Blessed are those who hunger and thirst for righteousness,
   for they will be filled.
Blessed are the merciful, for they will receive mercy.
Blessed are the pure in heart, for they will see God.
Blessed are the peacemakers, for they will be called children of God.
Blessed are those who are persecuted for righteousness' sake,
for theirs is the kingdom of heaven.
Blessed are you when people revile you and persecute you
and utter all kinds of evil against you falsely on my account.
Rejoice and be glad, for your reward is great in heaven, for in the same way they persecuted the prophets who were before you. —*Matthew 5: 1-12*

You have heard that it was said, "An eye for an eye and a tooth for a tooth." But I say to you, Do not resist an evildoer. But if anyone strikes you on the right cheek, turn the other also; and if anyone wants to sue you and take your coat, give your cloak as well; and if anyone forces you to go one mile, go also the second mile. Give to everyone who begs from you, and do not refuse anyone who wants to borrow from you.

   You have heard that it was said, "You shall love your neighbor and hate your enemy." But I say to you, Love your enemies and pray for those who persecute you, so that you may be children of your Father in heaven; for he makes his sun rise on the evil and on the good, and sends rain on the righteous and on the unrighteous. For if you love those who love you, what reward do you have? Do not even the tax collectors do the same? And if you greet only your brothers and sisters, what more are you doing than others? Do not even the Gentiles do the same? Be perfect, therefore, as your heavenly Father is perfect.
—*Matthew 5:38-48*

Beware of practicing your piety before others in order to be seen by them; for then you have no reward from your Father in heaven.

   So whenever you give alms, do not sound a trumpet before you, as the hypocrites do in the synagogues and in the streets, so that they may be praised by others. Truly I tell you, they have received their reward. But when you give alms, do not let your left hand know what your right hand is doing, so that your alms may be done in secret; and your Father who sees in secret will reward you.
—*Matthew 6:1-4*

In everything do to others as you would have them do to you; for this is the law and the prophets. —*Matthew 7:12*

When Jesus had come down from the mountain, great crowds followed him; and there was a leper who came to him and knelt before him, saying, "Lord, if you choose, you can make me clean." He stretched out his hand and touched him, saying, "I do choose. Be made clean!" Immediately his leprosy was cleansed. Then Jesus said to him, "See that you say nothing to anyone; but go, show yourself to the priest, and offer the gift that Moses commanded, as a testimony to them."

   When he entered Capernaum, a centurion came to him, appealing to him and saying, "Lord, my servant is lying at home paralyzed, in terrible distress." And he said to him, "I will come and cure him." The centurion answered, "Lord, I am not worthy to have you come under my roof; but only speak the word, and my servant will be healed. For I also am a man under authority, with soldiers under me; and I say to one, 'Go,' and he goes, and to another, 'Come,' and he comes, and to my slave, 'Do this,' and the slave does it." When Jesus heard him, he was amazed and said to those who followed him, "Truly I tell you, in no one in Israel have I found such faith. I tell you, many will come from east and west and will eat with Abraham and Isaac and Jacob in the kingdom of heaven, while the heirs of the kingdom will be thrown into the outer darkness, where there will be weeping and gnashing of teeth." And to the centurion Jesus said, "Go; let it be done for you according to your faith." And the servant was healed in that hour.

When Jesus entered Peter's house, he saw his mother-in-law lying in bed with a fever; he touched her hand, and the fever left her, and she got up and began to serve him. That evening they brought to him many who were possessed with demons; and he cast out the spirits with a word, and cured all who were sick. This was to fulfill what had been spoken through the prophet Isaiah, "He took our infirmities and bore our diseases." *—Matthew 8:1-15*

And as he sat at table in the house, behold, many tax collectors and sinners came and sat down with Jesus and the disciples. And when the Pharisees saw this, they said to his disciples, "Why does your teacher eat with tax collectors and sinners?" But when he heard it, he said, "Those who are well have no need of a physician, but those who are sick. Go and learn what this means, 'I desire mercy, and not sacrifice.'" *—Matthew 9:10-13*

When he went ashore, Jesus saw a great crowd; and he had compassion for them and cured their sick. *—Matthew 14:14*

Then Jesus called his disciples to him and said, "I have compassion for the crowd, because they have been with me now for three days and have nothing to eat; and I do not want to send them away hungry, for they might faint on the way." *—Matthew 15:32*

As Jesus and his disciples were leaving Jericho, a large crowd followed him. There were two blind men sitting by the roadside. When they heard that Jesus was passing by, they shouted, "Lord, have mercy on us, Son of David!" The crowd sternly ordered them to be quiet; but they shouted even more loudly, "Have mercy on us, Lord, Son of David!" Jesus stood still and called them, saying, "What do you want me to do for you?" They said to him, "Lord, let our eyes be opened." Moved with compassion, Jesus touched their eyes. Immediately they regained their sight and followed him. *—Matthew 20:34*

When the Pharisees heard that Jesus had silenced the Sadducees, they gathered together, and one of them, a lawyer, asked him a question to test him. "Teacher, which commandment in the law is the greatest?" Jesus said to him, "'You shall love the Lord your God with all your heart, and with all your soul, and with all your mind.' This is the greatest and first commandment. And a second is like it:

'You shall love your neighbor as yourself.' On these two commandments hang all the law and the prophets." —*Matthew 22:34-40*

When the Son of Man comes in his glory, and all the angels with him, then he will sit on the throne of his glory. All the nations will be gathered before him, and he will separate people one from another as a shepherd separates the sheep from the goats, and he will put the sheep at his right hand and the goats at the left. Then the king will say to those at his right hand, "Come, you that are blessed by my Father, inherit the kingdom prepared for you from the foundation of the world; for I was hungry and you gave me food, I was thirsty and you gave me something to drink, I was a stranger and you welcomed me, I was naked and you gave me clothing, I was sick and you took care of me, I was in prison and you visited me,. Then the righteous will answer him, "Lord, when was it that we saw you hungry and gave you food, or thirsty and gave you something to drink? And when was it that we saw you a stranger and welcomed you, or naked and gave you clothing? And when was it that we saw you sick or in prison and visited you?" And the king will answer them, "Truly I tell you, just as you did it to one of the least of these who are members of my family, you did it to me." Then he will say to those at his left hand, "You that are accursed, depart from me into the eternal fire prepared for the devil and his angels; for I was hungry and you gave me no food, I was thirsty and you gave me nothing to drink, I was a stranger and you did not welcome me, naked and you did not give me clothing, sick and in prison and you did not visit me. Then they will also answer, "Lord, when was it that we saw you hungry or thirsty or a stranger or naked or sick or in prison, and did not take care of you?" Then he will answer them, "Truly I tell you, just as you did not do it to one of the least of these, you did not do it to me." And these will go away into eternal punishment, but the righteous into eternal life. —*Matthew 25:31-36*

As he went ashore, he saw a great crowd; and he had compassion for them, because they were like sheep without a shepherd; and he began to teach them many things. —*Mark 6:34* [2]

"I have compassion for the crowd, because they have been with me now for three days and have nothing to eat. —*Mark 8:2*

As he was setting out on a journey, a man ran up and knelt before him, and asked him, "Good Teacher, what must I do to inherit eternal life?" Jesus said to him, "Why do you call me good? No one is good but God alone. You know the commandments: 'You shall not murder; You shall not steal; You shall not bear false witness; You shall not defraud; Honor your father and mother.'" He said to him, "Teacher, I have kept all these since my youth." Jesus, looking at him, loved him and said, "You lack one thing; go, sell what you own, and give the money to the poor, and you will have treasure in heaven; then come, follow me." When he heard this, he was shocked and went away grieving, for he had many possessions. —*Mark 10:17-22* [3]

He sat down opposite the treasury, and watched the crowd putting money into the treasury. Many rich people put in large sums. A poor widow came and put in two small copper coins, which are worth a penny. Then he called his disciples and said to them, "Truly I tell you, this poor widow has put in more than all those who are contributing to the treasury. For all of them contributed out of their abundance; but she out of her poverty has put in everything she had, all she had to live on." —*Mark 12:41-44*[4]

While he was at Bethany in the house of Simon the leper, as he sat at the table, a woman came with an alabaster jar of very costly ointment of nard,[5] and she broke open the jar and poured the ointment on his head. But some were there who said to one another in anger, "Why was the ointment wasted in this way? For this ointment could have been sold for more than three hundred denarii, and the money given to the poor." And they scolded her. But Jesus said, "Let her alone; why do you trouble her? She has performed a good service for me. For you always have the poor with you, and you can show kindness to them whenever you wish; but you will not always have me. She has done what she could; she has anointed my body beforehand for its burial. Truly I tell you, wherever the good news is proclaimed in the whole world, what she has done will be told in remembrance of her. —*Mark 14:6*[6]

He who has two coats, let him share with him who has none; and he who has food, let him do likewise. —*Luke 3:11*

When Jesus came to Nazareth, where he had been brought up, he went to the synagogue on the sabbath day, as was his custom. He stood up to read, and the scroll of the prophet Isaiah was given to him. He unrolled the scroll and found the place where it was written:
"The Spirit of the Lord is upon me,
    because he has anointed me
    to bring good news to the poor.
He has sent me to proclaim release to the captives
    and recovery of sight to the blind,
    to let the oppressed go free,
    to proclaim the year of the Lord's favor."
And he rolled up the scroll, gave it back to the attendant, and sat down. The eyes of all in the synagogue were fixed on him. Then he began to say to them, "Today this scripture has been fulfilled in your hearing." —*Luke 4:16-21*

Then he looked up at his disciples and said:
    Blessed are you who are poor,
        for yours is the kingdom of God.
    Blessed are you who are hungry now,
        for you will be filled.
    Blessed are you who weep now,
        for you will laugh.
Blessed are you when people hate you, and when they exclude you, revile you, and defame you on account of the Son of Man. Rejoice in that day and leap for joy, for surely your reward is great in heaven; for that is what their ancestors did to the prophets.
    But woe to you who are rich,
        for have received your consolation.

Woe to you who are full now,
     for you will be hungry.
Woe to you who are laughing now,
     for you will mourn and weep.
Woe to you when all speak well of you,
     for that is what their ancestors did to the false prophets.

But I say to you that listen, Love your enemies, do good to those who hate
you, bless those who curse you, pray for those who abuse you. If anyone strikes
you on the cheek, offer the other also; and from anyone who takes away your coat
do not withhold even your shirt. Give to everyone who begs from you; and if
anyone takes away your goods, do not ask for them again. Do to others as you
would have them do to you. *—Luke 6:20-31*

Give, and it will be given to you. A good measure, pressed down, shaken together,
running over, will be put into your lap; for the measure you give will be the
measure you get back. *—Luke 6:38*

Soon afterwards Jesus went to a town called Nain, and his disciples and a large
crowd went with him. As he approached the gate, a man who had died was being
carried out. He was his mother's only son, and she was a widow; and with her
was a large crowd from the town. When the Lord saw her, he had compassion
for her and said to her, "Do not weep." Then he came forward and touched the
bier, and the bearers stood still. And he said, "Young man, I say to you, rise!" The
dead man sat up and began to speak, and Jesus gave him to his mother.
—Luke 7:11-15

John summoned two of his disciples and sent them to the Lord to ask, "Are you
the one who is to come, or are we to wait for another?" When the men had come
to him, they said, "John the Baptist has sent us to you to ask, 'Are you the one
who is to come, or are we to wait for another?'" Jesus had just cured many people
of diseases, plagues, and evil spirits, and had given sight to many who were blind.
And he answered them, "Go and tell John what you have seen and heard: the
blind receive their sight, the lame walk, the lepers are cleansed, the deaf hear,
the dead are raised, the poor have good news brought to them."
—Luke 7:18-22[7]

Just then a lawyer stood up to test Jesus. "Teacher," he said, "what must I do to
inherit eternal life?" He said to him, "What is written in the law? What do you
read there?" He answered, "You shall love the Lord your God with all your heart,
and with all your soul, and with all your strength, and with all your mind; and
your neighbor as yourself." And he said to him, "You have given the right answer;
do this, and you will live."

But wanting to justify himself, he asked Jesus, "And who is my neighbor?"
Jesus replied, "A man was going down from Jerusalem to Jericho, and fell into
the hands of robbers, who stripped him, beat him, and went away, leaving him
half dead. Now by chance a priest was going down that road; and when he saw
him, he passed by on the other side. So likewise a Levite, when he came to the
place and saw him, passed by on the other side. But a Samaritan while traveling
came near him; and when he saw him, he was moved with pity. He went to him

and bandaged his wounds, having poured oil and wine on them. Then he put him on his own animal, brought him to an inn, and took care of him. The next day he took out two denarii, gave them to the innkeeper, and said, 'Take care of him; and when I come back, I will repay you whatever more you spend.' Which of these three, do you think, was a neighbor to the man who fell into the hands of the robbers?" He said, "The one who showed him mercy." Jesus said to him, "Go and do likewise." —*Luke 10:25-37*

Jesus said to the one who had invited him, "When you give a luncheon or a dinner, do not invite your friends or your brothers or your relatives or your rich neighbors, in case they may invite you in return, and you would be repaid. But when you give a banquet, invite the poor, the crippled, the lame, and the blind. And you will be blessed, because they cannot repay you, for you will be repaid at the resurrection of the righteous.

One of the dinner guests, on hearing this, said to him, "Blessed is anyone who will eat bread in the kingdom of God!" Then Jesus said to him, "Someone gave a great dinner and invited many. At the time for the dinner he sent his slave to say to those who had been invited, 'Come; for everything is ready now.' But all alike began to make excuses. The first said to him, 'I have bought a piece of land, and I must go out and see it; please accept my regrets.' Another said, 'I have bought five yoke of oxen, and I am going to try them out; please accept my regrets.' Another said, 'I have just been married, and therefore I cannot come.' So the slave returned and reported this to his master. Then the owner of the house became angry and said to his slave, 'Go out at once into the streets and lanes of the town and bring in the poor, the crippled, the blind, and the lame.' And the slave said, 'Sir, what you ordered has been done, and there is still room.' Then the master said to the slave, 'Go out into the roads and lanes, and compel people to come in, so that my house may be filled. For I tell you, none of those who were invited will taste my dinner.'" —*Luke 14:12-24*

There was a rich man who was dressed in purple and fine linen and who feasted sumptuously every day. And at his gate lay a poor man named Lazarus, covered with sores, who longed to satisfy his hunger with what fell from the rich man's table; even the dogs would come and lick his sores.

The poor man died and was carried away by the angels to be with Abraham. The rich man also died and was buried. In Hades, where he was being tormented, he looked up and saw Abraham far away with Lazarus by his side. He called out, "Father Abraham, have mercy on me, and send Lazarus to dip the tip of his finger in water and cool my tongue; for I am in agony in these flames." But Abraham said, "Child, remember that during your lifetime you received your good things, and Lazarus in like manner evil things; but now he is comforted here, and you are in agony. Besides all this, between you and us a great chasm has been fixed, so that those who might want to pass from here to you cannot do so, and no one can cross from there to us." He said, "Then, father, I beg you to send him to my father's house—for I have five brothers—that he may warn them, so that they will not also come into this place of torment." Abraham replied, "They have Moses and the prophets; they should listen to them." He said, "No, father Abraham; but if someone goes to them from the dead, they will repent." He said to him, "If they do not listen to Moses and the prophets, neither will they be convinced even if someone rises from the dead." —*Luke 16:19-31*

Jesus entered Jericho and was passing through it. A man was there named Zaccheus; he was a chief tax collector and was rich. He was trying to see who Jesus was, but on account of the crowd he could not, because he was short in stature. So he ran ahead and climbed a sycamore tree to see him, because he was going to pass that way. When Jesus came to the place, he looked up and said to him, "Zaccheus, hurry and come down; for I must stay at your house today." So he hurried down and was happy to welcome him. All who saw it began to grumble and said, "He has gone to be the guest of one who is a sinner." Zaccheus stood there and said to the Lord, "Look, half of my possessions, Lord, I will give to the poor; and if I have defrauded anyone of anything, I will pay back four times as much." Then Jesus said to him, "Today salvation has come to this house, because he too is a son of Abraham. For the Son of Man came to seek out and to save sinners. —*Luke 19:1-10*

Now before the festival of the Passover, Jesus knew that his hour had come to depart from this world and go to the Father. And during supper Jesus, knowing that the Father had given all things into his hands, and that he had come from God and was going to God, got up from the table, took off his outer robe, and tied a towel around himself. Then he poured water into a basin and began to wash the disciples' feet and to wipe them with the towel that was tied around him. He came to Simon Peter, who said to him, "Lord, are you going to wash my feet?" Jesus answered, "You do not know what I am doing, but later you will understand." Peter said to him, "You will never wash my feet." Jesus answered, "Unless I wash you , you have no share with me." Simon Peter said to him, "Lord, not my feet only, but also my hands and my head!" Jesus said to him, "One who has bathed does not need to wash, except for the feet, but is entirely clean. And you are clean.

After he had washed their feet, had put on his robe, and had returned to the table, he said to them, "Do you know what I have done to you? You call me Teacher and Lord—and you are right, for that is what I am. So if I, your Lord and Teacher, have washed your feet, you also ought to wash one another's feet. For I have set you an example, that you also should do as I have done to you.
—*John 13:1, 3-15*

Greater love has no man than this, that a man lay down his life for his friends.
—*John 15:13*

Acts of the Apostles

The book of Acts is the only history of the early church to be included in the Christian canon of scripture. It is written by the author of the Gospel of Luke, and is very much a "Volume Two" to that work.

Now the whole group of those who believed were of one heart and soul, and no one claimed private ownership of any possessions. With great power the apostles gave their testimony to the resurrection of the Lord Jesus, and great grace was upon them all. There was not a needy person among them, for as many as owned lands or houses sold them and brought the proceeds of what was sold. They laid it at the apostles' feet, and it was distributed to each as any had need. —*Acts 4:32–35*

[Addressing the elders of the church at Ephesus, Paul said:] "You know for yourselves that I worked with my own hands to support myself and my companions. In all this I have given you an example that by such work we must support the weak, remembering the words of the Lord Jesus, for he himself said, 'It is more blessed to give than to receive.'" —*Acts 20:34–35*

Epistles

Epistles are formal letters and discourses by Paul and other apostles of Jesus, often intended for public reading to an entire congregation of Christians. The Bible includes twenty-one; excerpts from several of these are included here.

Is there injustice on God's part? By no means! For he says to Moses,
  "I will have mercy on whom I have mercy,
  and I will have compassion on whom I have compassion."
So it depends not on human will or exertion, but on God who shows mercy. —*Romans 9:14b–16*

We have gifts that differ according to the grace given us: prophecy, in proportion to faith; ministry, in ministering; the teacher, in teaching; the exhorter, in exhortation; the giver, in generosity; the leader, in diligence; the compassionate, in cheerfulness. Let love be genuine; hate what is evil, hold fast to what is good; love one another with mutual affection; outdo one another in showing honor. Do not lag in zeal, be ardent in spirit, serve the Lord. Rejoice in hope, be patient in suffering, persevere in prayer. Contribute to the needs of the saints; extend hospitality to strangers. —*Romans 12:6–13*

At present, however, I, Paul, am going to Jerusalem in a ministry to the saints; for Macedonia and Achaia have been pleased to share their resources with the poor among the saints at Jerusalem. —*Romans 15:25–26*

Let no one seek his own good, but the good of his neighbor. —*I Corinthians 10:24*

If I speak in the tongues of mortals and of angels, but do not have love, I am a noisy gong or a clanging cymbal. And if I have prophetic powers, and understand all mysteries and all knowledge, and if I have all faith, so as to remove mountains, but do not have love, I am nothing. If I give away all my possessions, and if I hand over my body so that I may boast, but do not have love, I gain nothing.
  Love is patient; love is kind; love is not envious or boastful or arrogant or rude. It does not insist on its own way; it is not irritable or resentful; it does not rejoice

in wrongdoing, but rejoices in the truth. It bears all things, believes all things, hopes all things, endures all things.

Love never ends. But as for prophecies, they will come to an end; as for tongues, they will cease; as for knowledge, it will come to an end. For we know only in part, and we prophesy only in part; but when the complete comes, the partial will come to an end. When I was a child, I spoke like a child, I thought like a child, I reasoned like a child; when I became an adult, I put an end to childish ways. For now we see in a mirror, dimly, but then we will see face to face. Now I know only in part; then I will know fully, even as I have been fully known. And now faith, hope, and love abide, these three; and the greatest of these is love. —*I Corinthians 13*

Now, brothers and sisters, you know that members of the household of Stephanas were the first converts in Achaia, and they have devoted themselves to the service of the saints; I urge you to put yourselves at the service of such people, and of everyone who works and toils with them. —*I Corinthians 16:16*

For you know the generous act of our Lord Jesus Christ, that though he was rich, yet for your sakes he became poor, so that by his poverty you might become rich. —*II Corinthians 8:9*

Each of you must give as you have made up your mind, not reluctantly or under compulsion, for God loves a cheerful giver. And God is able to provide you with every blessing in abundance, so that by always having enough of everything, you may share abundantly in every good work. As it is written,

> "He scatters abroad, he gives to the poor;
> his righteousness endures forever." —*II Corinthians 9:7–9*

James and Cephas and John asked only one thing, that we remember the poor, which was actually what I, Paul, was eager to do. —*Galatians 2:10*

Bear one another's burdens, and so fulfill the law of Christ. —*Galatians 6:2*

Thieves must give up stealing; rather let them labor and work honestly with their own hands, so as to have something to share with the needy. —*Ephesians 4:28*

Render service with enthusiasm, as to the Lord and not to men and women, knowing that whatever good we do, we will receive the same again from the Lord, whether we are slaves or free. —*Ephesians 6:7–8*

For God is my witness, how I long for all of you with the compassion of Christ Jesus. —*Philippians 1:8*

If you have any encouragement from being united with Christ, if any comfort from his love, if any fellowship with the Spirit, if any tenderness and compassion, then make my joy complete by being like-minded, having the same love, being one in spirit and purpose. Do nothing out of selfish ambition or vain conceit, but in humility consider others better than yourselves. Each of you should look not only to your own interests, but also to the interests of others.

Your attitude should be the same as that of Christ Jesus:

Who, being in very nature God,
     did not consider equality with God something to be grasped,
but made himself nothing,
     taking the very nature of a servant,
     being made in human likeness.
And being found in appearance as man,
     he humbled himself
     and became obedient to death —
     even death on a cross! —*Philippians 2:1-8*

As God's chosen ones, holy and beloved, clothe yourselves with compassion, kindness, humility, meekness, and patience. —*Colossians 3:12*

For you had compassion for those who were in prison, and you cheerfully accepted the plundering of your possessions, knowing that you yourselves possessed something better and more lasting. Do not, therefore, abandon that confidence of yours; it brings great reward. —*Hebrews 10:34-35*

Do not neglect to show hospitality to strangers, for thereby some have entertained angels unawares. —*Hebrews 13:2*

My brothers and sisters, do you with your acts of favoritism really believe in our glorious Lord Jesus Christ? For if a person with gold rings and in fine clothes comes into your assembly, and if a poor person in dirty clothes also comes in, and if you take notice of the one wearing the fine clothes and say, "Have a seat here, please," while to the one who is poor you say, "Stand there," or, "Sit at my feet," have you not made distinctions among yourselves, and become judges with evil thoughts? Listen, my beloved brothers and sisters. Has not God chosen the poor in the world to be rich in faith and to be heirs of the kingdom that he has promised to those who love him? But you have dishonored the poor. Is it not the rich who oppress you? Is it not they who drag you into court?

   You do well if you really fulfill the royal law according to the scripture, "You shall love your neighbor as yourself." —*James 2:1-8*

Apocryphal Texts

The following passages come from a group of books found in the Greek version of the Hebrew Scriptures in use during the first century CE, but which were excluded from the Jewish canon by the Council of Jamnia in 100 CE. These writings give us a glimpse into the period between the most recent writings of the Hebrew Scriptures and the beginning of the Christian era, and contain much interesting material quite pertinent to this anthology. Today's Jews are often aware of these writings, but do not consider them sacred scripture. Neither do Protestant Christians, but Roman Catholic and Orthodox Christians accept them fully; Bibles published by these branches of Christianity include these books integrated among the other books of the Old Testament. Anglican Christians regard these writings as inspired and include readings from them in among those appointed for daily and weekly worship, but group them in a separate section of the Bible between the Old and New Testaments.

During Shalmaneser's reign I [Tobit] performed many charitable works for my kinsmen and my people. I would give my food to the hungry and my clothing to the naked; and if I saw the dead body of any of my people thrown out behind the wall of Nineveh, I would bury it. I also buried any whom King Sennacherib put to death when he came fleeing from Judea in those days of judgment that the king of heaven executed upon him because of his blasphemies. For in his anger he put to death many Israelites; but I would secretly remove the bodies and bury them. So when Sennacherib looked for them he could not find them. Then one of the Ninevites went and informed the king about me, that I was burying them; so I hid myself. But when I realized that the king knew about me and that I was being searched for to be put to death, I was afraid and ran away. Then all my property was confiscated; nothing was left to me that was not taken into the royal treasury except my wife Anna and my son Tobias.

During the reign of Esar-haddon I returned home, and my wife Anna and my son Tobias were restored to me. At our festival of Pentecost, which is the sacred festival of weeks, a good dinner was prepared for me and I reclined to eat. When the table was set for me and an abundance of food placed before me, I said to my son Tobias, "Go, my child, and bring whatever poor person you may find of our people among the exiles in Nineveh, who is wholeheartedly mindful of God, and he shall eat together with me. I will wait for you, until you come back." So Tobias went to look for some poor person of our people. When he had returned he said, "Father!" And I replied, "Here I am, my child." Then he went on to say, "Look, father, one of our own people has been murdered and thrown into the market place, and now he lies there strangled." Then I sprang up, left the dinner before even tasting it, and removed the body from the square and laid it in one of the rooms until sunset when I might bury it. When I returned, I washed myself and ate my food in sorrow. Then I remembered the prophecy of Amos, how he said against Bethel, "Your festivals shall be turned into mourning, and all your songs into lamentation." And I wept.

When the sun had set, I went and dug a grave and buried him. And my neighbors laughed and said, "Is he still not afraid? He has already been hunted down to be put to death for doing this, and he ran away; yet here he is again burying the dead!" —*Tobit 1:16-20; 2:2-8*[8]

Revere the Lord all your days, my son, and refuse to sin or transgress his commandments. Live uprightly all the days of your life, and do not walk in the ways of wrongdoing; for those who act in accordance with truth will prosper in all their activities. To all those who practice righteousness give alms from your possessions, and do not let your eye begrudge the gift when you make it. Do not turn your face away from anyone who is poor, and the face of God will not be turned away from you. If you have many possessions, make your gift from them in proportion; if few, do not be afraid to give according to the little you have. So you will be laying up a good treasure for yourself against the day of necessity. For almsgiving delivers from death and keeps you from going into the Darkness. Indeed, almsgiving, for all who practice it, is an excellent offering in the presence of the Most High. —*Tobit 4:5-11*

My child, do not cheat the poor of their living,
 and do not keep needy eyes waiting.
Do not grieve the hungry,
 or anger one in need.
Do not add to the troubles of the desperate,
 or delay giving to the needy.
Do not reject a suppliant in distress,
 or turn your face away from the poor.
Do not avert your eye from the needy,
 and give no one reason to curse you;
for if in bitterness of soul some should curse you,
 their Creator will hear their prayer.
Endear yourself to the congregation;
 bow your head low to the great.
Give a hearing to the poor,
 and return their greeting politely.
Rescue the oppressed from the oppressor;
 and do not be hesitant in giving a verdict.
Be a father to orphans,
 and be like a husband to their mother;
you will then be like a son of the Most High,
 and he will love you more than does your mother. —*Sirach 4:1-10* [9]

Stretch out your hand to the poor,
 so that your blessing may be complete. —*Sirach 7:32*

It is not right to despise one who is intelligent but poor,
 and it is not proper to honor one who is sinful. —*Sirach 10:23*

What are human beings, and of what use are they?
 What is good in them, and what is evil?
The number of days in their life is great if they reach one hundred years.
Like a drop of water from the sea and a grain of sand,
 so are a few years among the days of eternity.
That is why the Lord is patient with them
 and pours out his mercy upon them.
He sees and recognizes that their end is miserable;
 therefore he grants them forgiveness all the more.
The compassion of human beings is for their neighbors,
 but the compassion of the Lord is for every living thing.
He rebukes and trains and teaches them,
 and turns them back, as a shepherd his flock.
He has compassion on those who accept his discipline
 and who are eager for his precepts. —*Sirach 18:8-14*

Help the poor for the commandment's sake,
 and in their need do not send them away empty-handed.
—*Sirach 29:9*

Like one who kills a son before his father's eyes
 is the person who offers a sacrifice from the property of the poor.
The bread of the needy is the life of the poor;

whoever deprives them of it is a murderer. —*Sirach 34:24-25*

The one whose service is pleasing to the Lord will be accepted,
and his prayer will reach to the clouds. —*Sirach 35:20*

"Mother, embrace your children; bring them up with gladness, as does a dove; strengthen their feet, because I have chosen you," says the Lord. "Guard the rights of the widow, secure justice for the ward, give to the needy, defend the orphan, clothe the naked, care for the injured and the weak, do not ridicule the lame, protect the maimed, and let the blind have a vision of my splendor. Protect the old and young within your walls. When you find any who are dead, commit them to the grave and mark it, and I will give you the first place in my resurrection. Pause and be quiet, my people, because your rest will come."
—*II Esdras 2:15, 20-24*

ENDNOTES

1   See John 1:1-9, 14-18.
2   See also Matthew 9:36.
3   See also Matthew 19:16-22 and Luke 18:18-25.
4   See also Luke 21:1-4.
5   Nard is a sweet-smelling Middle Eastern plant. Ointment is made from its roots.
6   See also Matthew 26:6-11.
7   See also Matthew 11:2-5.
8   An early Jewish novella, *Tobit* is an example of the literature of the Diaspora.
9   *The Wisdom of Jesus Son of Sirach (Jesus ben Sira)*, also called *Ecclesiasticus*, dates from before 180 BCE.

Chapter Eight

Readings on Christianity and Service

Christians define ministry as meeting the needs of others in the name of Christ. Service to others is performed, not to earn one's salvation, but out of gratitude for what Christ has done for humanity through the life, ministry, crucifixion, and resurrection of Jesus. The entries in this chapter represent the diversity of the Christian spectrum: Roman Catholic, Eastern Orthodox, Anglican, and Protestant.

A Prayer
St. Francis of Assisi

Giovanni Francesco di Pietrodi Bernardone (1181–1226) founded orders of friars and nuns which espoused a lifestyle of poverty. His followers spent their time begging for their sustenance, preaching, and working on behalf of humanity. Although St. Francis's authorship of this prayer is disputed, it nevertheless remains a favorite among many Christians.

Lord, make us instruments of your peace. Where there is hatred, let us sow love; where there is injury, pardon; where there is discord, union; where there is doubt, faith; where there is despair, hope; where there is darkness, light; where there is sadness, joy. Grant that we may not so much seek to be consoled as to console; to be understood as to understand; to be loved as to love. For it is in giving that we receive; it is in pardoning that we are pardoned; and it is in dying that we are born to eternal life.

Discipline of Service
Richard J. Foster

The author is a professor of theology and writer in residence at Friends University. The following is his explanation of one of the eight classic spiritual disciplines of the Christian faith.

As the cross is the sign of submission, so the towel is the sign of service. When Jesus gathered his disciples for the Last Supper they were having trouble deciding who was the greatest. This was no new issue for them. "And an argument arose among them as to which of them was the greatest" *(Luke 9:46)*. Whenever there is trouble over who is the greatest, there is trouble over who is the least. That is the crux of the matter for us, isn't it? Most of us know we will never be the greatest; just don't let us be the least.

Gathered at the Passover feast, the disciples were keenly aware that someone needed to wash the others' feet. The problem was that the only people who washed feet were the least. So there they sat, feet caked with dirt. It was such a sore point that they were not even going to talk about it. No one wanted to be considered the least. Then Jesus took a towel and a basin and redefined greatness.

Having lived out servanthood before them, he called them to the way of service: "If I then, your Lord and Teacher, have washed your feet, you also ought to wash one another's feet. For I have given you an example, that you also should do as I have done to you" *(John 13:14, 15)*. In some ways we would prefer to hear Jesus' call to deny father and mother, houses and land for the sake of the gospel than his word to wash feet. Radical self-denial gives the feel of adventure. If we forsake all, we even have the chance of glorious martyrdom. But in service we must experience the many little deaths of going beyond ourselves. Service banishes us to the mundane, the ordinary, the trivial.

Jesus declares, "You know that the rulers of the Gentiles lord it over them, and their great men exercise authority over them. *It shall not be so among you.*"[1] He totally and completely rejected the pecking-order systems of his day. How then was it to be among Jesus' disciples? "Whoever would be great among you must be your servant . . . even as the Son of man came not to be served but to serve" *(Matt. 20:25-28)*. Therefore the spiritual authority of Jesus is an authority not found in a position or a title, but in a towel.

If true service is to be understood and practiced, it must be distinguished clearly from "self-righteous service." Self-righteous service comes through human effort. It expends immense amounts of energy calculating and scheming how to render the service. Sociological charts and surveys are devised so we can "help those people." True service comes from a relationship with the divine Other deep inside. We serve out of whispered promptings, divine urgings. Energy is expended but it is not the frantic energy of the flesh.

Self-righteous service is impressed with the "big deal." It is concerned to make impressive gains on ecclesiastical scoreboards. It enjoys serving, especially when the service is titanic. True service finds it almost impossible to distinguish the small from the large service. Where a difference is noted, the true servant is often drawn to the small service, not out of false modesty, but because he genuinely sees it as the more important task. He indiscriminately welcomes all opportunities to serve.

Self-righteous service requires external rewards. It needs to know that people see and appreciate the effort. It seeks human applause—with proper religious modesty of course. True service rests contented in hiddenness. It does not fear the lights and blare of attention, but it does not seek them either. Since it is living out of a new Center of reference, the divine nod of approval is completely sufficient.

Self-righteous service is highly concerned about results. It eagerly waits to see if the person served will reciprocate in kind. It becomes bitter when the results fall below expectations. True service is free of the need to calculate results. It delights only in the service. It can serve enemies as freely as friends.

Self-righteous service picks and chooses whom to serve. Sometimes the high and powerful are served because that will ensure a certain advantage. Sometimes the low and defenseless are served because that will ensure a humble image. True service is indiscriminate in its ministry. It has heard the command of Jesus to be the "servant of all" *(Mark 9:35)*.

Self-righteous service is affected by moods and whims. It can serve only when there is a "feeling" to serve ("moved by the Spirit" as we say). Ill health or inadequate sleep controls the desire to serve. True service ministers simply and faithfully because there is a need. It knows that the "feeling to serve" can often be a hindrance to true service. The service disciplines the feelings rather than allowing the feeling to control the service.

Self-righteous service is temporary. It functions only while the specific acts of service are being performed. Having served, it can rest easy. True service is a lifestyle. It acts from ingrained patterns of living. It springs spontaneously to meet human need.

Self-righteous service is insensitive. It insists on meeting the need even when to do so would be destructive. It demands the opportunity to help. True service can withhold the service as freely as perform it. It can listen with tenderness and patience before acting. It can serve by waiting in silence. "They also serve who only stand and wait."

Self-righteous service fractures community. In the final analysis, once all the religious trappings are removed, it centers in the glorification of the individual. Therefore it puts others into its debt and becomes one of the most subtle and destructive forms of manipulation known. True service builds community. It quietly and unpretentiously goes about caring for the needs of others. It draws, binds, heals, builds.

More than any other single way, the grace of humility is worked into our lives through the discipline of service. Humility, as we all know, is one of those virtues that is never gained by seeking it. The more we pursue it the more distant it becomes. To think we have it is sure evidence that we don't. Therefore, most of us assume there is nothing we can do to gain this prized Christian virtue, and so we do nothing.

But there is something we can do. We do not need to go through life faintly hoping that someday humility may fall upon our heads. Of all the classical Spiritual Disciplines, service is the most conducive to the growth of humility. When we set out on a consciously chosen course of action that accents the good of others and is, for the most part, a hidden work, a deep change occurs in our spirits.

A natural and understandable hesitancy accompanies any serious discussion of service. The hesitancy is prudent since it is wise to count the cost before plunging headlong into any Discipline. We experience a fear that comes out something like this: "If I do that, people will take advantage of me; they will walk all over me."

Right here we must see the difference between choosing to serve and choosing to be a servant. When we choose to serve, we are still in charge. We decide whom we will serve and when we will serve. And if we are in charge, we will worry a great deal about anyone stepping on us, that is, taking charge over us.

But when we choose to be a servant, we give up the right to be in charge. There is great freedom in this. If we voluntarily choose to be taken advantage of, then we cannot be manipulated. When we choose to be a servant, we surrender the right to decide who and when we will serve. We become available and vulnerable.

To stress the inward nature of service, however, is not enough. Service to be service must take form and shape in the world in which we live. Therefore, we must seek to perceive what service looks like in the marketplace of our daily lives. At the outset there is the service of hiddenness. Even public leaders can cultivate tasks of service that remain generally unknown. If all of our serving is before others, we will be shallow people indeed. Hiddenness is a rebuke to the flesh and can deal a fatal blow to pride.

At first thought it would seem that hidden service is only for the sake of the person served. Such is not the case. Hidden, anonymous ministries affect even people who know nothing of them. They sense a deeper love and compassion among people though they cannot account for the feeling. If a secret service is done on their behalf, they are inspired to deeper devotion, for they know that the well of service is far deeper than they can see. It is a ministry that can be engaged in frequently by all people. It sends ripples of joy and celebration through any community of people.

There is the service of small things. The following is a true story. During the frantic final throes of writing my doctoral dissertation I received a phone call from a friend. His wife had taken the car and he wondered if I could take him on a number of errands. Trapped, I consented, inwardly cursing my luck. As I ran out the door, I grabbed Bonhoeffer's *Life Together,* thinking that I might have an opportunity to read in it. Through each errand I inwardly fretted and fumed at the loss of precious time. Finally, at a supermarket, the final stop, I waved my friend on, saying I would wait in the car. I picked up my book, opened it to the marker, and these words:

> The second service that one should perform for another in a Christian community is that of active helpfulness. This means, initially, simple assistance in trifling, external matters. There is a multitude of these things wherever people live together. Nobody is too good for the meanest service. One who worries about the loss of time that such petty, outward acts of helpfulness entail is usually taking the importance of his own career too solemnly . . . [2]

There is the service of guarding the reputation of others or, as Bernard of Clairvaux put it, the service of "Charity." How necessary this is if we are to be saved from backbiting and gossip. The apostle Paul taught us to "speak evil of no one" *(Titus 3:2).* We may clothe our backbiting in all the religious respectability we want, but it will remain a deadly poison. There is a discipline in holding one's tongue that works wonders within us. Nor should we be a party to the slanderous talk of others. Guarding the reputation of others is a deep and lasting service.

There is the service of being served. When Jesus began to wash the feet of those he loved, Peter refused. He would never let his Master stoop to such a menial service on his behalf. It sounds like a statement of humility; in reality it was an act of veiled pride. Jesus' service was an affront to Peter's concept of authority. If Peter had been the master, he would not have washed feet! It is an act of submission and service to allow others to serve us. It recognizes their "kingdom authority" over us. We graciously receive the service rendered, never feeling we must repay it. Those who, out of pride, refuse to be served are failing to submit to the divinely appointed leadership in the kingdom of God.

There is the service of common courtesy. Such deeds of compassion have fallen on hard times in our day. But we must never despise the rituals of relationship that are in every culture. It is one of the few ways left in modern society to acknowledge the value of one another. We are "to be gentle, and to show perfect courtesy toward all men" *(Titus 3:2)*. The specific acts will vary from culture to culture, but the purpose is always the same: to acknowledge others and affirm their worth. The service of courtesy is sorely needed in our increasingly computerized and depersonalized society.

There is the service of hospitality. Peter urges us to "Practice hospitality ungrudgingly to one another" *(1 Pet. 4:9)*. Paul does the same and even makes it one of the requirements for the office of bishop *(1 Tim. 3:2; Titus 1:8)*. There is a desperate need today for Christians who will open their homes to one another.

There is the service of listening. We desperately need the help that can come through listening to one another. We do not need to be trained psychoanalysts to be trained listeners. The most important requirements are compassion and patience. We do not have to have the correct answers to listen well. In fact, often the correct answers are a hindrance to listening, for we become more anxious to give the answer than to hear. An impatient half-listening is an affront to the person sharing.

There is the service of bearing the burdens of each other. "Bear one another's burdens, and so fulfill the law of Christ" *(Gal. 6:2)*. The "law of Christ" is the law of love, the "royal law" as James calls it *(James 2:8)*. Love is most perfectly fulfilled when we bear the hurts and sufferings of each other, weeping with those who weep. And especially when we are with those who are going through the valley of the shadow, weeping is far better than words. If we care, we will learn to bear one another's sorrows.

Finally, there is the service of sharing the word of Life with one another. The "Poustinias" that were established by Catherine de Haeck Doherty have a rule: those who go into the deserts of silence and solitude do so for others. They are to bring back any word they receive from God and share it with others. This is a gracious service to be rendered for no individual can hear all that God wants to say. We are dependent upon one another to receive the full counsel of God. The smallest member can bring us a word—we dare not despise the service.

It is, of course, a fearful thing to proclaim these words to each other. The *fact* that God speaks to us does not guarantee that we rightly understand the message. We often mix our word with God's word: "From the same mouth come blessing and cursing" *(James 3:10)*. Such realities humble us and throw us in deep dependence upon God. But we must not draw back from this service for it is desperately needed today.

The risen Christ beckons us to the ministry of the towel. Such a ministry, flowing out of the inner recesses of the heart, is life and joy and peace. Perhaps you would like to begin by experimenting with a prayer that several of us use. Begin the day by praying, "Lord Jesus, as it would please you bring me someone today whom I can serve."

Comments on the story of the Good Samaritan
Donald K. Swearer

The text of this familiar parable is included in Chapter Seven.

The Synoptic Gospels[3] do provide us with a few specific ethical situations. There is the story of the good Samaritan (Luke 10:29–37) which not only praises people who go out of their way to help those in need but is also a lesson in race relations. The Samaritan who stopped to help the man by the side of the road was member of a race looked down upon by the Jews. This story contains some specific ethical advice, to be sure. It also exemplifies the general rule that neighborliness or humaneness demands that we offer a helping hand to those in need. Yet the striking fact about this story is not the general maxim that the *Christian* should help those in need but rather that the Christian helps those in need without reservation, hesitation, or calculation as a matter of his very being. At no point does the Samaritan pause to consider whether his status as a Samaritan should qualify his action, nor does he debate whether he should be out of pocket for the man's room and board at the inn. How does one develop this reflex action of self-giving love and concern? The story is silent at this point.

The Meaning and Nature of Diakonia
Metropolitan Paulos Mar Gregorios

Diakonia, the Greek word for service, has a particular nuance in the vocabulary of Christianity, as is explained in the article below. Metropolitan Gregorios is principal of the Orthodox Seminary, Kottayam, India. From 1983 to 1991, he served as one of the Presidents of the World Council of Churches.

The four necessary conditions of an authentic Christian *diakonia* are the following:

   a)   the willingness to suffer with those whom one serves and to give of oneself;

   b)   humility as.opposed to superiority about oneself, and respect as opposed to condescension towards those to be served;

   c)   not using diakonia as an occasion for domination, privilege and rank;

   d)   willingness to identify with the served to the point of laying down one's life for their sake.

Authentic diakonia should involve more than the giving of money or goods or services, more than the "sharing" of resources and personnel. It demands taking upon oneself the suffering of others. It demands laying aside the sense of self-sufficiency of the server, in order to feel and take on the sense of helplessness and need experienced by the served. The foreign missionaries of an earlier generation were better placed in this regard than the new interchurch aid and donor agency missionaries. The latter do not live among the people they serve, and only from a distance feel the pinch of the need of the poor. Their representatives in the field—those who handle "projects" and "programs"—are usually much better paid than routine church workers, serve out of their abundance and live lives far removed from that of the poor whom they are to serve.

We need a diaconic structure based in the people of the local church, rather than in the donor agencies or the project-holder networks they have created in their "field". Only then will the church in the locality be able to exercise its diakonia function, largely financed from the resources of the local church people, and largely involving the local Christians themselves suffering with and serving the poor.

Thus present money-and-project based interchurch aid should thus become more marginal, in order to permit the local church to exercise its diakonia of suffering with people and giving of oneself. If Christ our Lord is the model for authentic diakonia, then a diakonia which involves no cost to oneself, beyond "sharing money or personnel" can hardly be authentic.

We need constantly to repeat to ourselves that behind the New Testament concept of diakonia there are two distinct but related Old Testament concepts—the calling of Israel for the service of God, and the Old Testament model of the Suffering Servant of the Second Isaiah oracles as the true executor and fulfiller of that diakonia—the *servant of God* who suffers on behalf of others and by whose stripes they are healed.

This is the context in which Jesus Christ the true servant says constantly: "The Son of Man must suffer and be killed." Peter's avowal that this should not happen draws the Lord's most severe rebuke that it is no less than a Satanic temptation: "Get thee behind me, Satan." If our diakonia today becomes too comfortable, painless, riskless, unopposed, we will need to check whether we have fallen into the great temptation.[4]

It is in the same context that St. Paul speaks to the Corinthians about his own credentials as an ambassador of God. Those credentials are threefold:

   a)   constant suffering, affliction and humiliation;

   b)   total openness to all in unhypocritical love;

   c)   the capacity to take acceptance and rejection, approval and disapproval, with the same equanimity and rejoicing.

When I think of the church's diakonia in my own country, I find this rarely to be the case. Our credentials as a Suffering Servant in India are highly defective. Not only the official church, but even the action groups do not produce these credentials. Even Mother Teresa, who is tremendously successful Christian deacon, ambassador and servant to the poor, can hardly produce the credentials which St. Paul is talking about.

On the other hand there has been at least one suffering servant, with these credentials, whom I have encountered in India, in my own lifetime. But Mahatma Gandhi was not a baptized or believing Christian. He came to the people as a suffering servant of God, with all the three credentials. He walked into the village of Noakhali, where Hindus and Muslims were shooting and stabbing each other, in 1947. Clad in a loincloth, without sleep and without eating, with just the old man's walking stick in his hand, this frail and fragile servant walked into Muslim homes and Hindu homes, saying to the Muslims: "I am a Hindu; kill me if you want to kill a Hindu, but do not kill others." To the Hindu household, brimming with the same passionate and murderous hatred as the Muslim household, Gandhi walked in and said: "I am a friend of the Muslims; kill me first, but do not kill others." The fact that he succeeded in Noakhali shows only the power of love. The fact that he was shot by a Hindu at a joint prayer meeting of people of all religions confirms the truth that love does not always succeed, but that the true vocation of the Suffering Servant is to love to the point of laying down one's life for others.

Christians, I must say to the shame of my own community in India, should have seen, but did not acknowledge, their Lord as Suffering Servant, in this exceptionally free and dedicated "non-Christian," who held truth as his breast-plate and manifested the love of God in laying down his life that others may live.

Draw what lessons you can from this episode of a man of another faith fulfilling the role of the Suffering Servant in our time. I cannot compare a Camillo Torres or an Albert Schweitzer or a Livingstone with Gandhi. They too suffered in serving, but their credentials seem to me to have been incomplete.

Poem
Michel Quoist

Lord, why did you tell me to love all men, my brothers?
I have tried, but I come back to you, frightened. . .
Lord, I was so peaceful at home, I was so comfortably settled.
I was alone, I was at peace,
Sheltered from the wind, the rain, the mud.
I would have stayed unsullied in my ivory tower.
But, Lord, you have discovered a breach in my defences,
You have forced me to open my door,
Like a squall of rain in the face, the cry of men has awakened me.
Like a gale of wind a friendship has shaken me,
As a light slips in unnoticed, your grace has stirred me
. . . and, rashly enough, I left my door ajar. Now, Lord, I am lost!
Outside men were lying in wait for me.
I did not know they were so near; in this house, in this street, in this office; my
    neighbor, my colleague, my friend.

As soon as I started to open the door I saw them, with outstretched hands, burning eyes, longing hearts, like beggars on church steps.

The first ones came in, Lord. There was after all some space in my heart.

I welcomed them. I would have cared for them and fondled them, my very own little lambs, my little flock.

You would have been pleased, Lord, I would have served and honored you in a proper, respectable way.

Till then, it was sensible. . .

But the next ones, Lord, the other men, I had not seen them; they were hidden behind the first ones.

There were more of them, they were wretched; they overpowered me without warning.

We had to crowd in, I had to find room for them.

Now they have come from all over, in successive waves, pushing one another, jostling one another.

They have come from all over town, from all parts of the country, of the world; numberless, inexhaustible.

They don't come alone any longer but in groups, bound one to another.

They come bending under heavy loads; loads of injustice, of resentment and hate, of suffering and sin. . .

They drag the world behind them, with everything rusted, twisted, or badly adjusted.

Lord, they hurt me! They are in the way, they are everywhere.

I can't do anything any more; as they come in, they push the door, and the door opens wider. . .

Lord! my door is wide open!

I can't stand it any more! It's too much! It's no kind of a life! What about my job? my family? my peace? my liberty? and me?

Lord, I have lost everything, I don't belong to myself any longer;

There's no more room for me at home.

Don't worry, God says, you have gained all.
While men came in to you,
I, your Father,
I your God,
Slipped in among them.

You Give Them Something to Eat
Ray Buchanan

The author is a United Methodist clergyman, and the cofounder of the Society of St. Andrew, Big Island, Virginia.

It's time to face the truth. Thirty thousand of our brothers and sisters die of hunger every day. With each death the weight of guilt upon the church grows heavier. Martin Bell phrased it succinctly in The Way of the Wolf: "It is terrifying to see a starving child. It is more terrifying to be a starving child. Starvation is horrible. To be without food is hell." When we in the church choose not to act, not to alleviate the torment of the hungry, we sentence them to hell. But, let's understand. We pronounce the same sentence on ourselves.

We have to stop kidding ourselves. Every single hungry person on this planet is an indictment against a fat and prosperous church. Every malnourished child calls our bluff. "He who withholds but a pennyworth of worldly goods from his neighbor, knowing him to be in need of it, is a robber in the sight of God. Further, I declare, who spares a penny for himself to put it by against a rainy day, thinking, I may need that for tomorrow, is a murderer before God." This statement is just as true today as it was when originally written in the late thirteenth century by the German mystic, Meister Eckhart. Our idleness and lack of action in the face of millions of such needy children is a stark reflection of the emptiness of our spirituality. Our hope is as hollow as our faith if we think that a loving God would deign to bless us who sentence our brothers and sisters to the torture of hunger. To believe otherwise is an absurdity beyond comprehension.

Jesus said: "You give them something to eat." It is a simple command. It can be obeyed or it can be ignored. But it cannot be misunderstood. Spoken on a crowded hillside near Bethsaida nearly 2000 years ago, these words of Jesus place a divine mandate on all Christians to provide food for the hungry. For people of faith there is only one correct response to the cries of the hungry. That response is action. Anything less is immoral, irrelevant, and totally unacceptable. Action on behalf of our hungry brothers and sisters is where faithfulness and righteousness merge into justice, and justice demands that we share our resources with the poor and hungry. Whom do we think we are fooling? Mothers holding listless, malnourished infants are not interested in our platitudes. Fathers digging shallow graves to bury their emaciated sons do not care about our theology. The parents of the starving want one thing: food for their children. And Jesus still says to us, "You give them something to eat."

The numbers are staggering. United Nations calculations show that over 786 million people face "chronic malnutrition" in developing regions of the world. This extremely conservative estimate doesn't include either the hungry in the developed world or those of seventy-two countries with a population of less than 1,000,000. World Bank figures provide an even more frightening perspective on the numbers of hungry. In their estimates, over one billion people were under the poverty line of $1.00 a day in 1989. Since poverty is a root cause of hunger, these World Bank figures paint a horrifying picture of hunger in our world. It is difficult to imagine anyone in need of food in our own country. Yet, the vulgar reality is that over thirty million citizens of the United States are hungry on a regular basis. These are people who have nothing to eat two or more days each month. Again the question has to be raised: How can such obscenity exist in the midst of the richest, most affluent nation in the history of our planet? Am I missing something? Where are the people of faith?

The numbers of hungry in our country continue to escalate. How does that happen, especially in a country that has historically prided itself in its compassion and altruism? The latest US Census Bureau data confirm this grim picture. In October 1994, the bureau released data that should send a shock wave of revulsion through people of faith, regardless of their political stripe. In the wealthiest nation in the history of this glorious planet, over 15 percent of the population now lives in poverty. At the writing of this article over 39.3 million of our brothers and sisters are living under the poverty line. Over twelve percent of our elderly (65 and over) lives in poverty.

There is good news, however. No one needs to die from hunger. No more children must suffer from malnourishment and malnutrition. More than enough food to feed all the human family is already being grown. That's right. Enough food is available to feed all the world's hungry. That's the good news. But for our hungry brothers and sisters to be fed, these God–given resources must be equitably distributed.

Thirty thousand of our brothers and sisters are dying from hunger every single day, even when the food necessary for their survival is available. What is required is justice. This is where faithfulness and righteousness have to come together on behalf of the hungry. We who call ourselves Christian must act to implement a system of just distribution of food and other necessary resources. We in the church bear the responsibility for ensuring a just and equitable distribution. There is no one else to whom we can appeal, No other group is accountable. We in The United Methodist Church can begin to create a world where hunger is only a memory. The key is action. We must begin to act, and act now on behalf of the hungry. We who call ourselves Christians must act to implement a system of just distribution of food and other necessary resources. We in the church bear the responsibility for ensuring a just and equitable distribution. There is no one else to who we can appeal. No other group is accountable.

The key is action. We must begin to act, and act now on behalf of the hungry. We only have to look around us to see the faces of the poor and hungry. Every face is an invitation for faithfulness and righteousness to merge into justice. Forget the idea that before we can act we must pray and study and meditate on the correct course of action. All that is required is that we feed the hungry. Prayer, study, and meditation can wait until our brothers and sisters have taken their rightful place at the table with us. Just do it! That is all faithfulness requires. When that happens we will be part of a glorious explosion of spiritual power. We will see a world where hunger is only a distant memory. The Spanish poet Lorca envisioned such a world. He wrote: "The day hunger is eradicated from the earth, there will be the greatest spiritual explosion the world has ever known. Humanity cannot imagine the joy that will burst into the world on the day of that great revolution."

O God, My Heart is Ready: The St. Thomas Choir School Soup Kitchen
Gordon Clem

The only church-related boarding school of its kind remaining in the United States, the Choir School of St. Thomas Church, Fifth Avenue, is a tiny school with a big mission. Its student body of forty–fifty boys in grades four through eight must meet the demands of a rigorous academic curriculum. Each boy also takes his turn as a highly trained member of the soprano section of the renowned St. Thomas Choir of Men and Boys, which provides service music for worship many times per week, supplemented by a full schedule of concerts, tours, and recording sessions. The school's motto, taken from Psalm 108, is "O God, my heart is ready;" indeed, these boys are expected to be ready for an unrelenting schedule of activities. Daily evening prayer in the school's living room provides a quiet time for the boys to gather and reflect on their busy lives in New York City—a place fraught with as many oppressive problems as it is full of exciting possibilities. Gordon Clem, who joined the St. Thomas faculty in 1955 and served as its headmaster from 1955 until his retirement in 1995, recalls that on one such evening in 1983, the conversation centered on the overwhelming nature of the problems of the world at large: nuclear proliferation, wars, drugs, famine, AIDS . . . Could a small band of choirboys hope to do anything about any of this, or must it all be left in the hands of presidents and prime ministers? As the discussion continued, it became clear that, while they might not be able to solve the problem of hunger in Ethiopia or the Sudan, quite possibly the hunger which was quite literally on the Choir School doorstep could be alleviated by their efforts—if only for a few hours. They just might be able to give someone something to eat on a Saturday morning who might not otherwise have anything to eat. Choirboys might not be able to solve the problem of homelessness, but they might make a dent in the problem of hopelessness. Their hearts were ready; Mr. Clem reflects on the outcome.

Our first step was to do a survey of midtown Manhattan. We walked up and down all the avenues and streets between 40th Street and Central Park South, and between Park and Tenth Avenues. We weren't very good at looking for homeless people; we found only thirty. On the first Saturday of November, 1983, the boys made and delivered bag lunches to those thirty people. The St. Thomas Soup Kitchen was born.

Initially, the boys were assisted only by their teachers and some of the Choir School parents. The adults of the parish were a little slower to become involved. It quickly became clear that those individuals whom the Soup Kitchen served looked forward to their mobile lunch each week. However, our students were not always available every Saturday, and this troubled them. When the dilemma was brought to the St. Thomas Vestry, a partnership was formed; adults of the parish would take up the slack, and the boys could rest assured that their clients would not be forgotten when other duties called them away. About halfway through the Soup Kitchen's first year, a dozen other independent and parochial schools began to send teams of students, teachers, and parents regularly. Gradually, we have built up a wealth of volunteers from around the city who supplement our work force, especially when the boys are on vacation.

The thirty to whom we ministered on that first Saturday has grown to 300–400. That's the number we now try to feed each week, and I suspect that if we had enough volunteers and we made 3000 lunches, it still would not be enough. We meet every Saturday morning in the school's Dining Room to prepare lunches: a sandwich (usually ham and cheese, pot roast, or tuna salad), hot soup (fruit juice in the summer), and dessert (most often fruit). Working assembly-line fashion, many hands make light work, especially when most are familiar with the routine. Within half an hour, 300 sandwiches have been made, 300 cups of soup have been poured, capped, and the lids taped on to guard against spillage. Everything is put into individual paper bags; ten bags go into each of the bright red baskets with "St. Thomas" printed on the sides—a gift of Ernest Klein's

Market. The routes, which have been standardized with time and experience, are divided up. Then the morning's crew bundles up, grabs their baskets, and hits the sidewalks to deliver the lunchbags wherever they find the homeless: in doorways, parking garages, subway stations, bus and train terminals, and even the atrium of an office building.

We had to learn where to find the destitute, and how to approach them. The hungry had to learn to trust us. Joshua Mosher, Class of 1988, remembers the routine: "If we spotted people who seemed needy, we would go up to them and ask, 'Would you like a lunch?' Many accepted happily, but a good number refused to accept our gifts. Some even refused but then tried to grab a lunch while we weren't looking. The homeless can fiercely defend their self-respect." We have learned from practice, and from suggestions from those whom we serve. For instance, "Tony Bananas" of the 53rd Street subway station introduced us to Red Flynn and other regulars there. They make sure everyone is served. Whenever someone is missing, they tell us where we can find him. While usually our students don't encounter much jostling and pushing any more, some people still are aggressive, and even take more than one lunch. I remind the boys that not everyone who gets a lunch needs a lunch, but if 250 of them are delivered into the hands of truly needy people, it is worth the extra fifty.

At holidays, we try to make our lunches more special by adding things like handwritten cards, blueberry muffins, cranberry cake, and a chocolate Santa. Sometimes we are able to include toiletries or warm hats and scarves donated by the police department. While the homeless get handouts of used clothing from agencies like the Salvation Army, how wonderful it is to offer them a selection and let them choose something brand new! Jonathan Mosher, Class of 1994, remembers passing out blankets in the cold months. "Once St. Bartholomew's Church had a lot of stuffed animals left at the end of a tag sale; they gave them to us to give out with the lunches that week." Often, we also included brochures telling where in Manhattan to find meals each day of the week, where to get housing, and other such services.

Who pays for it? We get surplus food from the Human Resources Administration. Any time the Metropolitan Opera has a gala with food left over, they send it by. On those mornings, our lunches feature fantastic cheeses! Local restaurants also think of us when they have food they cannot use. Individuals and corporations sometimes donate money as well, including some of the homeless themselves. Sometimes a person will wait for us on the street and say, "Hey, I got a job now and you used to feed me," and give us a dollar or two to help with someone else's lunch.

As the project grew, so did discussions at the Choir School. One-on-one contacts had made the homeless and their concerns real to us; there were new friends for whom to pray. The boys saw how meaningful their lunches and their caring were to the people they served, how even a single kind word could help ward off despair. When they learned that unless one has a mailing address, one cannot receive Social Security payments, the boys decided to lobby the federal government for mail drops for the homeless. One of our regular patrons was an eighty-two-year-old gentleman who would wait for us on Ninth Avenue. For many years, he had been trying to get the documents he needed to qualify for Social Security benefits, a complicated task because he had entered the United States as an undocumented infant. One Saturday in February, he informed us that he would no longer need our lunches; he had received his first Social Security check the day before. He also said that he wanted to pay us back by joining us in making and distributing the lunches. What a privilege it was to share in his moment of happiness and to welcome him into our fold of volunteers.

Volunteers leave and others take their place. Choirboys have served and graduated. Some return to help the Soup Kitchen as adults; others have gone on to serve in other ways in other places. Some are moved by the experience; all seem to be affected by it. Joshua reflects: "When I was a student at the Choir School, participating in the Soup Kitchen was not something I did eagerly, nor at the time did I think too deeply about its purpose. I am sure that the adults had a fully-developed rationale, but we students were just asked to do our part. Beyond duty, I felt that it was a matter of compassion and fairness. Compassion, because the homeless obviously lacked much and few seemed to care about them or treat them as persons even for a moment, so shouldn't we as Christians do our best to love the homeless as ourselves? Fairness, because I believed that everybody had a right in our society to not go hungry, and we who had plenty had a responsibility to help those who had little."

Our Soup Kitchen ministry has not always been easy. There have been occasions when we have been kicked out of buildings, chased from storefronts, eyed suspiciously by those in authority. Familiar faces have disappeared from view; we are left wondering if they were helped or if they have fallen prey to further tragedy. Our students have responsibilities at three services every Sunday; the temptation to do something restful on Saturday morning is great! Some have asked why we keep doing the Soup Kitchen; our response to that evening of prayer and reflection in 1983 could have stopped with one Saturday— or one year—of lunch-making. The obvious answer is that there are many hungry people on the streets in our neighborhood and, as Joshua pointed out, Christians are called to feed the hungry and aid the homeless. Less obvious is the pleasure and satisfaction that comes to us all. For St. Thomas Choir School, the homeless have become real people with names, personalities, and stories to share. They greet us every day with beautiful smiles and a cheery "God bless you" as we walk the several blocks between school and church. We have formed friendships with those we serve and with those who serve with us. We have become family.

Mission on the Doorstep
William G. Carter

William Carter is now pastor of the First Presbyterian Church, Clarks Summit, PA.

One early November morning, the custodian rang the doorbell at the church manse. "Reverend," he said, "those kids are back! They're sleeping on the church steps. What are you going to do?"

He led me outside and pointed to a little alcove in the building next door. Two dirty figures were huddled on a concrete staircase, fast asleep.

"I thought you got rid of them," said the custodian, "but now they are back. What are you going to do?"

I didn't know.

It had been over a year since I had taken the young unmarried couple to a homeless shelter in nearby Bethlehem, Pennsylvania. Brad, 21, and Maria, 23, had lived on the street for about ten months. After landing in our small suburban town of Catasauqua, they had exhausted the patience of most of the ministers in our community.

The first time I ever saw them was the night they came looking for food. Not knowing much about them, I reached into the cupboard and pulled out some easy-to-fix dinners. Brad looked at one of the boxes and said, "I don't like macaroni and cheese."

Maria was more practical. "We're homeless," she said. "How are we going to cook something like this?" She stood to leave.

I asked her and Brad to remain and went inside to grab that morning's newspaper. We sat down on the porch together to look at the want ads. After a few minutes, Brad said, "I'm not sure I want a job." This time he stood to leave.

"Look," I said, pointing to an ad. "There's a fast food place that's hiring people at five dollars an hour."

"Didn't you hear us?" Maria said. "We're homeless. We have not washed for weeks. You expect somebody to hire us?" She stood to join Brad. They trudged away in silence.

The next morning I compared notes with neighboring pastors. All of them had tried to help Brad and Maria in their own ways. One after another pastor had offered food, shelter, and jobs, but to no avail. Apparently I was the last one to be approached. One colleague spoke for most, I think, when she said, "I want to help, but those two have either spurned my help or taken advantage of my generosity."

A few days later, our church's custodian was shocked to discover Brad and Maria sleeping in an alcove outside the sanctuary. Afraid to confront them, he called from a phone inside the building to tell me about it. I went next door and woke the young couple.

"Sorry," Maria said with embarrassment, "we must have overslept. We're usually awake and out of here by now."

"How long have you been sleeping here?" I asked.

"About a month."

I took them to a local restaurant for breakfast. Then we returned to the church office and called a number of homeless shelters in the area. One of them offered room and hot meals. Piling them into my car, I helped Brad and Maria gather up the belongings they had stashed in hiding places around town. Then I drove them to the shelter and we said goodbye. I didn't know if I would ever see them again.

Now a year had passed. Brad and Maria had returned to sleep on the church steps once again.

When the couple awoke, they told me about their many difficulties over the last year. "We tried to make it on our own," Brad said, "but we failed every time."

Much to their surprise, the couple had also become the parents of a child who was now two months old. Their daughter was staying with a relative some distance away while they were living on the street.

My own situation had also changed. Four weeks before Brad and Maria reappeared, I had told the congregation that I had accepted a call to another pastorate. The last month had been spent saying goodbye to a beloved congregation and attending to my family's needs. Because of my impending move, I could not offer any long-term help.

After taking the homeless couple to breakfast, I phoned some of the elders and told them about the situation. They knew the story of my prior attempts to help Brad and Maria. Two elders, George James and Lou Zerfass, promised to meet with Brad and Maria before the next week's Session[5] meeting. It would be my final meeting as moderator of the Catasauqua Session. "Don't worry," George James said, "we will do what we can."

After meeting with the homeless couple, George made a motion at the Session meeting. He said, "I move that we allocate five hundred dollars from undesignated funds as seed money for helping Brad and Maria find a new home in our community."

Lou Zerfass seconded the motion, adding, "This is a mission on our doorstep." After some debate over the exact use of the funds, the motion passed.

Within two days, the moving van carried my family's belongings to our new home. I could do nothing but pray for Brad and Maria.

Months went by. Friends from the Catasauqua congregation gave me occasional updates on Brad and Maria's situation. Yet geographical distance, excitement over a new position, and ongoing pastoral demands prevented my close contact. I did not know the full story until someone sent me a newspaper article dated six months after my departure.

After I left, the clipping said, the elders had mobilized the congregation to action. Arrangements were made for Brad and Maria to stay at a local motel until a reasonably priced apartment could be found. That took seven weeks. When a suitable apartment became available, the church loaned Brad and Maria the funds to cover the first month's rent.

Church members were invited to donate used furniture for the couple. Their gifts completely furnished the apartment. As Brad told the news reporter, "We've never met people who would do something for us like that."

George James and his family took a special interest in Brad and Maria. George took Brad for his first haircut in months and helped him get a job in a nearby shopping center. In lean times, he brought the young couple home for dinner. During the cold Pennsylvania winter, he took Brad to work each day and arranged for Brad to get a ride back to the apartment. Soon Brad and Maria paid back every dollar the Session had given them. Their daughter now lives with them.

In time, Brad and Maria chose to start attending worship in the Catasauqua church. They felt awkward at first, but discovered that the people of the congregation were both friendly and genuinely concerned about their welfare. The young couple asked the supply pastor, the Rev. Max Conley, to perform their wedding in March 1991. On Pentecost, May, 19, 1991, Brad and Maria joined the church. Their daughter was baptized on the same day. The church that once unknowingly offered physical shelter to Brad and Maria had now become their home.

Brad and Maria were not the only people whose lives were changed. As George James put it, "This has been an eventful time for our church. God placed a challenge literally on our doorstep that we could not turn down. When we baptized Brad and Maria's daughter, we promised to support that young family in the name of Jesus Christ. We intend to take our promise seriously."

I am proud of my former congregation. For them, homelessness is no longer an abstract social problem in some distant city. It is the plight of real people like Brad and Maria who once slept on the church's doorstep.

Yet a second lesson may be more important. As I learned from the Catasauqua congregation, homelessness is not a problem that a religious professional should try to "fix" alone. It is an opportunity for the church to be the church, for all baptized people to offer sanctuary for God's children.

Mother Teresa of Calcutta
Eileen Egan

Through Eileen Egan's own work at Catholic Relief Services with refugees and displaced persons, she met and became a supporter of Mother Teresa's efforts, serving as Vice–Chair of the International Co–Workers of Mother Teresa. She is also an associate editor of *Catholic Worker,* the paper founded by Dorothy Day. Egan's anecdotes and insights regarding Mother Teresa create an interesting counterpoint to those of Malcolm and Kitty Muggeridge, in that she herself has been highly acclaimed for her own relief work. It is time well spent to read the remainder of her essay on Mother Teresa.

At the shrine of the goddess Kali in Calcutta is a caravanserai. It is ivory in color and from its roof rise eight bulbous, fluted cupolas topped by slender spires. The structure is built around a large inner courtyard, after the manner of the traditional *serai,* or hostel for pilgrims and merchants. Such hostels marked the old Middle East caravan routes and the ancient Silk Route to Asia. This hostel was intended to serve the poorest pilgrims who make their *puja,* their act of worship, to Kali, goddess of death and destruction. Her image, with its necklace of skulls, stood nearby in its shrine, a squat, silver-domed temple.

It was the least likely place in which to find a Catholic nun, yet it was there that Mother Teresa took me in 1955. It had become a hostel for pilgrims of the ultimate moment, men and women barely alive, picked up from the alleyways and gutters of a scourged city. The small unknown woman, then in her mid-forties, moved with gentle care in a hall filled with raging diseases, of which the all-conquering one was starvation.

The same small woman I had seen leaning over a skeletonized man in the hostel for the dying was, barely a quarter of a century later, the focus of all eyes as she mounted the platform of the Aula Magna of the University of Oslo. Then I had stood frozen with fear as she had stroked the brown, stick-like arm and murmured consoling words. On December 10, 1979, before a king and a hall filled with diplomats, politicians, members of the academy and the press, the same woman, her white cotton sari shining under the spotlights, stood framed against the sunrise mural of Edvard Munch. She had been named as the recipient of the ultimate accolade, the Nobel Prize for Peace.

The anthem of praise for Mother Teresa as the choice for the 1979 Nobel Award had been preceded by world attention never accorded to a nun in history. She had been pictured on the cover of *Time* magazine as an exemplar of a "living saint." A book on her work in Calcutta by Malcolm Muggeridge had been translated into many languages and a film based on it had been shown around the world. Universities from Cambridge to Yale had vied to present her with honorary degrees. A jury of the world's major religions had voted her the Templeton Prize for Progress in Religion, a prize which brought to the poor as significant a sum as that which accompanied the Nobel Prize. Pope Paul VI had given her the Pope John XXIII Prize for Peace and the Vatican had placed her on their delegation to the World Congress for International Women's Year. The United Nations had struck a medal depicting her image as a world figure in the struggle against hunger.

In October 1955, Mother Teresa took me through the thronged street leading to the caravanserai that had become a hostel for the dying. The door to which Mother Teresa brought me was outlined with the fanciful tracery of the Mongul scalloped arch. I looked up to see some lettering in Bengali script, and over that the fateful words, "Home for the Destitute Dying, *Nirmal Hriday.*" Over all were the words, "Corporation of Calcutta."

When we entered the immense, high-ceilinged hall, I found myself in a dropped cement walkway, between parapets raised on both sides to a height of somewhat over two feet. About sixty figures lay on pallets, thirty on each side, their heads against the walls and their feet against the walkway. The pallets were placed on metal stands, hardly above the cement floor. A sister, a large apron over her sari, was laboriously feeding a prone man, gently turning his head so that he would not suffocate. She kept drying his chin and neck as one would do to a tiny infant. Mother Teresa sat down on the parapet to take a man's hand in hers. He smiled and tried without success to raise his head. She stepped on the parapet to kneel and talk quietly to a man having difficulty breathing. Sometimes she would just listen and stroke a wasted arm or place her strong hand on a head as if in blessing. Once she slipped into English to talk to a man who must have been Anglo-Indian.

I felt that among the men in the hall there must have been all the diseases known to man. The open, infected sores, the cavernous cheeks, the faces with the terrible grin of death already upon them, paralyzed me. But what was heart-stopping was that, as Mother Teresa could not stop at every pallet, some hands were held out to me. Fear held me frozen. I wondered how she and the sisters could come there day after day. Did they not want at times to turn away?

Mother Teresa said many things to me during those days in 1955, but one thing branded itself deep in my psyche. It expressed her vision of her work and the ground of conviction behind it.

"How could we turn away from Jesus? Each one is Jesus, only Jesus in a distressing disguise. Sometimes we meet Jesus rejected and covered with filth in the gutter. Sometimes we find Jesus stuffed into a drain, or moaning with the pain of sores or rotting with gangrene—or even screaming from the agony of a broken back. The most distressing disguise calls for even more love from us."[6]

Something Beautiful For God
Malcolm Muggeridge

Although journalist Malcolm Muggeridge was baptized a Christian late in life, at the point that he wrote the following, he was very much an agnostic. He fell under Mother Teresa's spell while making a film about her for the BBC. *Something Beautiful for God* is an attempt to tell more than could the film about the Missionaries of Charity, the order Mother Teresa founded to work with the poorest of the poor. All royalties from the sale of this book have gone to benefit that work. Muggeridge succeeded in getting Mother Teresa to articulate her theology and philosophy of service. A few of her remarks follow his.

What the poor need, Mother Teresa is fond of saying, even more than food and clothing and shelter (though they need these, too, desperately), is to be wanted. It is the outcast state their poverty imposes upon them that is the most agonizing. She has a place in her heart for them all. To her, they are all children of God, for whom Christ died, and so deserving of all love. If God counts the hairs of each of their heads, if none are excluded from the salvation the Crucifixion offers, who will venture to exclude them from earthly blessings and esteem; pronounce this life unnecessary, that one better terminated or never begun? I never experienced so perfect a sense of human equality as with Mother Teresa among her poor. Her love for them, reflecting God's love, makes them equal, as brothers and sisters within a family are equal, however widely they differ in intellectual and other attainments in physical beauty and grace. Mother Teresa is fond of saying that welfare is for a purpose—an admirable and a necessary one—whereas Christian love is for a person. The one is about numbers, the other about a man who was also God. Herein lies the essential difference between welfare services and the service of Christ.

Mother Teresa speaks

Let there be no pride or vanity in the work. The work is God's work, the poor are God's poor. Put yourself completely under the influence of Jesus, so that he may think his thoughts in your mind, do his work through your hands, for you will be all-powerful with him who strengthens you.

Without our suffering, our work would just be social work, very good and helpful, but it would not be the work of Jesus Christ, not part of the Redemption. Jesus wanted to help by sharing our life, our loneliness, our agony, our death. Only by being one with us has he redeemed us. We are allowed to do the same; all the desolation of the poor people, not only their material poverty, but their spiritual destitution, must be redeemed, and we must share it, for only by being one with them can we redeem them, that is, by bringing God into their lives and bringing them to God.

The biggest disease today is not leprosy or tuberculosis, but rather the feeling of being unwanted, uncared for and deserted by everybody. The greatest evil is the lack of love and charity, the terrible indifference towards one's neighbor who lives at the roadside assaulted by exploitation, corruption, poverty and disease. As each one of this Society is to become a Co-Worker of Christ in the slums, each ought to understand what God and the Society expect from her. Let Christ radiate and live his life in her and through her in the slums. Let the poor seeing her be drawn to Christ and invite him to enter their homes and their lives. Let the sick and suffering find in her a real angel of comfort and consolation, let the little ones of the streets cling to her because she reminds them of him, the friend of the little ones. Our life of poverty is as necessary as the work itself. Only in heaven we will see how much we owe the poor for helping us to love God better because of them.

I believe the people of today do not think that the poor are like them as human beings. They look down on them. But if they had that deep respect for the dignity of poor people, I am sure it would be easy for them to come closer to them, and to see that they, too, are the children of God, and that they have as much right to the things of life and of love and of service as anybody else. In these times of development everybody is in a hurry and everybody's in a rush, and on the way there are people falling down, who are not able to compete. These are the ones we want to love and serve and take care of.

Muggeridge concludes

Doing something beautiful for God is, for Mother Teresa, what life is about. Everything, in that it is for God, becomes beautiful, whatever it may be; as does every human soul participating in this purpose, whoever he or she may be. In manifesting this, in themselves and in their lives and work, Mother Teresa and the Missionaries of Charity provide a living witness to the power and truth of what Jesus came to proclaim. His light shines in them. When I think of them in Calcutta, as I often do, it is not the bare house in a dark slum that is conjured up in my mind, but a light shining and a joy abounding. I see them diligently and cheerfully constructing something beautiful for God out of the human misery and affliction that lies around them. One of their leper settlements is near a slaughterhouse whose stench in the ordinary way might easily make me retch. There, with Mother Teresa, I scarcely notice it; another fragrance had swallowed it up. It will be for posterity to decide whether she is a saint. I only say of her that in a dark time she is a burning and shining light; in a cruel time, a living embodiment of Christ's gospel of love; in a godless time, the Word dwelling among us, full of grace and truth. For this, all who have the inestimable privilege of knowing her, or knowing of her, must be eternally grateful.

Mother Teresa and Politics
Kitty Muggeridge

Author and translator Kitty Muggeridge is also the wife of social critic Malcolm Muggeridge. The following are excerpts from her own testimonial to the life and works of Mother Teresa.

Politics are irrelevant for Mother Teresa. "There are those," she says, "who struggle for justice in the world and for human rights and try to change structures. Our mission is to look at the problem individually. If a person feels that God wants him to pledge for the collective change of the social structures, this is a question between him and God." For her, revolution "comes from God and is made of love." Mother Teresa is not a woman who judges others. The harshest comment she ever makes about even the most villainous person is that she has met "Jesus in a *very* distressing disguise." And so the Missionaries of Charity have opened houses in the third world, among the victims of consumerism who are suffering from surfeit and in even greater need of their loving care. They have opened houses in communist countries such as East Germany and Yugoslavia, and in South America, and, indeed, in countries all over the world. The one exception is Belfast, Northern Ireland, where, after a short stay, the sisters were asked to leave. As it happened, Mother Teresa, as always on the lookout for where her sisters might be needed, had just applied for permission from Haile Selassie for her Missionaries of Charity to work in Ethiopia, which was suffering from a disastrous drought at the time. Before this was granted, she was asked these questions:

"What do you want from the Government?"

"Nothing. I have only come to offer my sisters to work among the poorest suffering people."

"What will your sisters do?"

"We give wholehearted free service to the poorest of the poor."

"What qualifications do you have?"

"We try to bring tender love and compassion to the unwanted and the unloved."

"I see you have quite a different approach. Do you preach to the people, trying to convert them?"

"Our work reveals to the suffering poor the love of God for them."

In the short interview that followed, the eighty-year-old Emperor's response was: "I have heard about the good work you do. I am very happy you have come. Yes, let your sisters come to Ethiopia."

So Mother Teresa was able to write to her sisters in Belfast, telling them that through the intervention of divine providence the sisters who were excluded from Ireland were now to go to Ethiopia to "feed the hungry Christ . . . [to give] His love and compassion to the suffering people of Ethiopia."

In December 1979, the Nobel Prize Committee awarded the Nobel Prize for Peace to Mother Teresa. When her name was first put up the response was: "What has this woman done for peace?" The question is best answered by Mother Teresa herself in her Nobel Lecture. Having requested beforehand that the usual banquet should not be held and that the money which would have been spent on it be used to feed the hungry, she addressed her distinguished audience, which included the King of Norway. She spoke simply with her usual unsophisticated eloquence which went straight to the heart of her listeners.

> As we have gathered her together to thank God for the Nobel Peace Prize, I think it will be beautiful that we pray the prayer of St. Francis of Assisi which always surprises me very much and I always wonder that 400 or 500 years ago when St. Francis of Assisi composed it they had the same difficulties that we have today. As we compose this prayer that fits very nicely us also, I think some of you know it—so we will pray together. . . Let us thank God for the opportunity that we all have together today for this gift of peace that reminds us that we have been created to live in peace and that Jesus became man to bring the good news to the poor.[6]

Peace and Power
Malcolm Muggeridge and William F. Buckley, Jr.

The following dialogue was part of an interview taped February 19, 1983, in Sussex, England, for the television news program, *Firing Line.*

Mr. M: When we were trying to get the Nobel peace prize for Mother Teresa, which we had to do several years in succession to get, and then she finally got it, and the question came back from Oslo, which is where the thing is settled by these rather sombre Norwegian senators who decide who is the person of peace, that—the question came back, "What does Mother Teresa do for peace?" In other words, where does she sort of march and recite slogans and hold hands around missile sites and so on and so on; what has she done for peace?

Mr. B: She gives it a sense of priority.

Mr. M: Yes; well, the point is that she lives in the opposite proposition.

Mr. B: That's right.

Mr. M: I mean, those two great forces in our existence of power and love. She is the one who lives in terms of love. Now, that is really working for peace. That is really overcoming the menace of people who are going to totally destroy our world and ourselves. But it struck me as very humorous in a way that somebody should want to be given some point in her activities which you could say, "That is definitely in the direction of peace," and I suppose, for people who put that question, if she had actually joined this so-called peace movement that would have met the case. But of course it's much more than that.

Mr. B: Yes.

Mr. M: In her, one can see why the Christian can confront the danger of a nuclear holocaust without undue fear.

Mr. B: Well, surely in the case of Mother Teresa you have an example of somebody who is carrying out so explicitly the injunction that she should love her neighbors as to entitle you to say, "If everybody loved their neighbors as she loves her neighbors, you could not crank up the kind of hostility that would bring on belligerence."

Mr. M: Exactly.

Mother Teresa, Religion, and Society
Malcolm Muggeridge

The Universe Provides A Stage; Jesus Is The Play: Once when I was in Calcutta with Mother Teresa she picked up one of the so-called 'unwanted' babies which had come into the care of her Missionaries of Charity. It had been salvaged from a dustbin, and was so minute that one wondered it could exist at all. When I remarked on this, a look of exultation came into Mother Teresa's face, "See," she said, "there's life in it!" So there was; and suddenly it was as though I were present at the Bethlehem birth, and the baby Mother Teresa was holding another Lamb of God sent into the world to lighten our darkness.

The Prospect of Death: Mother Teresa, with characteristic audacity, calls the place where derelicts from the streets of Calcutta are brought by her Missionaries of Charity (actually a former Hindu temple), a home for dying destitutes, whereas the sanctuaries for the more affluent derelicts of the west are called rest homes.

Nobel Laureate: Along with a vast multitude of people all over the world, I rejoiced over the award of the Nobel Peace Prize to Mother Teresa. Not, obviously, because the award, as such, enhanced her, though she may well have enhanced the award; funded, as it is, by conscience money provided by the inventor of dynamite. After all, previous recipients were the Prime Minister of North Vietnam and Dr. Kissinger; not exactly doves of peace, I should have thought. No, the glory of the award was precisely the glow of satisfaction it gave to all of us who love and respect Mother Teresa, in the knowledge that it would serve to spread yet further afield awareness of the ministry of love and compassion in which she and her Missionaries of Charity are so valiantly engaged.

The True Crisis of Our Time: Again there is Mother Teresa and her ever-growing Missionaries of Charity, going about their work of love with their own special geography of compassion moving into country after country. Sisters, now of many nationalities, arriving in twos and threes in the troubled places of this troubled world with nothing to offer except Christ, no other purpose than to see in every suffering man or woman, the person of their Savior and to heed his words "Insofar as ye did it unto the least of these my brethren ye did it unto me."

A Prayer
Mother Teresa of Calcutta

Make us worthy, Lord,
To serve our fellowmen throughout the world
    who live and die in poverty or hunger.
Give them, through our hands this day their daily bread,
And by our understanding love, give joy and peace.

Dorothy Day: A Radical Devotion
Robert Coles

Dorothy Day was a feisty woman with the courage of her convictions. This is apparent the moment we learned that she was arrested several times: the first time when she was twenty, for picketing the White House on behalf of women's right to vote; the last time when she was seventy-five, for protesting with Caesar Chavez and the United Farmworkers. She was in the forefront of social justice efforts for over a half–century, founded the Catholic Worker Movement with her friend, Peter Maurin, and is said to have had more of an impact on American Catholicism than any other lay person.

Robert Coles is a renown psychiatrist, author, and teacher. His long friendship with Dorothy Day began when, while he was a young medical student, he wandered into one of her Catholic Worker soup kitchens. Here follow some of his impressions of her and her work.

It was on that afternoon, almost thirty-five years ago, that I first met Dorothy Day. She was sitting at a table, talking with a woman who was, I quickly realized, quite drunk, yet determined to carry on a conversation. The woman to whom Dorothy Day was talking had a large purple-red birthmark along the right side of her forehead. She kept touching it as she uttered one exclamatory remark after another, none of which seemed to get the slightest rise from the person sitting opposite her.

I found myself increasingly confused by what seemed to be an interminable, essentially absurd exchange taking place between the two middle-aged women. When would it end—the alcoholic ranting and the silent nodding, occasionally interrupted by a brief question, which only served, maddeningly, to wind up the already overtalkative one rather than wind her down? Finally, silence fell upon the room. Dorothy Day asked the woman if she would mind an interruption. She got up and came over to me. She said, "Are you waiting to talk with one of us?"

One of us! With those three words she had cut though layers of self-importance, a lifetime of bourgeois privilege, and scraped the hard bone of pride: "Vanity of vanities; all is vanity." With those three words, so quietly and politely spoken, she had indirectly told me what the Catholic Worker Movement is all about and what she herself was like. There would be other lessons, many just as hard to absorb and keep alive within myself. Dorothy Day was a most determined teacher, well aware that in those, like me, who came to learn from her, modesty and humility are poses difficult to sustain for long stretches of time.

A Life Remembered

Dorothy Day's early tumultuous, aimless years included several relationships with men, one culminating in an abortion. Having been jailed before for suffrage activities, she found herself behind bars again—this time for her involvement with the Wobblies (International Workers of the World). Coles notes that although she found comfort in reading the Bible during this imprisonment, "organized religion" did not yet appeal to her.

As she continued her political activism, Dorothy Day's ability as a writer blossomed. Her unconventional lifestyle now included a common law marriage to scientist Forster Batterham, whose politics leaned toward anarchism and whose theology was decidedly atheistic. Their relationship came to an end over Dorothy Day's decision to have their infant daughter, Tamar Teresa, baptized in the Catholic Church, and her eventual decision to become a Catholic herself. From that point onward, she endeavored to be "not only a Catholic, but a Catholic who wanted to learn how to live her life according to the teachings of Jesus Christ, whom the church claims as its founder. Put differently, her conversion was not nominal." Her next turning point came as a result of the Great Depression.

Dorothy could not ignore what she saw around her everywhere—the poverty and pain of men and women who walked the streets hoping for a handout, anything. As she watched so many people endure humiliation and jeopardy, she began to wonder why the major institutions of the nation were unwilling, she believed, to respond to the need for food, shelter, and clothing. America was a rich and powerful nation, and in New York, as well as in other American cities, she had seen how much wealth was available: blocks and blocks of fancy townhouses and apartment houses and stores and churches, including Catholic ones, to which came flocks of well-dressed, well-fed parishioners. She could not simply accept the disparities of "the facts of life." She read the Bible and went to church every day; she read papal encyclicals or books devoted to Catholic social teaching, and she felt that Christ's words, His example, and His admonitions had somehow been forgotten, even by priests and nuns, bishops and cardinals. Her response was not to turn on the church, but rather to pray for it, as she prayed for her friends and for herself.

Turning-point

Dorothy Day despaired the lack of help forthcoming from state or church agencies. Coles notes her mentioning many times that in 1929, when Canon Cardijn was organizing Belgian workers, Pope Pius XI had remarked sadly: "The workers of the world are lost to the Church," a statement which had a profound effect on her.

She would never forget that papal statement. It can be said that her entire life from 1932 until her death was dedicated to working against its assumptions. It was in November of 1932 that she learned of a "hunger march" to Washington, an effort to make known loudly and clearly to the nation's leaders what was happening to millions of its citizens. She had, by then, written many pieces for *Commonweal,* a liberal Catholic magazine, and she wanted very much to record what happened to the hundreds who assembled in Union Square, her old political haunt, in order to take their cause to the steps of America's Capitol Building.

While in Washington, on December 8, 1932, saddened and angered by what she saw in Union Square, on the way to Washington, and in that city—a small army of desperately impoverished and vulnerable people who were pleading for food, for a chance to work, to assert their dignity as citizens—she went to the National Shrine of the Immaculate Conception at Catholic University and prayed with all her heart and soul for a chance to "use what talents" she could find within herself for her "fellow workers, for the poor." On her return to New York City she found a man named Peter Maurin waiting for her. George M. Shuster, then *Commonweal's* editor, had come to know Maurin, and of course had admired his contributor Dorothy Day for some time. He recognized their similarity of views and shared willingness to mix religion and politics as activists. Maurin was quick to accept Shuster's suggestion that he meet Dorothy Day, talk with her, and determine with her what might be done on behalf of the poor.

On many occasions Dorothy made it quite clear that for her Peter's "spirit and ideas" were utterly essential to the rest of her life. She was inspired by his struggle to make the principles of Jesus incarnate in the kind of life he lived, to rescue them from those who had turned Him into an icon of Sunday convenience. The Catholic Worker Movement became their shared initiative.[7]

The newspaper came first, of course; they were both writers. On May Day 1933 the two of them had 2,500 copies of *The Catholic Worker* available for distribution. They had not opened an office, hired a staff, secured mailing lists, or planned elaborate promotion. They had raised $57 from two priests and a nun and from their own almost empty pockets, and with the help of a printer had put out a small eight-page edition. Then came the attempt to attract readers, by a long march from the Lower East Side to Union Square, where they joined the political crowds assembled there and peddled their paper, no doubt to the surprise of many onlookers, for whom the juxtaposition of "Catholic" and "worker" seemed anomalous.

In a way, as Dorothy Day herself once put it, "the rest was history." She was not being grandiose, as she made clear by her immediate qualifications. "I mean by 'history' the history of all of us who have been part of the Catholic Worker family. That's what happened, that's what we became, a family spread across all the cities and states of this country." Within a few years, *The Catholic Worker* had a circulation of over a hundred and fifty thousand, with many more readers than that figure suggests, because it has always been a paper that is handed from person to person.

Yet Dorothy Day and Peter Maurin were not content simply to write about what they believed the Catholic church has to offer the ordinary worker, to publish their moral and political philosophy. They both believed in the importance of "works." Together they founded the hospitality houses that became part of the American social scene for men and women who had no other place to go, nothing to eat, and were at the mercy of whatever secular or religious charity happened to be available. Peter Maurin envisioned a twentieth-century version of the ancient notion of hospice, a place where "works of mercy" were offered and acknowledged in a person–to–person fashion, as opposed to the faceless, bureaucratic procedures of the welfare state. He shared that vision with Dorothy Day. Together they started to make the vision real, by renting a store, an apartment, buying bread and butter, making coffee, preparing soup, serving food to the homeless, finding clothes for them, offering them, when possible, a place to sleep, and very important, sitting with them, trying to converse, hoping in some way to offer them friendship and affection. Other people joined to help, and in time there would be over thirty "houses of hospitality" across the nation. Over the years more have started, folded, and sometimes got going again.

The Catholic Worker has dwelt often on the moral as well as political significance of agriculture. Beyond its obvious purpose of growing food, it is also an antidote to the alienation caused by industrialism, which separates us from the barebones of life and makes us spend entire lives in offices or on assembly lines. Farms were built up by the men and women and children who became part of the Catholic Worker family in New England and New York State, in Appalachia, in the Midwest, and on the Pacific Coast. In all those places knots of kindred souls became centers of action. Newspapers appeared in Chicago, Buffalo, St. Louis, Seattle, Houston, Los Angeles, and as far away as England and Australia. There was no party line, no set of rules or positions handed down to the various hospitality houses or farms or newspapers. Thousands of men and women the world over responded in various ways to the example and determination of two Catholic laypersons, Dorothy Day and Peter Maurin.

From May Day 1933 until November 29, 1980, when she died, Dorothy Day lived without interruption as a Catholic Worker. She edited the paper of that name, she lived in the hospitality houses of that name, and she traveled by bus across the United States, teaching and speaking, helping to cook, and sitting with people the rest of us call bums or homeless or drunks. She also kept saying her prayers, going through devotional rhythms, reading and rereading the books she loved and writing her *Catholic Worker* column, "On Pilgrimage." Tamar grew up at her side, then left, married, and made her mother a grandmother numerous times.

During those years Dorothy Day took on many a controversy. She stood up to Franco when he started the Spanish civil war, thereby losing lots of Catholic readers who saw Franco as a godsend who was leading a Catholic charge against the atheists, the Communists who had taken over Spain. She argued the case for pacifism during the Second World War, a lonely stance, indeed, and one that many of her closest friends, her most enthusiastic coworkers adamantly rejected. After the war, she continued her work among the poor and on behalf of those whom we now call minorities. (One of the first efforts she and Peter Maurin made was in Harlem, at the very start of their work together.) I well remember her, during the 1960s, riding buses in the South, involving herself in the civil rights struggle, and showing up on the West Coast alongside Cesar Chavez. By then she was a veteran of marches and demonstrations and picket lines and jails, someone who had learned to live simply, travel lightly. Wherever she was she found time every day for prayer, for reading the Bible, for attending Mass, taking Communion, and saying confession.

The last time I saw her, not long before her death, I had taken a group of my students to the Catholic Worker office, to St. Joseph's House, and to Maryhouse, where she lived. She was frail, but she stood straight and was gracious as she had been years earlier when she had the strength to serve personally the hundreds of homeless people who came daily to the Catholic Worker kitchen for soup and coffee and bread.

An Inquiring Idealism

Over the past half century many young men and women have been drawn toward the Catholic Worker Movement, considering its principles and approach to social problems compelling enough to warrant serious study or a commitment of time and energy. By no means have all of them been professing Catholics or Christian or even religious in any conventional or explicit sense of the word. Agnostics and atheists in significant numbers have found their way to the hospitality houses and devoted time to them.

The hospitality houses are places where one can do concrete work on behalf of others. Many young men and women who feel within themselves surges of idealism don't know what to do about it. A skeptic might say that they don't look hard enough, but it isn't always easy for people to find opportunities for charity in the biblical sense of the word, free from the implication of condescension. In the hospitality houses there is an immediacy to the charitable gesture, a directness, unmediated by bureaucracy and self-consciousness, that many young people find appealing.

Dorothy Day began her social activism on the campus of the University of Illinois and for years was willing to go talk with young people, wherever and whenever they invited her to come, within the limits of her own obligations. She never ceased being interested in young people, responsive to their questions, and aware of their hungers and thirsts. "When young people come here," she said,
we are grateful for their interest. I have watched some of them, trying so hard to talk with those men and women standing in line or sitting with their coffee and soup. The students know so much, and yet they are learning. The poor who come here feel there is little they have to offer anyone, and yet they have a lot to offer. The giving and the receiving is not only going on in one direction.

A House of Hospitality

Nothing mattered more to Dorothy Day than the way she lived her life. For almost a half century she chose to live alongside the urban poor. She and her fellow Catholic Workers are not the kind of reformers who live in one world while hoping to change another. The Catholic Worker houses of hospitality are meant to be communities in which the so-called helpers merge with those who, in the conventional sense, would be regarded as needing help. During stays in these houses, I've felt that the aim is for the workers and the guests to be indistinguishable.

She was always trying to reach others, to encourage them to do a stint of work on behalf of the needy. In *House of Hospitality* she tells of "thousands," men and women all over the country, who became involved as Catholic Workers. Not all of them, of course, made that most serious commitment of living for a while in one of the houses. Many came, were touched, and went back to campus or job, but with a determination to help in their own way. Some offered to do volunteer work, to prepare or serve food, to distribute clothes. Some got closer and became day-to-day members of a Catholic Worker community: a life immersed in service, prayer, and reflection.[8]

Habitat for Humanity: 'No More Shacks'
Kerra Davis

Habitat for Humanity International (HFHI) is a nonprofit, ecumenical Christian housing ministry. HFHI seeks to eliminate poverty housing and homelessness from the world, and to make decent shelter a matter of conscience and action. Habitat invites people from all walks of life to work together in partnership to help build houses with families in need. Habitat has built more than 40,000 houses around the world, providing some 250,000 people with safe decent, affordable shelter.

Habitat is a grassroots movement. Concerned citizens from all walks of life come together as volunteers to form a HFHI affiliate in their community. Fund-raising, house construction, family selection and other key decisions are carried out by the local affiliates. HFHI headquarters, located in Americus, GA, provides information, training, prayer support and other services to Habitat affiliates worldwide.

An ecumenical, international board of directors determines policy and monitors operations in conjunction with a board of advisors. Board members are dedicated volunteers who are deeply concerned about the problems of poverty housing around the world. HFHI headquarters operates with an administrative staff, assisted by a core group of professional, clerical and support employees and supplemented by long-term and short-term volunteers. Each Habitat for Humanity affiliate is managed by a volunteer board.

Through volunteer labor and tax-deductible donations of money and materials, Habitat builds and rehabilitates simple, decent houses with the help of the homeowner (partner) families. Habitat houses are sold to partner families at no profit, financed with affordable, no-interest loans. The homeowners' monthly mortgage payments go into a revolving Fund for Humanity that is used to build more houses. Habitat is not a give-away program. In addition to a down payment and the monthly mortgage payments, homeowners invest hundreds of hours of their own labor—sweat equity—into building their houses and the houses of others.

In 1996, a three-bedroom Habitat house in the United States cost the homeowner an average of $38,000. Prices differ slightly depending on location and the costs of land, professional labor and materials. In developing nations, a Habitat house costs $500–$5,000, depending on design, materials and location.

Habitat houses are affordable for low-income families because there is no profit included in the sale price and no interest charged on the mortgage. The average length of a Habitat mortgage in the United States is twenty years. Internationally, mortgage length varies from seven to thirty years.

Whether in the U.S. or overseas, families in need apply to local Habitat affiliates. The affiliate's family selection committee chooses homeowners based on their level of need, their willingness to become partners in the program and their ability to repay the no-interest loan. Every affiliate follows a nondiscriminatory policy of family selection. Neither race nor religion is a factor in choosing the families who receive Habitat houses. There are now more than 1,200 active affiliates located in all fifty states and the District of Columbia. There also are more than 200 international affiliates coordinating some 800 building projects in nearly fifty nations around the world.

Due to the extreme poverty found in many developing nations, Habitat affiliates in developing countries often receive funds for house-building from HFHI headquarters. However, international affiliates are required to raise as much of their funding locally as possible. All Habitat affiliates are asked to tithe—to give ten percent of their unrestricted cash contributions to fund house building work in developing nations.

Donations, whether to a local Habitat affiliate or to HFHI headquarters, are used as designated by the donor. Gifts received by HFHI headquarters that are designated to a specific affiliate or building project are forwarded to that affiliate or project. Any undesignated gifts are used where most needed and for administrative expenses.

Habitat does not accept government funds for the construction of new houses or for the renovation or repair of existing houses. Habitat does accept government funds for the acquisition of land or houses in need of rehabilitation. Habitat also accepts government funds for streets, utilities, and administrative expenses, so long as the funds have no strings attached that would violate Habitat's principles or limit its ability to proclaim its Christian witness. Former President Jimmy Carter has lent considerable support to Habitat For Humanity International, on organization whose motto is: "Unless the Lord builds the house, those who build it labor in vain." *(Psalm 127:1a)* [9]

After a day of nonstop activity, the familiar trek toward home begins. Driving around the bend, the welcome sight of home comes into view with smoke wafting from the chimney and the warm glow of light streaming from the window. Most would agree that almost nothing compares to the comforts of home. And yet millions of families around the world live in substandard housing that is unsanitary, unhealthy and unsafe. Thoughts of home paint quite a different picture for these people.

One of the most visible signs of poverty is poor housing or no housing. Poverty often causes despair, a lack of interest in anything except one's own worries. And this poverty causes a vicious cycle where children also begin to feel the same helplessness and hopelessness that their parents feel. Habitat for Humanity, founded in Georgia in 1976, offers hope that many have never had. It gives them more than a home. It also provides them with a goal and a vision for their lives.

Clarence Jordan was an inspiration to Habitat for Humanity International's founder, Millard Fuller. Jordan, the founder of Koinonia Farm, believing there was great need for suitable housing worldwide, launched "partner housing" by setting up a "Fund for Humanity." In a letter written to friends, he said, "What the poor need is not charity but capital, not caseworkers but coworkers. And what the rich need is a wise, honorable and just way of divesting of their overabundance. The Fund for Humanity will meet both of these needs." The first house was under construction when Mr. Jordan died in 1969 at the age of 57. But the dream had spread and others continued to build.

Linda and Millard Fuller moved their family to Africa to build houses and do other work with the Church of Christ in Zaire. Upon returning to Koinonia Farm, a Christian Community near Americus, Georgia, they began to lay plans for Habitat for Humanity. Since then, Habitat has grown across the country and around the world. With the goal of "No More Shacks," Habitat for Humanity International realized a wonderful goal on May 1, 1992, with the approval of the Central Peninsula of Alaska. This affiliate's confirmation established Habitat for Humanity in all fifty states and the District of Columbia. By 1992, Habitat for Humanity had completed more than 15,000 houses. Habitat projects are in over 700 U.S. and Canadian communities, and in more than 100 locations in 34 other countries.

It is estimated that a modest home can be built for $25,000 to $35,000. The home is sold to a low-income family at no profit and with no interest on a 20-year mortgage. This family becomes a partner by the fact that they must also invest 500 hours of "sweat equity" by helping in the land-clearing, construction and finishing of the home. The mortgage payments made by the family are recycled into the Fund for Humanity to help in the building of more homes. There is a nondiscriminatory family selection criterion for all Habitat projects, both in the United States and abroad. This simply means that neither race nor religion determines who receives Habitat housing. The criterion is need.

Funds that are raised stay within the local community—except the "tithe" which goes to Habitat for Humanity International. This money is used to build houses abroad. For example, when $30,000 is used in the United States to build a house, $3,000 goes international. In India, $3,000 will build three houses. Habitat always has been committed both to reasonable salaries and to stringent efforts to hold all administrative expenses to as low a level as possible. The highest salary at Habitat for Humanity International is less than a third of the average top salary at similar nonprofit service organizations. Further, many of the staff at headquarters in Americus, Georgia, are volunteers who are given only room and utilities plus a modest check ($40) each week to use in purchasing food.

"The simplest answer I can offer to the question of how to eliminate poverty housing in the world is to make it a matter of conscience," says Millard Fuller. "We must do whatever is necessary to cause people to think and act to bring adequate shelter to everyone." A return to the idea of neighbor helping neighbor, people helping people, and "doing unto others as you would have them do unto you," is exciting, refreshing and contagious. Habitat for Humanity embodies these ideals and has given thousands of people everywhere opportunities to apply them. What projects currently are under way for Habitat for Humanity?

- New affiliates in Poland and Hungary during the spring of 1992 expanded the ministry for the first time ever in Europe.
- 100 new homes built in Tijuana, Mexico
- 7 homes in San Diego, California.
- 29 homes in Kasese, Uganda.
- 21 wooden frame houses built in one week in Evansville, Indiana.
- Rehabilitation of 10 row houses in Baltimore, Maryland. Plans for 100 rehabs in the next five years.
- 80 new homes in the Rocky Mountain Habitat area.
- In Durham, North Carolina, the fund-raising and construction of a Habitat project are being done completely by young people from the Northern High School campus chapter.

And this list could fill page after page. In Americus and Sumter County, Georgia, where Habitat got started, bold plans have been laid to eliminate substandard housing within the county by the year 2000. "For the first time ever, a definite date is being set to eliminate poverty housing in a specific area," says Millard Fuller, "and we believe we can set an example that will be emulated by others in the US and abroad. For the sun never sets on our work. Somewhere in the world, no matter what the hour, there is work proceeding on a Habitat house."

Economic Justice for All
A Pastoral Message from The National Conference of Catholic Bishops

Monsignor Daniel F. Hoye, General Secretary of the National Conference of Catholic Bishops, explains that following their November 1980 general meeting, the Council appointed an ad hoc committee to draft a pastoral letter on the U.S. economy. The first draft of this letter was submitted to the bishops in November 1984, with subsequent drafts presented and discussed in November 1985 and June 1986. The body gave its final approval of the text—most of which is included here—during their plenary assembly in Washington, D.C. in November 1986.

Brothers and Sisters in Christ:

We are believers called to follow Our Lord Jesus Christ and proclaim his Gospel in the midst of a complex and powerful economy. This reality poses both opportunities and responsibilities for Catholics in the United States. Our faith calls us to measure this economy, not only by what it produces, but also by how it touches human life and whether it protects or undermines the dignity of the human person. Economic decisions have human consequences and moral content: they help or hurt people, strengthen or weaken family life, advance or diminish the quality of justice in our land.

This is why we have written *Economic Justice for All: A Pastoral Letter on Catholic Social Teaching and the U.S. Economy.* This letter is a personal invitation to Catholics to use the resources of our faith, the strength of our economy, and the opportunities of our democracy to shape a society that better protects the dignity and basic rights of our sisters and brothers, both in this land and around the world.

The pastoral letter has been a work of careful inquiry, wide consultation, and prayerful discernment. The letter has been greatly enriched by this process of listening and refinement. We offer this introductory pastoral message to Catholics in the United States seeking to live their faith in the marketplace—in homes, offices, factories, and schools; on farms and ranches; in boardrooms and union halls; in service agencies and legislative chambers. We seek to explain why we wrote this pastoral letter, to introduce its major themes, and to share our hopes for the dialogue and action it might generate.

We write to share our teaching, to raise questions, to challenge one another to live our faith in the world. We write as heirs of the biblical prophets who summon us "to do the right, and to love goodness, and to walk humbly with your God" (Micah 6:8). We write as followers of Jesus who told us in the Sermon on the Mount: "Blessed are the poor in spirit. . . . Blessed are the meek. . . . Blessed are they who hunger and thirst for righteousness. . . . You are the salt of the earth. . . . You are the light of the world" (Matthew 5:1-6, 13-14). These words challenge us not only as believers but also as consumers, citizens, workers, and owners. In the parable of the Last Judgment, Jesus said, "For I was hungry and you gave me food, I was thirsty and you gave me drink. . . . As often as you did it for one of my least brothers, you did it for me" (Matthew 25:35-40). The challenge for us is to discover in our own place and time what it means to be "poor in spirit" and "the salt of the earth" and what it means to serve "the least among us" and to "hunger and thirst for righteousness."

Followers of Christ must avoid a tragic separation between faith and everyday life. They can neither shirk their earthly duties nor, as the Second Vatican Council declared, "immerse [them]selves in earthly activities as if these latter were utterly foreign to religion, and religion were nothing more than the fulfillment of acts of worship and the observance of a few moral obligations" (*Pastoral Constitution on the Church in the Modern World,* no. 43).

Economic life raises important social and moral questions for each of us and for society as a whole. Like family life, economic life is one of the chief areas where we live out our faith, love our neighbor, confront temptation, fulfil God's creative design, and achieve our holiness. Our economic activity in factory, field, office, or shop feeds our families—or feeds our anxieties. It exercises our talents—or wastes them. It raises our hopes—or crushes them. It brings us into cooperation with others—or sets us at odds. The Second Vatican Council instructs us "to preach the message of Christ in such a way that the light of the Gospel will shine on all activities of the faithful" (*Pastoral Constitution,* no. 43). In this case, we are trying to look at economic life through the eyes of faith, applying traditional church teaching to the U.S. economy.

In our letter, we write as pastors, not public officials. We speak as moral teachers, not economic technicians. We seek not to make some political or ideological point but to lift up the human and ethical dimensions of economic life, aspects too often neglected in public discussion. We bring to this task a dual heritage of Catholic social teaching and traditional American values.

As *Catholics,* we are heirs of a long tradition of thought and action on the moral dimensions of economic activity. The life and words of Jesus and the teaching of his Church call us to serve those in need and to work actively for social and economic justice. As a community of believers, we know that our faith is tested by the quality of justice among us, that we can best measure our life together by how the poor and the vulnerable are treated. This is not a new concern for us. It is as old as the Hebrew prophets, as compelling as the Sermon on the Mount, and as current as the powerful voice of Pope John Paul II defending the dignity of the human person.

As *Americans,* we are grateful for the gift of freedom and committed to the dream of "liberty and justice for all." This nation, blessed with extraordinary resources, has provided an unprecedented standard of living for millions of people. We are proud of the strength, productivity, and creativity of our economy, but we also remember those who have been left behind in our progress. We believe that we honor our history best by working for the day when all our sisters and brothers share adequately in the American dream.

As bishops, in proclaiming the Gospel for these times we also manage institutions, balance budgets, meet payrolls. In this we see the human face of our economy. We feel the hurts and hopes of our people. We feel the pain of our sisters and brothers who are poor and vulnerable are on our doorsteps, in our parishes, in our service agencies, and in our shelters. We see too much hunger and injustice, too much suffering and despair, both in our own country and around the world.

As pastors, we also see the decency, generosity, and vulnerability of our people. We see the struggles of ordinary families to make ends meet and to provide a better future for their children. We know the desire of managers, professionals, and business people to shape what they do by what they believe. It is the faith, good will, and generosity of our people that gives us hope as we write this letter.

The pastoral letter is not a blueprint for the American economy. It does not embrace any particular theory of how the economy works, nor does it attempt to resolve the disputes between different schools of economic thought. Instead, our letter turns to Scripture and to the social teachings of the Church. There, we discover what our economic life must serve, what standards it must meet. Let us examine some of these basic moral principles.

Every economic decision and institution must be judged in light of whether it protects or undermines the dignity of the human person. The pastoral letter begins with the human person. We believe the person is sacred—the clearest reflection of God among us. Human dignity comes from God, not from nationality, race, sex, economic status, or any human accomplishment. We judge any economic system by what it does *for* and *to* people and by how it permits all to *participate* in it. The economy should serve people, not the other way around.

Human dignity can be realized and protected only in community. In our teaching, the human person is not only sacred but also social. How we organize our society—in economics and politics, in law and policy—directly affects human dignity and the capacity of individuals to grow in community. The obligation to "love our neighbor" has an individual dimension, but it also requires a broader social commitment to the common good. We have many partial ways to measure and debate the health of our economy: Gross National Product, per capita income, stock market prices, and so forth. The Christian vision of economic life looks beyond them all and asks, Does economic life enhance or threaten our life together as a community?

All people have a right to participate in the economic life of society. Basic justice demands that people be assured a minimum level of participation in the economy. It is wrong for a person or group to be excluded unfairly or to be unable to participate or contribute to the economy. For example, people who are both able and willing, but cannot get a job are deprived of the participation that is so vital to human development. For, it is through employment that most individuals and families meet their material needs, exercise their talents, and have an opportunity to contribute to the larger community. Such participation has a special significance in our tradition because we believe that it is a means by which we join in carrying forward God's creative activity.

All members of society have a special obligation to the poor and vulnerable. From the Scriptures and church teaching, we learn that the justice of a society is tested by the treatment of the poor. The justice that was the sign of God's covenant with Israel was measured by how the poor and unprotected—the widow, the orphan, and the stranger—were treated. The kingdom that Jesus proclaimed in his word and ministry excludes no one. Throughout Israel's history and in early Christianity, the poor are agents of God's transforming power. "The Spirit of the Lord is upon me, therefore he has anointed me. He has sent me to bring glad tidings to the poor" (Luke 4:18). This was Jesus' first public utterance. Jesus takes the side of those most in need. In the Last Judgment, so dramatically described in St. Matthew's Gospel, we are told that we will be judged according to how we respond to the hungry, the thirsty, the naked, the stranger. As followers of Christ, we are challenged to make a fundamental "option for the poor"—to speak for the voiceless, to defend the defenseless, to assess life styles, policies, and social institutions in terms of their impact on the poor. This "option for the poor" does not mean pitting one group against another, but rather, strengthening the whole community by assisting those who are most vulnerable. As Christians, we are called to respond to the needs of *all* our brothers and sisters, but those with the greatest needs require the greatest response.

Human rights are the minimum conditions for life in community. In Catholic teaching, human rights include not only civil and political rights but also economic rights. As Pope John XXIII declared, "all people have a right to life, food, clothing, shelter, rest, medical care, education, and employment." This means that when people are without a chance to earn a living, and must go hungry and homeless, they are being denied basic rights. Society must ensure that these rights are protected. In this way, we will ensure that the minimum conditions of economic justice are met for all our sisters and brothers.

Society as a whole, acting through public and private institutions, has the moral responsibility to enhance human dignity and protect human rights. In addition to the clear responsibility of private institutions, government has an essential responsibility in this area. This does not mean that government has the primary or exclusive role, but it does have a positive moral responsibility in safeguarding human rights and ensuring that the minimum conditions of human dignity are met for all. In a democracy, government is a means by which we can act together to protect what is important to us and to promote our common values.

These six moral principles are not the only ones presented in the pastoral letter, but they give an overview of the moral vision that we are trying to share. This vision of economic life cannot exist in a vacuum; it must be translated into concrete measures. Our pastoral letter spells out some specific applications of Catholic moral principles. We call for a new national commitment to full employment. We say it is a social and moral scandal that one of every seven Americans is poor, and we call for concerted efforts to eradicate poverty. The fulfillment of the basic needs of the poor is of the highest priority. We urge that all economic policies be evaluated in light of their impact on the life and stability of the family. We support measures to halt the loss of family farms and to resist the growing concentration in the ownership of agricultural resources. We specify ways in which the United States can do far more to relieve the plight of poor nations and assist in their development. We also reaffirm church teaching on the rights of workers, collective bargaining, private property, subsidiarity, and equal opportunity.

We believe that the recommendations in our letter are reasonable and balanced. In analyzing the economy, we reject ideological extremes and start from the fact that ours is a "mixed" economy, the product of a long history of reform and adjustment. We know that some of our specific recommendations are controversial. As bishops, we do not claim to make these prudential judgments with the same kind of authority that marks our declarations of principle. But, we feel obliged to teach by example how Christians can undertake concrete analysis and make specific judgments on economic issues. The Church's teachings cannot be left at the level of appealing generalities.

In the pastoral letter, we suggest that the time has come for a "New American Experiment"—to implement economic rights, to broaden the sharing of economic power, and to make economic decisions more accountable to the common good. This experiment can create new structures of economic partnership and participation within firms at the regional level, for the whole nation, and across borders.

Of course, there are many aspects of the economy the letter does not touch, and there are basic questions it leaves to further exploration. There are also many specific points on which men and women of good will may disagree. We look for a fruitful exchange among differing viewpoints. We pray only that all will take to heart the urgency of our concerns; that together we will test our views by the Gospel and the Church's teaching; and that we will listen to other voices in a spirit of mutual respect and open dialogue.

We should not be surprised if we find Catholic social teaching to be demanding. The Gospel is demanding. We are always in need of conversion, of a change of heart. We are richly blessed, and as St. Paul assures us, we are destined for glory. Yet, it is also true that we are sinners; that we are not always wise or loving or just; that, for all our amazing possibilities, we are incompletely born, wary of life, and hemmed in by fears and empty routines. We are unable to entrust ourselves fully to the living God, and so we seek substitute forms of security in material things, in power, in indifference, in popularity, in pleasure. The Scriptures warn us that these things can become forms of idolatry. We know that, at times, in order to remain truly a community of Jesus' disciples, we will have to say "no" to certain aspects in our culture, to certain trends and ways of acting that are opposed to a life of faith, love, and justice. Changes in our hearts lead naturally to a desire to change how we act. With what care, human kindness, and justice do I conduct myself at work? How will my economic decisions to buy, sell, invest, divest, hire, or fire serve human dignity and the common good? In what career can I best exercise my talents so as to fill the world with the Spirit of Christ? How do my economic choices contribute to the strength of my family and community, to the values of my children, to a sensitivity to those in need? In this consumer society, how can I develop a healthy detachment from things and avoid the temptation to assess who I am by what I have? How do I strike a balance between labor and leisure that enlarges my capacity for friendships, for family life, for community? What government policies should I support to attain the well-being of all, especially the poor and vulnerable?

The answers to such questions are not always clear—or easy to live out. But, conversion is a lifelong process. And, it is not undertaken alone. It occurs with the support of the whole believing community, through baptism, common prayer, and our daily efforts, large and small, on behalf of justice. As a Church, we must be people after God's own heart, bonded by the Spirit, sustaining one another in love, setting our hearts on God's kingdom, committing ourselves to solidarity with those who suffer, working for peace and justice, acting as a sign of Christ's love and justice in the world. The Church cannot redeem the world from the deadening effects of sin and injustice unless it is working to remove sin and injustice in its own life and institutions. All of us must help the Church to practice in its own life what it preaches to others about economic justice and cooperation.

The challenge of this pastoral letter is not merely to think differently, but also to act differently. A renewal of economic life depends on the conscious choices and commitments of individual believers who practice their faith in the world. The road to holiness for most of us lies in our secular vocations. We need a spirituality that calls forth and supports lay initiative and witness not just in our churches but also in business, in the labor movement, in the professions, in education, and in public life. Our faith is not just a weekend obligation, a mystery to be celebrated around the altar on Sunday. It is a pervasive reality to be practiced every day in homes, offices, factories, schools, and businesses across our land. We cannot separate what we believe from how we act in the marketplace and the broader community, for this is where we make our primary contribution to the pursuit of economic justice.

We believe that the Christian view of life, including economic life, can transform the lives of individuals, families, schools, and our whole culture. We believe that with your prayers, reflection, service and action, our economy can be shaped so that human dignity prospers and the human person is served. This is the unfinished work of our nation. This is the challenge of our faith.

It Was Life : Outreach Ministry in New York City
James Goodmann

Jim Goodmann, of the Council for Religion in Independent Schools, spent approximately four years in a mission in New York City's Times Square district. The following piece contains some reflections on the nature of outreach ministry in an urban setting.

He was overwhelmed by the belated suspicion that it was life, more than death, that had no limits. —Gabriel Garcia Marquez

There is a quality to the life of service that can make it an instrument of conversion. At least, that is what I discovered in the midst of Times Square from 1980 to 1984, where I served as an outreach minister to the homeless, the elderly, runaway teenagers, single mothers, and hundreds of others who—often without category—came to us in their various states of need. It was my first engagement of active ministry and the end of intellectual involvement only, as far as my spiritual life was concerned. I lived and worked in the old Lamb's Club on West 44th Street, a building bought in 1975 by the Church of the Nazarene. It was also home to an off-Broadway theatre which was the main source of income for this particular congregation. So, what was a Catholic from the Midwest doing there? Making use of an opportunity offered by a friend from my home town, B.J. Weber, to serve the poor and to learn some things I might otherwise never have learned. That is the short answer. The longer answer involves a perception of the most enduring quality about God: love, which is God's essence.

I cannot measure or recount how much of a leap forward or, more properly, a leap into another dimension my four years of outreach ministry was. It is one thing to imagine and romanticize from the portals of a graduate school classroom the life of those who serve the poor. It is another thing to enter that domain and, far from having these imaginings diffused, to find that God is the last romantic: the one whose ambition it is to tie every soul to Godself and who will not suffer to lose the least occasion of showing that Self to those who have just one eye open. Coming to an understanding of this God (who is love and nothing but love) in the company of friends and strangers in New York City was the beginning of what I am sure is a lifelong lesson for me.

I lived in the company of other outreach workers and missionaries, in the company of actors, writers, artists, teachers, bankers and socialites. . . and in the company of people who spent their days at the Off-Track Betting Center at the Port Authority Bus Station, who slept in the doorways of theatres and spent their days at *Roy Rogers* fast-food restaurant, who lived on old-age pensions in Single Room Occupancy hotels and managed (some of them) to compose poetry, who stood on street corners and shouted at people hoping to find an audience or some form of attention, whose lives were so rich with stories and memories but who had never found the opportunity to share it with someone. Some had lived their entire lives in New York and, in most cases, had never left the island of Manhattan. Then there were others who just arrived in the city from North Carolina, Tennessee, Florida, Wisconsin and North Dakota, from Albania, Yugoslavia, Central America, Viet Nam, Afghanistan, the Middle East—any place in the United States where the economy was bad or any place in the world where life or freedom was endangered; people with lives of such variation of geography and experience that one could spend hours, if not days, getting acquainted with them and their stories. In some cases it seemed that just *listening* to them was a work of mercy, a mercy that extended both ways, I should add. There were some days when, either sitting in my office or standing on the front stoop of our building on 44th Street, I felt the entire world was literally passing by.

New York was the city in which all the ills of society as all the opulence were the most visible. At that time, it and the country as a whole were in the first days of the homeless crisis. The first symptoms of a society divided between the affluent and the indigent were beginning to show themselves. What now seems to be all too normal on our city streets was then still a novelty. To put this situation down to just institutional or bureaucratic failure was, I have always thought, a great mistake. I believed then, and still do that the real failure was one of *will*. Somewhere in the 1970s, the country decided that it would no longer be responsible for a number of people who had previously been wards of the state, pushing many of the institutionalized into the streets. The upshot of this failure of will was that it spread to include much of the urban poor and their neighborhoods. When I left New York in July, 1984, the second wave of this "benign neglect" was in full force.

The time in between, however, was rich with occasions of compassion, demonstrated by those of great wealth to the needy and vice versa. Sometimes, the distinctions of social status, so highly prized by our world, seemed utterly erased. That often seemed to be the object of my being in New York for those four years: that I might understand that I was part of a larger world, in fact and not in imagination only; that this larger world included a population of which two–thirds were ill-housed, illiterate, and hungry; that I was here to learn from them as much as I was there to minister to them.

One such tutor from among the poor was Lawrence Moten, or *Brother Lawrence* as we called him, a man who had known the life of the streets for the better part of his life. This man was a convert in the truest sense of the word. Having survived a brutal upbringing which included being sent away by his own mother, life in several foster homes, and run-ins with juvenile authorities, he later testified that "it had to have been the Lord who was with me all that time. . . there is no other explanation for it." He came to this state of conversion shortly after the age of fifty when I made his acquaintance. With little difficulty, I discovered that when in his presence, it was my turn to listen. As Frank Herbert, the author of *Dune* puts it, ". . . beginnings are such delicate things." So, I listened—with as much care as I could muster. Conversation would come later: ongoing, four-year conversation which touched on such things as the Scriptures, the matter of service, the nature of church politics, and interracial black/white relationships. He was my main companion in ministry for that period of time and probably the most formative example of humble service I have ever known. To encounter him was not unlike, I surmise, encountering God: a mixture of awe, some fear, admiration and, inevitably, joy and laughter.

The greater part of the wisdom Brother Lawrence imparted had to do with the nature of service. First, he made clear, we should identify our service as, purely and simply, "the Lord's work," not our own. Over and over, he would say, "We're not doing anything! There is nothing for us to be proud of." With that in mind, the little we were doing became rather light work: feeding hot lunches to transients, runaway teenagers, mothers in welfare hotel accommodations; distributing clothes to those in need; and arranging for housing for those few we managed to shelter.

The second thing that comes to mind regarding Lawrence's counsel is that, if it is God's work we do, then anxiety should not attend it—even when there were painful and perplexing situations to deal with and people of whom one could be nothing but wary. Lawrence's knowledge of people, garnered from years of practice, always seemed to be supplemented by his faith: "Those whom the Lord sends your way you should help insofar as is possible. Spare your ambitions to save them. That's not your role. Remember, '. . . all this is from God who has reconciled the world to himself through Christ and entrusted to us the message of reconciliation' (2 Cor. 5:17)." It is important that messengers not confuse themselves with the Source of the message, since they are recipients of the same reconciling power at work in the world. We can identify with the compassion of Christ, with his love, but we all qualify for his saving grace— which should make of any service "an easy yoke, a burden that is light," in sharing company with others who have received mercy.

One incident which will always remain with me illustrates Lawrence's humility toward the men he served. It was dismissal time at the end of a luncheon, a time when order was often at the breaking point. I and several others were particularly intent on an orderly exit by all—probably at the more-than-suggestion of the main office upstairs. When the rush for the doors began, I interjected with a little anxiety that everyone must leave in an orderly fashion. Then Lawrence added his two-cents, which turned out to be worth much more. "Men," he said quietly, "we are pleased to have you here as our guests in the name of Our Lord, and no one has authority over you. We do not seek that. We just ask that you leave in a calm manner and go with God's blessing." Like magic, a pleasant meekness stole through the crowd and opened a window on eternity for a moment. Like magic, I was reminded—somewhat embarrassingly— that the authority of the Gospel has nothing whatever to do with authority as it is imagined by the world. Like magic, we were reminded that the kingdom of God is embodied where the adversarialism of the world is vanquished.

One thing I will say for this kind of service is that it certainly gives you an insight into the life of the poor—more, perhaps, than one might wish. During my last winter at the Lamb's, petty cash funding for some of our programs ran low to nonexistent. Lawrence and I took to providing for some folks out of our own thin pockets—a valuable lesson in contingency and solidarity with "the other $^2/_3$." It certainly turned the "prosperity Christianity" preached from some pulpits in the early 1980s neatly on its head.

For me, it took an active engagement of ministry for things in the head to sink into the heart I had to allow time for this to happen; a genius I may have been in the classroom but a babe in the woods I was definitely on the streets of New York, at least for a while. I learned what limitless life there was to be had in a city so often assumed to be cold and unfriendly, if not hostile. When I poked my nose into a museum, took a walk or run through Central Park, strolled on the Upper East Side or rode the Staten Island Ferry I not only was recharged, I met some pretty remarkable people.

I also began to realize that a spiritual life has a flesh and blood reality and he who neglects these concrete realities in favor of things ethereal will have neither for a while. (Exhaustion *can* make you forget to eat.) Or one will have to bear listening to one's friends reminders that God's love for us is what inspires a ministerial presence to those in need, and that duty, while a helpmate in constructing one's daily calendar, is not or should not be the rule of life. Within a couple of months of my arrival, I already had burned out and needed to go to Fr. Benedict Groeschel's Trinity Retreat House in Larchmont, NY. He saw my exhaustion and said, "Well, pay the price of sin [overwork] and relax; and take as much time to relax as you need."

I began to learn the detachment from what J. D. Salinger calls the need "to comb the other person's face for some sign of gratitude" when rendering any form of service. That is probably the most trying experience for a young person venturing on any type of community outreach. We can't believe that people in such need could be so ungrateful. Beginning to accept this trait in others is a step toward understanding the "self-emptying" of Christ who became a slave for the sake of the world. Such detachment also reminds us of the reason why we stand in the place of service. This is one of the little prices of striving for union with God—you win the chance to see what it is like to love as God does.

Above all, I think I learned something of the patience of God. This is no small thing. The world has taken a long time in getting itself out of order. Even with the help of God, it is going to take some time to put even a few things back into place—a good thing to keep in mind when you set about to "fix" things, including your own life. And things remain only temporarily in place anyway, awaiting the great resurrection as the final putting in place of all that is out of joint, broken, or dislocated. Patience, with practice, can become what the writers of the New Testament referred to as "waiting patiently for God to reveal Himself"—a good thing, also, to keep in mind with regard to prayer. During my New York years, I learned some things about contemplative prayer which have stayed with me since then. Some months before my arrival, a Dominican priest had told me—quoting St. Teresa of Avila—that prayer is the practice of "being in the presence of one who loves us utterly." From 1980-84, I began to discover just what this meant. It certainly does not mean that prayer would make me a paragon of moral perfection, but I did begin to learn what little I could do without it.

I left New York City with so many gifts, especially the memories: of the people I worked with, of those who served and took care of me, and of the paradox of an experience that at once seemed larger than life yet contracted and small. There were times when prayer and action appeared almost indistinguishable, times when the presence of God was so tangible that no force or interruption or anxiety could dampen or negate it. There were times when the mass of humanity seemed almost as accessible as any individual human being, and other times when neither mass nor individual seemed accessible at all. I felt as though I were growing and learning in so many directions that my own memory was incapable of accounting for this sudden expansion of experience and, to some degree, of maturity.

"Human things," said Blaise Pascal, "must be known to be loved but divine things must be loved to be known." That was a part of his famous "wager": that God is, and that He is also good—even more good, I think, than Pascal suspected. My life in New York for those four years was something of a wager, too. God took me up on a bet, as it were, and planted something within me that, thankfully, will not go away. It was more, much more, than an engagement of service. It was an encounter with life that teaches me more each time I recall it.

The Beatitudes
Elias Chacour

Father Elias Chacour is a Palestinian Melkite priest and thus a member of a branch of Christianity which traces its activity back to the Apostle James in Jerusalem. He has spent over thirty years working educational and spiritual wonders in Galilee, building libraries, schools, and community centers for Palestinians. He is especially pleased that Prophet Elias Community College—which he founded—includes Israeli Jews as well as Israeli Christians and Muslims on its faculty, and hopes the day will come soon when Jews will join its student body. Fr. Chacour has said that as a boy he could see only two choices in the face of oppression: "surrender to abuse, or turn to violence." When, however, he left home for seminary study, his gentle father urged him to learn all he could, saying, "If you become a true man of God, you will know how to reconcile enemies—how to turn hatred into peace. Only a true man of God, servant of God can do that." That Fr. Chacour has become such a servant is affirmed in that he has received several nominations for the Nobel Peace Prize.[11]

Knowing Aramaic, the language of Jesus, has greatly enriched my understanding of Jesus' teachings. Because the Bible as we know it is a translation of a translation, we sometimes get a wrong impression. For example, we are accustomed to hearing the Beatitudes expressed passively:

Blessed are those who hunger and thirst for justice,
    for they shall be satisfied.
Blessed are the merciful,
    for they shall obtain mercy.
Blessed are the pure in heart,
    for they shall see God.
Blessed are the peacemakers,
    for they shall be called children of God.

"Blessed" is the translation of the word *makarioi,* used in the Greek New Testament. However, when I look further back to Jesus' Aramaic, I find that the original word was *ashray,* from the verb *yashar. Ashray* does not have this passive quality to it at all. Instead, it means "to set yourself on the right way for the right goal; to turn around, repent; to become straight or righteous."

How could I go to a persecuted young man in a Palestinian refugee camp, for instance, and say, "Blessed are those who mourn, for they shall be comforted," or "Blessed are those who are persecuted for the sake of justice, for theirs is the kingdom of heaven"? That man would revile me, saying neither I nor my God understood his plight, and he would be right.

When I understand Jesus' words in the Aramaic, I translate like this:

Get up, go ahead, do something, move, you who are hungry and thirsty
    for justice, for you shall be satisfied.
Get up, go ahead, do something, move, you peacemakers,
    for you shall be called children of God.

To me this reflects Jesus' words and teachings much more accurately. I can hear him saying, "Get your hands dirty to build a human society for human beings; otherwise, others will torture and murder the poor, the voiceless, and the powerless." Christianity is not passive but active, energetic, alive, going beyond despair.

One day two bats fell into a pot of milk. The pessimistic bat said, "What can I do? Will I struggle and sink, and die so very tired? I will not die tired." He sank and drowned immediately. The optimistic bat said, "I will strive to the end, and at least they will say I tried everything." She struggled and struggled, trying to fly, until she fainted. Later she awakened and found herself resting safely on a big roll of butter. This is not giving in to despair, but going beyond despair.

"Get up, go ahead, do something, move," Jesus said to his disciples.

ENDNOTES

1   The italics are Foster's.

2   Dietrich Bonhoeffer, *Life Together* (NY: Harper & Row, 1952), p. 99.

3   "Synoptic" means to see things the same way, literally, "with the same eye." The Synoptic Gospels—Matthew, Mark, and Luke—are those which tell the story of Jesus' life and teachings in a similar fashion, even sharing much of the actual wording.

4   Scripture quotes are from Matthew 16:21-23.

5   In the hierarchy and political organization of the Presbyterian Church, the "session" is that group which makes policy decisions and solves problems for the local congregation.

6   The prayer of St. Francis, to which Mother Teresa refers, is found at the beginning of this chapter, p. 112.

7   In Chapter Four, Coles remarks that "Peter Maurin offered Dorothy Day a new respect for the possibilities within the Catholic church, for the Franciscan tradition. He offered her his own relentless insistence that the spirit of the Catholic church has to be fought for—that the fate of the Church rests in each Catholic's heart and mind and soul, in each Catholic's daily deeds. Again and again her new teacher insisted that it is foolish and sinful to accept the reality of a particular society by sitting back and railing against its great power and awesome resources, thereby abdicating one's responsibility to use one's God-given capacity for independent initiatives." p. 72.

8   For a more complete understanding of Dorothy Day's life and character, read all of Robert Coles' excellent biography. William D. Miller is another significant biographer of Dorothy Day. For his perspective on her life and work, see his essay, "Dorothy Day," in *Saints Are Now: Eight Portraits of Modern Sanctity,* John J. Delaney, ed. (New York: Doubleday & Company, Inc., 1981), as well as his books, *Dorothy Day: A Biography* (San Francisco: Harper & Row, 1982), and *A Harsh and Dreadful Love: A History of the Catholic Worker Movement* (New York: Doubleday & Company, Inc.).

9   The introductory material is taken from the Habitat For Humanity International brochure, *A Decent House in a Decent Community for God's People in Need.*

10   Mr. Goodmann expresses his appreciation for Andrew Greeley whose book, *St. Valentine's Night,* first brought this quote to his attention.

11   The introductory material is a passage from *Living Stones: A Jerusalem Seminar Journal & Reflections on the Israeli-Palestinian Peace Process* by Lucinda Allen Mosher (Pomfret Press, 1994). The words of Chacour's father are from *Blood Brothers* by Elias Chacour with David Hazard (Grand Rapids, Michigan: Chosen Books, 1984), p. 75. Melkite Christians are also sometimes called Greek Catholics. They retain the Greek Orthodox liturgy and theology, but are in communion with the Vatican. Their language of worship is Arabic.

Chapter Nine

Islam: Qur'ān, Ḥadīth and Social Justice

I t is difficult to overestimate the importance of the Qur'ān to Muslims. According to Islam, the Qur'ān is the very *words* of God, revealed to humanity through the prophet Muḥammad, the Seal—the final one—of the prophets of God. Muḥammad then recited these revelations to his followers, who memorized them and/or wrote them down and later codified them into a single book of sacred scripture. Thus, according to Islam, God—not Muḥammad—is the author of the Qur'ān. Islam acknowledges that other scriptures exist for other religions, but believes that the Qur'ān supersedes them all.

The Qur'ān contains a total of one hundred fourteen chapters, which are called *sūras*. These are arranged roughly according to length from longest to shortest—except for the first *sūra*, which is quite short. Scholars have been able to deduce which *sūras* date from Muḥammad's life in Mecca, and which from the time he spent in Medina. Some editions indicate this at the beginning of each sūra. The name of each sūra, and the numbering of the verses within them, are part of the revelation. However, they have been omitted here to make the text read more smoothly.

The Qur'ān was revealed to Muḥammad in the rhymed prose of the Arabic language; therefore, Arabic is also sacred to Islam. Muslims believe that the Qur'ān preserves its revealed nature only if read and recited in Arabic; thus, it is in this language that the Qur'ān is used in worship. Translations do exist, but are not considered authoritative.[1]

All Arabic-speaking monotheists—be they Christians, Jews, or Muslims—refer to God as Allāh. Therefore, in this chapter, Allāh has been translated consistently as "God" in order to clarify that the reference is not to some separate, specifically Muslim deity.

The Qur'ān makes many pronouncements on matters of social justice, mostly in terms of the obligation for Muslims of almsgiving: *zakāt* and *sadāqa*. The *zakāt* is one of the Five Pillars of Islam, and refers to the giving of two-and-one-half percentage of one's annual disposable income to those in need. It is equivalent in importance to the other four primary religious obligations: the witness of faith in God and belief in Muḥammad's prophethood, regular prayer, fasting during the sacred month of *Ramaḍān*, and making a pilgrimage to Mecca. *Sadāqa* refers to charitable giving beyond the legal requirement of the *zakāt*. *Sūra* 2.261–74 is a lengthy explanation of this concept.

From the Qur'ān

Be firm in devotion; give zakāt the due share of your wealth for the welfare of others, and bow with those who bow before God.
—Sūra 2.43: *al-Baqarah (The Cow)*

Piety does not lie in turning your face to East or West:
Piety lies in believing in God, the Last Day and the angels, the Scriptures and the prophets, and disbursing your wealth out of love for God among your kin and the orphans, the wayfarers and mendicants, freeing the slaves, observing your devotional obligations, and in paying the zakāt and fulfilling a pledge you have given, and being patient in hardship, adversity, and times of peril. These are the men who affirm the truth, and they are those who follow the straight path.
—Sūra 2.177: *al-Baqarah (The Cow)* [2]

They ask you of what they should give charity. Tell them: "What you can spare of your wealth as should benefit the parents, the relatives, the orphans, the needy, the wayfarers, for God is not unaware of the good deeds that you do."—Sūra 2.215: *al-Baqarah (The Cow)*

Those who expend their wealth in the way of God are like a grain of corn from which grow seven ears, each ear containing a hundred grains. Truly God increases for whomsoever He will, for God is infinite and all-wise. Those who spend in the way of God, and having spent do not boast or give pain by word or deed, will get their reward from their Lord, and will neither have fear nor regret. Saying a word is kind, and forgiving is better than charity that hurts.

Do not forget that God is affluent and kind. O believers, do not nullify your charity by giving to oblige and flaunting your favors like a man who spends of his wealth only to show off, but does not believe in God and the Last Day. He is like a rock covered with earth which is washed away by rain exposing the hard rock bare. So they gain nothing from their earnings.

God does not guide a people who do not believe. But those who expend their wealth to please God with firm and resolute hearts, are like a garden on a height on which the rain falls and it yields its fruits twice as much; and even if the rain does not fall the dew will suffice. For God sees all that you do.

Does any of you wish to have an orchard full of date-palms and vines, and streams of running water and fruits of all kinds, and then old age should overtake him while his children are small, and a scorching whirlwind should smite and burn it down? Thus God makes His signs clear to you that you may reflect.

O believers, give in charity what is good of the things you have earned, and of what you produce from the earth; and do not choose to give what is bad as alms, that is, things you would not like to accept yourself except with some condescension. Remember that God is affluent and praiseworthy.

Satan threatens you with want, and orders you to commit shameful acts. But God promises His pardon and grace, for God is bounteous and all-knowing. He gives wisdom to whomsoever He pleases; and those who are bestowed wisdom get good in abundance. Yet none remembers this save men of wisdom.

Whatsoever you give away in alms or vow as offering, is all known to God; but the wicked will have none to help them. If you give alms openly, it is well; but if you do it secretly and give to the poor, that is better. This will absolve you of some of your sins; and God is cognizant of all you do.

It is not for you to guide them: God guides whom He will. Whatever you spend you will do so for yourself, for you will do so to seek the way that leads to God; and what you spend in charity you will get back in full, and no wrong will be done to you. Give to the needy who are engaged in the service of God who are not able to move about in the land, whom the ignorant consider to be affluent as they refrain from asking. You can know them from their faces for they do not ask of men in a persteringly troublesome manner.

God is surely cognizant of good things that you spend. Those who spend of their wealth in the way of God, day and night, in secret or openly, have their reward with the Lord, and have nothing to fear or regret.
—Sūra 2.261-274: *al-Baqarah (The Cow)*

You will never come to piety unless you spend of things you love; and whatever you spend is known to God.
—Sūra 3.92: *Āli-ʿImrān (The Family of Imrān)*

Pay homage to God and make none His equal, and be good to your parents and relatives, the orphans and the needy and the neighbors who are your relatives, and the friend by your side, the traveller and your servants and subordinates. God does not surely love those who are arrogant and boastful, who are miserly and bid others to be so, and hide what God has given them in His largesse.
—Sūra 4.36-37a: *an-Nisāʾ (The Women)*

Those who believe and perform good deeds will not be held guilty for what they have eaten in the past if they fear God and believe, and do good things and are conscious of God and believe, and still fear and do good, for God loves those who do good. —Sūra 5.93: *al-Māʾidah (The Feast)*

Charities are meant for the indigent and needy, and those who collect and distribute them, and those whom you wish to win over, and for redeeming slaves and captives and those who are burdened with debt, and in the cause of God, and the wayfarers: So does God ordain. God is all-knowing and all-wise. —Sūra 9.60: *at-Tawbah (Repentance)*

There is good for those who do good in this world.
—Sūra 39.10: *az-Zumar (The Small Groups)*

Do not bestow favors in expectation of return and persevere in the way of your Lord. —Sūra 74.6-7: *al-Muddaththir (The Enfolded)*

And feed the needy for the love of Him, and the orphans and the captives, saying: "We feed you for the sake of God, desiring neither recompense nor thanks. We fear the dismal day calamitous from our Lord."
—Sūra 76. 8-10: *ad-Dahr (Time)*

But save him who fears and gives of his wealth that he may grow in virtue, and is under no one's obligation to return his favor, other than seeking the glory of his Lord, most high, will surely be gratified.
—Sūra 92. 17-21: *al-Layl (The Night)*

In the name of God, most benevolent, ever merciful.

When the world is shaken up by its cataclysm, and the earth throws out its burdens, and man enquires: "What has come over it?"
    That day it will narrate its annals, for your Lord will have commanded it. That day people will proceed separately to be shown their deeds. Whosoever has done even an atom's weight of good will behold it; and whosoever has done even an atom's weight of evil will behold that.
—Sūra 99: *az-Zilzāl (The Earthquake)*

In the name of God, most benevolent, ever merciful.

Have you seen him who denies the Day of Judgement?
It is he who pushes the orphans away, and does not induce others to feed the needy. Woe to those who pray but who are oblivious of their moral duties, who dissimulate and withhold things of common use from others.
—Sūra 107: *al-Māʿūn (Things of Common Use)*

From the Ḥadīth

Ḥadīth are the prophet Muhammad's *sunna*—his sayings and deeds during those times when he was not serving as a vehicle of divine revelation. Reports of these statements and actions were collected by his followers and eventually compiled in written form. These writings are considered to have authority second only to the Qurʾān; this authority is underscored by citing the chain of witness leading back to Muhammad himself.
    Specific ḥadīth are identified by the name of the compiler of the collection in which they appear. Selections below include some from the collection compiled by Muhammad Ismāʾil al-Bukhārī in the ninth century. His has long been considered the most meticulously researched, the most comprehensive in scope, and thus, the most authentic. In the 13th century CE, Imām Yahyā ʾibn Sharaf ad-Dīn an-Nawawī chose forty ḥadīth, primarily from al-Bukhārī, to include in a small but comprehensive and highly respected volume. Several entries from this collection are included as well.

According to Abū Huraira, the Prophet said: Camels in better condition than they were on earth will advance on their owner who failed to pay zakāt on them and will trample him under foot, and sheep will butt him with their horns. You should milk your animals when they have drunk and give some of the milk as charity. On the Day of Resurrection none of you need come to me with a bleating sheep round his neck and plead "Muhammad intercede for me," for I shall tell him, "I can't do anything for you. I told you before what you should do." Nor need anyone come with a grumbling camel round his neck and make the same plea, for I shall simply reply, "I can't influence God in your favor. I told you before what you should do." —*al-Bukhārī*

According to Abū Dharr, the Prophet said: I wouldn't want to have a heap of gold the size of Mount Uhud, unless I could spend it all in God's cause, bar the last three dinars. —*al-Bukhārī*

According to ʿAbbullah ʾibn ʿUmar, the Prophet said: The higher hand is better than the lower hand. The higher hand is the one that gives; the lower hand is the one that receives. —*al-Bukhārī*

According to Hāritha ʾibn Wahb, the Prophet said: Give charity because a time will come when a man will go round with his charity and not find anyone willing to accept it. The person to whom he offers it will say, "Ah! If you had come yesterday I would have accepted it, but today I don't need it any more." —*al-Bukhārī*

According to Asmā, the Prophet said: Give generously and do not keep an account; God will keep an account for you. Put nothing to one side; God will put to one side for you. —*al-Bukhārī*

According to ʿAdiyy ʾibn Hātim, the Prophet said: Avoid Hell by giving charity, even if it means sharing your last date. If you have nothing at all, give charity by speaking a kind word. —*al-Bukhārī*

ʿAʾisha said, "Messenger of God, I have two neighbors. To which one ought I to give charity?" He replied, "The one whose door is nearest yours." —*al-Bukhārī*

Someone asked the Prophet (peace be upon him) which is the greatest charity. The Prophet replied, "The charity you perform while you are healthy, afraid of poverty, and eager for wealth. Do not wait to give charity until you are on your deathbed, and then say, 'Give this portion to this person, and that portion to that person.' By then it is too late; it is already theirs!" —*al-Bukhārī*

According to Jarīr ʾibn ʿAbdullah, the Prophet said: God will have no sympathy for the person who showed no sympathy for humanity. —*al-Bukhārī*

According to ʾIbn ʿAbbās, the Prophet said: A person who reneges on a gift he has given is like a dog which returns to its vomit. —*al-Bukhārī*

According to Abū Huraira, the Prophet said: Every single day each person has two angels near him who have descended from heaven. The one says, "O God, remunerate the person who gives charity;" the other says, "O God, exact payment from the person who withholds his money." —*al-Bukhārī*

According to Abū Huraira, the Prophet said: The charitable person and the stingy person are like two men clothed in armor from the breast to the shoulders. Every time the charitable man gives charity this tunic stretches over his skin until soon it extends to the tips of his fingers and

protects his whole body. On the other hand, each time the stingy person wants to give charity each link of his armor rusts where it is. When he tries to stretch it, it remains rigid.
—*al-Bukhārī*

According to Abū Huraira, the Prophet said: Muslim women, don't avoid giving a gift to your neighbor even if all you can spare is a sheep's foot.
—*al-Bukhārī*

According to Abū Huraira, the Prophet said: Ah! How fine a thing is the loan of a she-camel with its udders swollen with pure milk, or a ewe which yields a bowlful of pure milk in the morning and another in the evening! —*al-Bukhārī*

According to Abū Huraira, the Prophet said: Each joint of a believer's body should give charity. Every day that the sun rises, anyone who establishes justice among people performs a charitable act. —*al-Bukhārī*

According to Abū Huraira, the Prophet said: The truly poor person is not the one whom you send on his way after giving him a couple of dates or a few bites of food. The really poor person is the one who dares not even ask for such charity. —*al-Bukhārī*

According to Abū Huraira, once when a man sought out the Messenger of God, the Prophet asked his wives for something to give the man to eat.
    "We have absolutely nothing," they replied, "except water."
    "Who wants to share his meal with this man?" asked the Prophet.
    One of the Companions replied, "I do;" then he led this man to his wife and said to her, "Treat generously the guest of the Messenger of God."
    She replied, "We have nothing except our children's supper."
    "Oh, well," he replied, "get your meal ready, light your lamp, and when the children want supper, put them to bed."
    So the woman prepared the meal, lit the lamp, put the children to bed, then, getting up as if to trim the lamp, she extinguished it. The Companion and his wife then made as if to eat, but in fact they spent the night with empty stomachs.
    The next day when the Companion went to visit the Messenger of God, the Prophet said to him, "Last night God smiled." It was then that God revealed these words, "and they take care of others before themselves, even though they be in the midst of poverty." —*al-Bukhārī*

ʿAbdullah ʾibn ʿAmr remembers that someone once asked the Prophet what was the best thing in Islam, and was told, "It is to feed the hungry and to give the greeting of peace both to those one knows and to strangers." —*al-Bukhārī*

Abū Mūsā reported that the Prophet (peace and blessings of God be on him) said: "Every Muslim is required to give charity." They said, O Prophet of God! And what about someone who has nothing? He said: "He should work with his hand and benefit himself and then give charity." They said, What if he still has nothing? He said: "He should help those who are needy." They said, What if he can't even do this? He said: "He

should work for good and not for evil—this is charity for him."
—*al-Bukhārī*

Abū Huraira reported, The Prophet (peace and blessings of God be on him) said: "Charity is required of every bone of each of your fingers every day: Charity includes helping someone mount his beast so he can ride, or lifting his provisions to the back of that animal; charity also includes saying a good word, and every step which one takes on the way to prayer; and showing the way of Islam to someone else is charity, also.
—*al-Bukhārī*

Abū Huraira reported, The Prophet (peace and blessings of God be on him) said: "Removing harm from the path is charity." —*al-Bukhārī*

Abū Huraira said on the authority of the Prophet, (peace and blessings of God be on him), who said: "When someone does a charitable thing for someone else, he hides it so that his left hand does not know what his right hand spends." —*al-Bukhārī*

According to ʿAbdullah, the Prophet (peace and blessings of God be on him), said: "The *zakat* due on the crops from lands watered by natural resources such as rainfall and springs or by ground-water is one-tenth of what is harvested, and from land watered by well–water (or artificial means), one-twentieth of the yield." —*al-Bukhārī*

On the authority of Abū Hurayra, the Messenger of God (may the blessings and peace of God be upon him) said: The person who gives to a family a female camel (which can supply them with a large portion of milk each morning and evening) earns a great reward. —*Salih Muslim*

On the authority of Abū ʿAbd ar-Raḥmān ʿAbdullah, the son of ʿUmar ʾibn al Khaṭṭāb (may God be pleased with them both), who said: I heard the Messenger of God (may the blessings and peace of God be upon him) say: Islam has been built on five pillars: testifying that there is no god but God and that Muhammad is the Messenger of God, performing the prayers, paying the zakāt, making the pilgrimage to the Kaʾaba, and fasting during Ramaḍān. It was related by al-Bukhārī and Muslim. —*an-Nawawī*

On the authority of Abū Hamza Anas ʾibn Mālik (may God be pleased with him), the servant of the Messenger of God (may the blessings and peace of God be upon him), that the Prophet (may the blessings and peace of God be upon him) said: None of you [truly] believes until he wishes for his brother what he wishes for himself. It was related by al-Bukhārī and Muslim. —*an-Nawawī*

On the authority of Abū Huraira (may God be pleased with him), that the Messenger of God (may the blessings and peace of God be upon him) said: Let him who believes in God and the Last Day either speak good or keep silent, and let him be generous to his neighbor, and let him who believes in God and the Last Day be generous to his guest. It was related by al-Bukhārī and Muslim. —*an-Nawawī*

On the authority of Abū Huraira (may God be pleased with him), that the Prophet (may the blessings and peace of God be upon him) said: Whoever removes a worldly grief from a believer, God will remove from him one of the griefs on the Day of Judgment. Whosoever alleviates the lot of a needy person, God will alleviate his lot in this world and the next. Whosoever shields a Muslim, God will shield him in this world and the next. God will aid a servant of His so long as the servant aids his brother. It was related by a Muslim in these words. —*an-Nawawī*

Abū Huraira said that the Apostle of God (may God's blessings and peace be upon him) said: "The best house among Muslims is one in which there is an orphan who is treated well, and the worst house among Muslims is one in which there is an orphan who is treated badly. — *Ibn Mājah*

'Anas and 'Abdullah said that the Messenger of God (may God's blessings and peace be upon him) said, "Humanity is the family of God, and whoever acts kindly toward His family is most favored by God." —*al-Baihaqī*

'Ibn 'Abbas heard the Messenger of God (may God's blessings and peace be upon him) say: he is not a believer who eats until he is full while his neighbor beside him goes hungry. —*al-Baihaqī*

Jābir said that the Messenger of God (peace and blessings of God be on him) said: "Every good deed is charity, and it is a good deed to meet your brother with a happy face and—if you have a pail of water and your brother's is empty—to pour water from your pail into his." —*Musnad of Aḥmad*

'Ibn 'Umar said: The Messenger of God (peace and blessings of God be on him) said: There is no *zakāt* due on wealth one has acquired until a year has passed over it." —*Tirmidī*

Samurah reported that it was by order of the Messenger of God, (peace and blessings of God be on him) that we must pay *zakāt* out of what we sell. —*Abū Dāwūd*

ENDNOTES

[1] Sometimes a word or two not found in the original Arabic is added in parentheses by the translator to enhance the sense of the English translation. In this volume, the parentheses have been removed in order to make these passages smoother to read.

[2] This piety code lists the proper recipients of the zakāt: relatives, orphans, the needy, travellers, beggars, and for the ransom of slaves—that is, to free political prisoners.

Chapter Ten

Readings on Islam and Social Welfare

Islam clearly encourages a narrowing of the disparity between society's rich and poor. Both major holidays of Islam—the celebration marking the end of the month-long fast of Ramaḍān, and that which marks the conclusion of the annual period of the Ḥajj—include a special monetary offering on behalf of those in need. "Just think of it," a Muslim friend remarked recently, "When we celebrate the end of the Ḥajj, every Muslim man, woman, and child is expected to give an offering of $5.00. When you multiply that times six million Muslims in America, that's $30 million straight to charity!" As the number of Muslims in America has grown larger, so has an Islamic network of charitable institutions. Among them are the Chechnya Relief Fund, the Holy Land Foundation, ICNA Relief, ISNA Indian Muslim Relief, the Kashmiri Relief Committee, Mercy International, and the Somali Relief Committee, all of which strive to alleviate suffering resulting from political struggles. There are, as well, a growing number of Islamic groups providing assistance to victims of natural disasters, as well as to the homeless and hungry. The articles presented here seek to clarify Islam's theology of charity, as well as to offer some examples of Muslims in action on behalf of others.

The Qurʾān on Man in Society
Fazlur Rahman

A native of what is now Pakistan, Fazlur Rahman held an M.A. degree from Punjab University in Lahore, and a doctorate from Oxford University. He served on the faculties of Durham and McGill Universities, and for six years was the Director of Pakistan's Central Institute of Islamic Research. From 1969 until his death in 1988 at the age of 68, Dr. Rahman was Professor of Islamic Thought at the University of Chicago. A prolific author who was respected internationally, he received many awards for his distinguished contributions to the realm of scholarship.

There is no doubt that a central aim of the Qurʾān is to establish a viable social order on earth that will be just and ethically based. There is no such thing as a societiless individual. Whenever there is more than one human being, God enters directly into the relationship between them and constitutes a third dimension which can be ignored by the two humans only at their risk:

> Do you not see that God knows everything in the heavens and the earth? There is no secret cliquing of three but that God is their fourth, nor of five but that He is their sixth, nor of less than these or more but that He is with them wherever they be. *(58:7)*

The immediate meaning is that no matter how secret they talk, God knows what they say, the more general idea obviously is that God is present wherever two or more persons are present.

The Qur'ān's goal of an ethical, egalitarian social order is announced with a severe denunciation of the economic disequilibrium and social inequalities prevalent in contemporary commercial Meccan society. The Qur'ān began by criticizing two closely related aspects of that society: the polytheism or multiplicity of gods which was symptomatic of the segmentation of society, and the gross socioeconomic disparities that equally rested on and perpetuated a pernicious divisiveness of mankind. The two are obverse and converse of the same coin: only one God can ensure the essential unity of the human race as His creation, His subjects, and those responsible finally to Him alone. The economic disparities were most persistently criticized, because they were the most difficult to remedy and were at the heart of social discord.

The Qur'ān bears eloquent testimony to a situation characterized by selfish and callous uncharitableness and boastful conspicuous consumption on the one hand and grinding poverty and helplessness on the other:

> Competition in accumulating wealth keeps you preoccupied until you visit your graves. Nay, you shall find out soon; nay, nay, you shall find out soon. (102:1–4)

> Woe betide every fault-finder, back-slider, who collects wealth and counts it. He thinks his wealth will bestow eternal life upon him! Nay, he shall certainly be thrown in *hutama* and do you know what *hutama* is? It is God's fire that He lights and that descends upon the hearts of callous miserly people. (104:1–6)

The Qur'ān is certainly not against earning wealth. On the contrary, it sets a high value on wealth. It counts peace and prosperity among the highest blessings of God:

> How accustomed have the *Quraysh* [the mercantile tribe of Mecca] become to their winter journey to Byzantium and their summer journey to the Indian Ocean so that they take them for granted. Let them, then, serve the Lord of this House [the Kaʿba] Who has given them plenty instead of hunger, and peace instead of war. (106:1–4)

But the abuse of wealth prevents man from pursuing higher values and renders it "a pittance of this world" and a "delusion of this world."[1]

In the absence of concern for the welfare of the poor, even prayers became hypocritical:

> Did you see the one who gives the lie to the Faith? It is he who maltreats orphans and works little for the feeding of the poor. Woe betide, then, those who pray, yet are neglectful of their prayers—those who pray for show and even deny the use of their utensils to the poor. (107:1-7)

This lack of consideration for the economically needy is the ultimate expression of pettiness and narrowness of mind—the basic weakness of man.

The Meccans contended that they had earned their wealth, which they, therefore, rightfully owned and which they could spend or dispose of as they wished. The Qur'ān insisted, first, that not all wealth earned was rightfully the earner's; the needy had also a "right" in it: "In their wealth there is a definite right of the indigent and the deprived."[2] Secondly, the Qur'ān told the Meccans that even the wealth they rightfully owned they could not spend just as they wished, for they could not become islands of plenty in a sea of poverty: "Does man think that none can put reins on his wealth when he says, 'I have thrown away stacks of money on such-and-such'?"[3]

The Qur'ān exhorted Muslims "to spend in the cause of Allah" and thus "establish credit with God, so that God may repay you manifold," rather than invest money in usury in order to suck the blood of poor people.[4] In a lengthy Medinan passage (2:260-74), the Qur'ān states that expenditure on the needy is like a single grain that grows seven ears of corn, each ear containing a hundred or more grains, that those who spend in order to show off or who want recognition from their beneficiaries are like rocks upon which there is a thin layer of earth which is easily washed away by a torrential rain, leaving the bare rock that grows nothing, while those who spend "seeking God's pleasure" are like the highlands which, if watered by rains, bring forth plenty but which even in the absence of rains get enough dew because of their height to grow a crop. It then states: "Satan inspires you with fear of poverty for investing in society and commands you obscenities; God, on the other hand, promises you forgiveness and prosperity for such investment." (2:268) Indeed, the Qur'ān holds that one major cause of the decay of societies is the neglect into which they are cast by their prosperous members:

> When God tests man and raises his position and gives him plenty, he says, My Lord has favored me; but when God tests him and puts strict reins on his means of sustenance, he says, My Lord has forsaken me! Nay it is not so, but you do not do good to orphans nor work for the weal of the poor; you wrongfully devour inheritances wholesale and are excessively attached to wealth. (89:15-20)

Two important measures taken were the banning of usury and the imposition of the *zakāt* tax. The prohibition of usury was essential for the public welfare; the medieval lawyers of Islam, however, drew the conclusion from this that all forms of interest are banned, a stand to which even today the vast majority of

Muslims still cling, despite the fundamental change in the role of modern banking in the context of a "developmental economy."

With regard to distributive justice, the Qur'ān laid down the principle that "wealth should not circulate only among the rich" (59:7). Although these words were spoken in the context of the distribution of booty among the poor Meccan immigrants to Medina to the exclusion of more well-to-do Medinese, who consequently raised complaints, they point to a central theme in the general economic policy of the Qur'ān. Thus, after the Qur'ān denounced the Meccans for hoarding wealth and exploiting the poor classes, in Medina the zakāt tax was imposed. Its purposes are detailed in 9:60:

> The *zakāt* is not for the rich but only for the indigent and the poor, those who collect the tax, those whose hearts are to be won over for Islam, for ransoming war-captives, for the relief of those who are in chronic debt, for the "cause of God" (*jihād* and social welfare purposes like education and health) and for the wayfarer (to facilitate travel).

These categories of expenditure, including social welfare in a wide sense and comprising relief from chronic indebtedness, wages for the administrative service (tax-collectors), diplomatic expenditure ("for the winning of hearts"), defense, education, health, and communications, are so broad that they comprise all the activities of a state.

Social Justice
Ibrahim Abu-Rabi'

Dr. Abu-Rabi', a native of Nazareth, is the co-director of Hartford Seminary's Duncan Black Macdonald Center for the Study of Islam and Christian-Muslim Relations. He has the distinction of being the first Muslim to serve as a full member of the faculty of an American Christian seminary. He writes and lectures extensively on Islamic resurgence. In the article below, which is adapted from a longer entry in the *Oxford Encyclopedia of The Modern Islamic World,* several references are made to the *'ulamā'.* They are experts in Islamic law, the religious elite of Islamic societies.

The *Nahḍah* (renaissance; rebirth), which began in the latter part of the nineteenth century, is a vast intellectual, cultural, religious, and political movement that sought to translate the main principles of Western progress into an Arab and Muslim environment, and as a result, it stood against the degeneration of Islam while attempting to rescue the achievements of classical Islamic civilization from centuries of decline and oblivion.

Representatives of the *Nahḍah* movement in the Arab world discussed the need of their societies to overcome decadence and stagnation and find answers to the increasing Western challenge, in both its technical and intellectual aspects. One such challenge was the necessity of attaining a new Muslim social and political order that would put an end to poverty and helplessness in Muslim societies. In many ways, one must see the issue of social justice in nineteenth century Muslim thought as a product of two interchangeable factors: prevailing backward social and economic conditions that did not attract the serious attention of the traditional *'ulamā'* class, and Western domination that neglected to ameliorate the social conditions of the dominated people as a whole. *Nahḍah* thinkers criticized these two factors.

Social justice was closely bound with a host of religious, political, and educational issues and questions facing the Arab and Muslim world of the nineteenth century. Nevertheless, because of the existing political conditions, that is, the formidable challenge of colonialism, the *Nahḍah* movement was unable to attain its immediate social and political goals. This failure placed the issue of social justice at the forefront of Muslim debate in the twentieth century.

In order to analyze the position of Islamic resurgence on the issue of social justice, one must distinguish between three broad phases of resurgence: resurgence as a reaction to imperialism and colonialism; resurgence as a reaction to the emerging nation-state, especially in the 1950s and 1960s; and resurgence as a reaction to the contemporary situation. In the first stage, Islamic resurgence reacted to issues of social justice in the context of imperialism. This warrants us to consider resurgence as a modern phenomenon that uses Islamic concepts and motifs in order to respond to a formidable modern situation. The Islamic resurgence produced a number of outstanding thinkers, such as Ḥasan al-Bannā' and Sayyid Quṭb, among others, who carried the banner of social justice both in writings and through activism.

In twentieth-century Islamic thought, the issue of social justice became more sharply defined, especially with the influx of a large number of peasants from the countryside to the urban areas of the Muslim world. This migration created social and demographic tensions that, to a large extent, gave religion, that is, Islam, a definite ideological and political role in society. . . . The foundation by Ḥasan al-Bannā' of the Muslim Brotherhood in Egypt in 1928, and its spread to the rest of the Arab world soon after, was a reflection of an endemic social crisis in Egyptian and Arab societies. The Muslim Brotherhood has always thought of itself as an organizational and religious response to the plight of the poor and downtrodden in society.

Ḥasan al-Bannā' used the mosque as a medium to spread his social and economic message. His perception of the mosque as a dynamic domain for the propagation of Islam and the preparation of an active Muslim group developed in the social context of the early days of the Muslim Brotherhood. At the time, the Muslim Brotherhood attracted the poor and the uneducated. Therefore, the mosque, as a sacred place, and as a place that gives emotional comfort and security to the poor, was the ideal medium for the preaching and transmission of the Muslim Brotherhood's ideas. Al-Bannā', according to a contemporary theorist, was aware of the total dependency of the Third World in general, and the Muslim world in particular, on the West. He understood Islam as primarily a movement aiming at social improvement rather than one which was predominantly philosophical or cultural.

This phase of Muslim reaction also witnessed a major controversy around issues of religion and social justice between the Islamist camp, represented by Muḥammad al-Ghazālī, and the liberal camp, represented by Khālid Muḥammad

Khālid. In *From Here We Start,* Khālid maintains that one major reason behind
the deteriorating social and economic conditions in Egypt at the time (late 1940s),
besides Western hegemony, was the existence of a Muslim priesthood "pregnant
with pernicious doctrines and deadly principles." According to Khālid, the sole
aim of this class has been to exploit people's spirituality and devotion to religion,
while maintaining its social prestige.

As a liberal thinker who believes that social justice can be only achieved in
the context of state–religion separation, Khālid also criticizes the Muslim
Brotherhood's doctrine of religion–society and religion–state compatibility. He
notes that any "priestly class," ancient or modern, *ʿulamāʾ*-oriented or Muslim
Brotherhood-oriented, is the embodiment of social injustice and exploitation of
the poor, one which promotes superstitions instead of rationalism and poverty
instead of wealth. Muḥammad al-Ghazālī, a leading Muslim Brotherhood
thinker, also held the view that some of the *ʿulamāʾ* he knew acted just like
parasites sucking the blood of the poor.

In 1948, Sayyid Quṭb wrote a major work that has shaped the thought of many
Islamists on social and economic issues. One must view Quṭb's *Social Justice in
Islam* as a critical comment on the social, economic, cultural, and educational
conditions and policies of the Egyptian state in the interwar period. In this book.
Quṭb lays down the theoretical framework of proper conduct in social, legal, and
political affairs. Notwithstanding his normative analysis and his idealistic
solutions, Quṭb's main goal is to dissect the socioeconomic and political problems
in the light of what he perceives as "genuine Islam." In a sense, he takes it for
granted that there is a widespread malaise in Egyptian society, and he offers the
"true" Islamic solution to remedy this situation. Quṭb's arguments reflect the
thoughts of a complex man in transition, as well as a complex situation in flux.
Furthermore, Quṭb's arguments underlie the foundations of many theoretical
arguments in the Muslim Brotherhood movement and its different offshoots in
the 1960s and 1970s. No doubt it is a major work with a significant influence on
a generation of Arab and Muslim intelligentsia in the post–World War II period.

Quṭb points out that the past independence of Islam as a socio-religious and
political system stands in sharp contrast to its present manifestations. In other
words, he argues that the current secular state's monopoly over religion must be
dismantled. One way of doing that is to attack the privileges of the religious
hierarchy that, to his mind, was always linked with the state. Quṭb contends that
the *ʿulamāʾ*, as the established Muslim clergy, have robbed the poor of their social
prestige and economic growth, Islamic history has known *ʿulamāʾ* who have
exploited religion for their worldly benefits and have kept the workers and lower
classes drugged by means of religion.

Quṭb's argument is that the Islamic notion of social justice is all embracing;
it takes account of the material as well as the spiritual dimensions of man's well-
being. Quṭb enumerates the following principles as the foundations of the Islamic
theory of social justice: absolute freedom of conscience; complete equality of all
men; and the permanent mutual responsibility of society. The individual is the
supreme example of social justice. The individual, according to Quṭb, has to place

his trust in Divine and not human authority. To him, divine authority is indivisible. Therefore, man has nothing to fear in this life; he should not allow anxiety to run his life; neither should he be afraid of transient matters in life. Yet, in spite of all this encouragement, Qutb draws our attention to an important aspect in man's life: the material need for food and shelter. He says that "the empty belly cannot appreciate high-sounding phrases. Or else he is compelled to ask for charity, and all his self-esteem leaves him lost, forever." Therefore, the main conclusion Qutb reaches is that social justice cannot prevail in a society if the material foundations of society are not sound and if the minority exploits the majority. One way then of insuring the material well-being of the members of society is through mutual responsibility. The individual must care about the community, which should, in turn, be responsible for feeding the poor and destitute members. That is why, maintains Qutb, Islam has instituted the *zakāt* as well as individual as well as a social responsibility in order to combat poverty.

Although Islam, according to Qutb, respects the individual's property, justice is not always concerned to serve the interests of the individual. The individual is in a way a steward of property on behalf of society. And therefore, property in the widest sense is a right which can belong only to society, which in turn receives it as a trust from God who is the only true owner of anything. Thus, although the individual has the right to possess property, the community's interest is supreme. Communal property is a distinguishing mark of Islam, and therefore communal wealth cannot be limited to individuals. One honest way of gaining money is through work. Therefore, Islam, according to Qutb, is against monopoly, usury, corruption, wastefulness, and dishonest commercial practices. Above all Islam stands against luxury-loving people. Luxury is both an individual as well as a social disease.

In his search for a historical foundation of what he calls "the true spirit of Islam," Qutb finds that Abū Dharr, a companion of the Prophet, was the true embodiment of this spirit. Abū Dharr was unpopular with the corrupt rulers, and any person emulating his example at present will find the same treatment from "the present-day exponents of exploitation." According to Qutb, Abū Dharr stood against the system of preferential treatment instituted by the third caliph, Uthmān, and he was for a complete system of justice like the one instituted by ʿAlī. When Muʿāwiyah came to power, he used public money for bribes and gifts, buying the allegiance of others. Also the Umayyad rulers, in his view did not distinguish between their private funds and public money.

In short, social and political corruption is an old story. Qutb traces it all the way down to the early Islamic state. The deviation from the Islamic ideal begins early on, Qutb, in a sense, considers present history to be the culmination of all that complexity beginning with early Islam. Present Muslim history is unfaithful to its origins. The pious have always been the steadfast few, from Abū Dharr in the first century of Islam to Qutb in the present century. Is most Muslim history, then, just a story of deviation from and betrayal of the ideal? What about the creative tension throughout Islamic history?

Social Justice in Islam by Sayyid Quṭb contains the theoretical principles and foundations of the Muslim Brotherhood's social thought. Quṭb's line of analysis, although grounded in idealistic solutions, dispels the notion of social and human harmony in Egyptian society. It is a society torn apart between feudalists and exploiters, including the professional men of religion, on the one hand, and foreign imperialists, on the other. A radical criticism of this state of affairs, therefore, necessitates the criticism of two parallel, but equally hegemonic mentalities and forces, one indigenous and the other foreign.

Social justice has proven to be a pivotal issue in modern Islamic thought, at least in the Arab world. Any increase in social and economic gaps in Arab society is not likely to push the issue to the side.

On Zakāt
Suzanne Haneef

Haneef is active in the field of Islamic education and has traveled widely in the Muslim world. *What Everyone Should Know About Islam and Muslims* is the outgrowth of her years of studying and living Islam.

In practical terms, *zakāt* is the sum of money which is to be paid on various categories of property—notably savings and investments, produce, inventory of goods, salable crops and cattle—which is to be used to assist the poor of the community, or for the welfare of Muslims and the propagation of Islam. *Zakāt* is usually calculated at two-and-a-half percent, although there is some difference in the amounts due on various categories of " *zakāt*-able" property. *Zakāt* can be paid directly, in such a way that it does not hurt feelings, to needy, deserving Muslims in one's own community; it can be sent to Islamic organizations or centers in one's country of residence to be distributed at their discretion; or it can be sent to individuals or organizations in the Muslim world for distribution.

On Charity
ʿAbdullah Yūsuf ʿAlī

ʿAlī's English translation of the Qurʾān, with commentary on the text, is widely respected and extensively used. Below is his commentary on Sūra 2:215.[6]

Three questions arise in charity: (1) What shall we give? (2) to whom shall we give? and (3) how shall we give? The answer is here. Give anything that is good, useful, helpful, valuable. It may be property or money; it may be a helping hand; it may be advice; it may be a kind word; "whatever ye do that is good" is charity. On the other hand, if you throw away what is useless, there is no charity in it. Or if you give something with a harmful intent, *e.g.,* a sword to a madman, or a drug or sweets or even money to someone whom you want to entrap or corrupt, it is no charity but a gift of damnation. To whom should you give? It may be tempting to earn the world's praise by a gift that will be talked about, but are you meeting the needs of those who have the first claim on you? If you are not, you are like a person who defrauds creditors: it is no charity. Every gift is judged by its unselfish character: the degree of need or claim is a factor which you should consider; if you disregard it, there is something selfish behind it. How should it be given? As in the sight of God; this shuts out all pretence, show, and insincerity.

Compulsory
Shamal Zamaluddin

Among Muslims, it is customary that when one mentions the name of the Prophet Muḥammad, one adds, "peace be upon him." When writing, this is often abbreviated—as it is in this article—as "pbuh."

Relief or charity. By whatever name you choose to call helping the poor, this vital aspect of Islam is woefully short of Muslim manpower and Islamic institutions. *Zakāt* is an institution in Islam for helping the needy. This money is strictly used on the poor and certain other categories of people. We give this money to our mosques, Islamic centers and known charities. It goes to relieve the sufferings of the poor. We trust our imams and leaders, don't we? We should. We know what would happen on the Day of Judgment if they do not carry out their responsibility. But is this good enough? Shouldn't we make an effort to see where the money goes and perhaps even let the mosques know of any area where help is desperately needed? Let us zero in on some of the teachings of our Holy Messenger (pbuh), and after this self-education which leads to awareness of this moral duty, let us act.

The Messenger (pbuh) said, "He is not a true believer who eats his fill while his neighbor goes hungry." We all know that the Messenger (pbuh) gave us comprehensive teachings in regard to the way we should behave and our moral and spiritual obligations. Why should people go on quoting this great and truthful personality if there is no benefit? The Qur'ān reminds us: "Keep on warning, for the warning might benefit." How many of us are guilty of neglecting our neighbors while reaching deep into pockets for our brothers and sisters in faraway lands. Both are important, at all times. But why is it always easier for us to help internationally rather than locally? Let us heed the advice of our Messenger (pbuh) and consider our neighbors.

"Do you know what the rights of neighbors are?" asked the Messenger (pbuh). "Help him if he asks your help. Give him relief if he seeks your relief. Lend him if he needs a loan. Show him concern if he is distressed. Nurse him when he is ill. Attend his funeral if he dies. Congratulate him if he meets any good. Sympathize with him if any calamity befalls him. Do not block his air by raising your building high without his permission. Do not harass him. Give him a share when you buy fruits, and if you do not, bring what you buy quietly and let not your children take them out to excite the jealousy of his children."

This *ḥadīth* is like a laden fruit tree with the fruits ripened by the life-giving sun waiting to be picked. Taste it, savor it. Drink its nectar. So sweet. Which pair of eyes could read such words and just pass them by? Certainly from the eyes these words would reach the innermost being and it would soften, and actions would be forthcoming.

The first command by the Messenger (pbuh) to the small band of Muslims in Medina was "Spread peace and distribute food." To everyone without exception, whether Muslim or non-Muslim. The first command was relevant then and more than relevant now. With the current events of terrorism hovering over our heads we need to spread peace. Allah has permitted fighting and Islam lays down guidelines for war so let us adhere to them. Let us establish justice in all our dealings. Distribute food. Those in need must be given sustenance. There is no excuse for not wanting to help the needy, the hungry. We must help. Not once, not twice, but all the time. Remember that "He who waits to do a great deal of good at once, will never do anything."

"There is no person who does not have the obligation of doing charity every day that the sun rises." The Messenger (pbuh) was then asked: "Messenger of God, from where would we get something to give in charity so often?" He said: "Indeed the gates to goodness are many: glorifying God, praising Him, magnifying Him, saying 'There is no god but Allah,' enjoining good and forbidding wrong, removing any source of harm from the road, listening to the aggrieved, guiding the blind, showing the seeker his need, striving as far as your two legs could carry you and with deep concern to give succor to him who asks, carrying with the strength of your arms the burdens of the weak. All these are acts of charity which are an obligation on you. Also, your smiling in the face of your brother is a charity, your removing of stones and thorns from people's paths is charity and your guiding a man gone astray in the world is charity for you." If this wisdom has not caused us to have love for our less fortunate brothers and sisters, then we are in the category of people like those found in this quote by Bob Hope: "If you have not got any charity in your heart, you have the worst kind of heart trouble." Let us be of those who having gained knowledge and wisdom have charitable hearts.

Charity has many shades and hues. For Muslims, charity is not just feeding the poor. We should not look at charity as having pity on someone who is less fortunate than us. Charity for the poor should be the stepping stone for these people to move on. Unfortunate circumstances at some period in life should not be translated into a lifelong tragedy. We, as Muslims, must help our unfortunate brothers and sisters to climb out of whatever rut they are in, using charity (our charity) as the ladder to climb on.

There is a Chinese proverb that says, "Give a person a fish and you feed just one person; teach a person to fish and he can then feed hundreds." Once a man came to the Messenger (pbuh) seeking charity. The Messenger (pbuh) gave him an axe and told him to use that for cutting wood and to sell the wood. The man came back a few days later and happily told the Messenger (pbuh) that he had been able to earn enough to maintain his family. The helping hand of the Messenger (pbuh) made his society better off by granting the man the ability to earn. In so doing the man was not made homeless, penniless and worst of all to a human, hopeless. Let us come to the realization that a helping hand never takes anything away from society. It builds it.

The Messenger (pbuh) has said that poverty can lead to *kufr* (the rejection of God). So let us struggle to lift humanity, one person at a time, from poverty, and in so doing steer him/her away from the greatest sin in the sight of God.

Keep these thoughts with you: "As the purse is emptied, the heart is filled." "Happiness adds and multiplies as we divide it with others." And from Islam comes this action-pill. You can take it with the tears of compassion: "Prayer carries us halfway to God, fasting brings us to the door of His palace and charity procures us admission."

On Islamic Festivals and Observances
Suzanne Haneef

The pre-Islamic Arabs of Mecca observed numerous festivals which revolved around their polytheistic religion. After the advent of Islam, the Holy Prophet, Muḥammad (peace be on him), abolished all these. In their place Muslims were given two major feasts, *'Id al-Fitr* and *'Id al-Adha,* the celebration of which, with the worship of God and with joy and happiness, is a religious obligation for Muslims.

'Id al-Fitr, the Feast of Fast–Breaking, the festival which marks the end of Ramadān, occurs on the 1st of *Shawwal,* the first day of the following month, and its celebration extends over a period of three days. This occasion is a time of great joy and thankfulness for Muslims because they have completed their obligation of fasting, a month-long discipline of the body and appetites, and it is an occasion for celebration. The festival is characterized by a special *salat,* visiting and exchanging greetings and good wishes, and it is a time of special happiness for the children.

Before the time of the *'Id salat,* which is held in the morning usually shortly after sunrise, a special obligatory charity must be given. This is a specified amount of grain or other foodstuff, or alternatively a sum of money equivalent to the cost of one meal, to be given on behalf of every member of one's family to needy Muslims, either directly or through some Islamic organization.

'Id al-Adha—the Feast of Sacrifice—is the greater of the two major festivals, the period of its celebration extending over four days. This festival marks the annual completion of the ḥajj. It falls on the tenth of the month of *Dhul-Ḥijjah* approximately two-and-a-half months after *'Id al-Fitr,* rotating clockwise around the year and occurring twelve days earlier annually, as do all dates.

At this time, those who have gone to ḥajj are completing their observances in Minā with the slaughter of an animal (although this is not a requirement for all pilgrims) and the termination of their state of *ihrām.* At the same time, as part of their celebration of *'Id al-Adha,* countless Muslims throughout the world are sacrificing animals (this is *sunnah* rather than obligatory) in commemoration of Prophet Abraham's sacrifice of a sheep in the place of his son Ishmael, as commanded by God. The example of Prophet Abraham (peace be on him) is recalled on this occasion as a model of total obedience and surrender to God for Muslims of all times to follow.

Then what happens to the slaughtered animal? Its meat is divided into three equal portions—one for the use of the family, one to be given to neighbors and friends, and one to be given away to the poor, to be used as food; the portions which are distributed are given away as meat (not cooked or prepared). This giving of meat constitutes the special charity of this *'Id* in the place of a monetary one, due to which *'Id al-Adha* is one time in the year—in many places perhaps the only time—when the poor may have meat to eat.

In addition to these two festivals, Muslims observe the Night of Power *(Lailat al-Qadr)*, the night on which the first revelation of the Holy Qur'ān came to the Prophet Muhammad (may God's peace and blessings be on him). Although its exact date is not known with certainty, it falls during one of the odd-numbered nights during the last ten days of Ramaḍān. On this night, according to the Prophet's *Hadīth,* the doors of God's mercy and forgiveness are open to all who call upon Him. The night during which it is commemorated, usually the night preceding the twenty-seventh day of Ramaḍān, is observed by devout Muslims by the performance of *taraweeh salat* [the special sixth prayer of the day added by Muhammad to be said only during Ramaḍan], night-long devotions, recitations of the Qur'ān and acts of charity.

Ramaḍān, Struggle, Compassion and Joy
Ernest Hamilton

Hamilton served as managing editor of *The Muslim World,* a journal published by Hartford Seminary's Duncan Black Macdonald Center for the Study of Islam and Christian–Muslim Relations. He has written and lectured frequently on Islam.

Although it is rarely stated in this way, Ramaḍān, which is the month of fasting for Muslims, may be more accurately called the *Month of Jihād*— of striving hard in one's journeying toward God, for that is the ultimate goal of an ideal Muslim. This, I feel, is the best way to express the significance of Ramaḍān for Muslims, for Ramaḍān is nothing if not a *jihād.*

Fasting in Ramaḍān is a requirement of all Muslims above the age of puberty, but younger members of the population are not exempt from its many ancillary activities—unaware as they may be of the deep meaning of Ramaḍān. They find it to be a month of excitement and reward.

Ramaḍān is the ninth month of the Muslim (lunar) year, and, therefore, the exact starting date may vary a little from country to country. At sighting the new moon, prominent religious leaders announce the start of Ramaḍān through both modern media and word of mouth—town criers.

Fasting begins at dawn the next day. People wake up as early as 3 or 4 a.m., in order to cook and finish eating the meal by sunrise. As families usually cook some of their most favorite dishes during Ramaḍān, children get to enjoy the special meals that begin the fast at sunrise and end it at sunset each day for a whole month, in addition to getting their favorite dishes at the regular times. They also look forward to the end of Ramaḍān, when they expect to get new clothes, new shoes, and the *muᶜayada*— the festival pocket money—to spend at the carnivals and fairs held during *ᶜĪd al-Fiṭr,* the three-day "Feast of the Breaking of the Fast" which marks the end of Ramaḍān.

In a different way, Ramaḍān is a special time for adults, too. It is, indeed, a time of *jihād.* Ideally, a Muslim's life is a continual *jihād* (the Arabic term *jihād* comes from *jahada,* literally, to strive, to struggle) to be in the company of God; and the Muslim who sincerely strives to do so is, therefore, called *mujāhid* (fem. *mujāhida*).

The ideal Muslim is seen, in the Qurᵓān, as a continual striver. As such, he or she strives *for* living in the presence of God (5:35; 13:22; 30:38), and, at the same time, strives *against* all those things that hinder him or her from being in the company of God (49:13)

One who would see the face of God and live in His company, the Qurᵓān warns, must be willing to engage in a long, hard struggle *(jihād)* in this world to purify one's own self; for a human being cannot live in God's company until he or she has purified his or her own self in order to be admitted into the presence of the divine (20:74-6; 34:37).

How does one purify one's self? To be sure, one is not automatically purified by merely believing in God and in the "right" creed (49:14) or by faithfully performing the prescribed rituals (2:177). The only way to purify one's self is through what the Qurᵓān calls the process of "the ascent" (*al-aqaba,* literally, the steep uphill path), that is, by taking the steep uphill path of striving to serve one's fellow human beings—as the following verses make clear:

Ah, what will convey unto thee what the Ascent is!
(It is) to free a slave.
And to feed in the day of hunger.
An orphan near of kin.
Or some poor wretch in misery.
And to be of those who believe and exhort one another to perseverance
and exhort one another to compassion.
Their place will be on the right hand (90:12-18).

In other words, one cannot be admitted into the presence of God until one's self is purified, and one's self cannot be purified unless one takes the steep uphill path of serving one's fellow human beings and entering into a supportive and caring relationship with them. That is what the word *tazakka* (to purify) implies in the Qurᵓanic usage: to purify one's self is to grow in goodness by being good to one's fellow beings ("And whosoever grows [in goodness], grows only for himself." 35:18).

In essence, the Qurᵓān is saying that each sincere act of kindness, care, concern, support, protection, and compassion that we *strive* to do for our fellow beings leads to our self-growth and, thus, to our self-purification, bringing us ever nearer to God (29:6). The Qurᵓān holds that the nearer the concerns of our fellow human beings are to us, the nearer our concerns are to God; the closer we are to our fellow human beings, the closer we are to God.

"O you who believe! Fasting is prescribed for you, even as it was prescribed for those before you, that you may ward off evil *(tattaquna)*" (2:183)—with these words the Qur'ān exhorts Muslims to set aside a time for taking an opportunity, individually and collectively, for self-growth through abstaining from food, drink, and sexual intercourse from sunrise to sunset for an entire month.

They are asked first to engage in the *jihād* of *empathizing* with the hungry and the thirsty by voluntarily undergoing their experience daily. Then, with the breaking of fast each day, they are asked to engage in the *jihād* of *giving* by actually sharing their food and water with the less fortunate on the streets.

The month of Ramaḍān may also be called the Month of the Deprived, for in depriving themselves of the blessings of the most basic necessities of life willingly, Muslims may come to know and feel the sting of their absence in the lives of those who have come to know and feel it unwillingly.

The month of Ramaḍān thus directs the attention of the whole Muslim community to its poor and its destitute. It not only evokes a sense of empathy, but also stirs the community to compassionate action.

The morning after the last day of fasting, all Muslims gather at a designated place to pray together and give thanks to God for His infinite bounties to humankind. Parents and children all dressed in new clothes leave the mosques after the prayers, ready to feast and to entertain their relatives, friends and strangers alike.

For three days, festivities go on. Old friendships are renewed, new friends are made, and family bonds are strengthened. A sense of newness prevails. For many Muslims the joy of sharing and the warmth of family and friends that the experience of Ramaḍān affords bring a renewed sense of closeness to their fellow beings and give a new strength to continue on the steep uphill path to God.

Where's the Beef?
The Message News Staff

About seven years ago, a mere handful of ICNA members in Chicago loaded up the backs of their station wagons with donated meat and distributed it to needy families in the Windy City area. Little could they have envisioned that today (1996), their annual Eid-ul-Adha Meat Drive would collect over 15,000 pounds of halal meat and provide it to more than 350 area families, Bosnian and Afghānī refugees, as well as foster homes with large numbers of children.

ICNA Chicago unit president, Ikhram Ḥussain, observed that although the annual meat drive is sponsored by ICNA, several local masjids actively support the project. He explained that the bulk of the meat comes from brothers and sisters who donate the third portion of meat designated to the poor from their Eid-ul-Adha sacrifice. The Meat Drive is advertised widely on radio stations and by extensive distribution of fliers.

This year, ICNA New York Unit collected over 7000 pounds of beef, goat, and lamb meat for distribution to the needy following Eid-ul-Adha. The first-time project for the New York Unit was considered successful, according to Unit president Zahid Bukhari, who acknowledged the tremendous cooperation on the part of area individuals, grocery stores and meat markets. The meat was distributed throughout the various boroughs of New York by Al-Markaz, the national headquarters of ICNA and various other member masjids and organizations of the Majlis-ash-Shura of New York. Br. Bukhari stated that the Eid-ul-Adha Meat Drive in New York is expected to develop into a year-round project, *inshallah* [God willing].

🎋

What Was Done About Alcohol With The Coming Of Islam?
B. Aisha Lemu

Because Islam's position on the matter is so clear, Muslims have often been quite successful in controlling alcoholism and drug abuse. Imam Qasim Shareef, of Masjid Muhammad, Hartford, Connecticut, relates proudly how, during the summer of 1995, members of his mosque staged an initiative in the city's Bellevue neighborhood. For two months some twenty to thirty men kept a vigil outside a known crack house. "It was dangerous," Imam Qasim stresses; "the drug-sellers were relentless." Nevertheless, the vigil was successful. The house was boarded up, and the neighborhood is now drug-free.

The following is an excerpt from a lecture on "Islam and Alcohol" presented as the Advanced Teachers' College of Minna (Saudi Arabia), February, 1981.

Alcohol was very popular with the Arabs before Islam. It was as much an accepted part of social life in pagan Arabia as it is in the West today, and for similar reasons—social relaxation, release of inhibitions, forgetfulness of problems, proof of manliness and so on. And of course among them were its victims—the drunkards and alcoholics and their families.

The approach of Islam to this problem has many lessons for us. The aim was total prohibition, but the method was step by step. If total prohibition had been introduced arbitrarily and without any prior preparation of people's minds, the Prophet would have had great difficulty in imposing it. But by the method employed the people were so ready for the prohibition when it came that the obedience was immediate and positive.

The first hint of what was to come was in Mecca when the Qur'anic verse was revealed:

> They question you about alcohol and gambling. Say: In both is great sin and some utility for men; but the sin of them is greater than their usefulness. . . . (Sūra 2:219)

This hint was already enough for some of the Muslims, who stopped drinking on the advice of this verse alone. This was followed some years later in Medina by the revelation: "O believers, do not pray when you are drunken until you know what you are saying. . . ." (Sūra 4:43).

In view of the frequency of the Muslim prayers at five specific times of the day and night, this condition imposed a further restraint on drinking, particularly in respect of quantity, and was enough to stop many more Muslims from drinking at all.

The final prohibition came in Medina with the revelation:

> O you who believe, intoxicants and gambling and idolatrous practices and divination of the future are an abomination of Satan's handiwork. Avoid it, so that you may prosper. The devil wants only to cast among you enmity and hatred by means of intoxicants and gambling, and to turn you from remembering God and from prayer. Will you not then desist? (S. 5:90–1)

The effect of this revelation was dramatic. The remaining wine in the houses and stores and jars and cups was poured away in the streets and from that moment alcohol had no legal or acceptable place in Muslim society. *Khamr* [alcohol] was cursed, together with anyone who thenceforth might make it, sell it, buy it, store it or serve it.

Moreover, *Khamr* was defined as anything which would, if taken in large quantity, intoxicate, and of such drinks or substances it was forbidden to take even a small quantity. It therefore covers all intoxicating drugs.

From this condition of an alcoholic society to an alcohol-free society we have seen the steps, and need to look more closely at the process involved.

The Islamic policy on alcohol is that prevention is better than cure. From what we have seen of the difficulty of a cure for alcoholism, and the damage already done to the alcoholic and his family, before a cure is even sought, we can see that the Islamic policy is valid. Prevention is indeed far better than cure.

Islam therefore attacks the alcohol problem root and branch, and as we have seen, it began with the root. Where is the root? It is in the mind of man—in his understanding and in his belief in Allah and the Day of Judgment. A Muslim who has submitted to God learns to be conscious of God at all times. Therefore he will not drink something that will interfere with or remove is consciousness of God. A Muslim believes that the whole of his life is a test of his conduct. Therefore he will not drink something that will cause him to fail that test. In particular he is aware of his responsibility to his family and of the *hadīth* of the Prophet that "The best of you is the one who is kindest to his family." Then how can he go and drink the thing that will destroy his family? A Muslim is aware of the *hadīths* on modesty, for example "Each religion has its characteristic, and the characteristic of Islam is modesty," and "Modesty and faith go together: when the one is lost the other is lost." Therefore he will not drink what will cause him to be boastful and shameless.

These are among the basic teachings of the Qur'ān and *Hadīth* where we find great emphasis on intelligence, knowledge, understanding, consciousness of God, unity of mankind, brotherly love, kindness to the weak, kindness within the family, consideration for others, and also strong condemnation of boastfulness, aggression, sexual irregularity, harshness and unreason.

Therefore alcohol is clearly identified for the Muslim as something that will completely destroy his chances of the blessings of Allah when his life on earth comes to an end, if not earlier. Alcohol was called "the Mother of Sins" because of all the sins that are born of it.

It is this consciousness that for most Muslims is [a] sufficient deterrent against having anything whatsoever to do with alcohol. Whatever the problems of alcohol in some Muslim countries today, this consciousness still prevents the situation from being anything like as bad as in non-Muslim countries.

What did the Prophet do about those Muslims who ignored Allah's prohibition of alcohol—either because of the insincerity of their belief in the divine revelation or because they were already alcoholic addicts? It is recorded that the Prophet used three basic methods with such people, depending on the individual case. The first and mildest was group pressure and persuasion by the Muslim's brother Muslims. The second method was for the Prophet himself to reprimand or indicate his disapproval—on one occasion he threw dust in a drunkard's face as an indication of his disapproval. But he never allowed people to curse a drunkard—the aim was always to reclaim them from alcohol, not to disown them. The third method was by public beating. In the Prophet's time the type of beating was not specified—it might be with the hands, sandals, clothes or sticks. He was instructed by revelation to give this punishment, although it was not part of the Qur'anic revelation.

Concerning the Muslim alcoholics of our own day and age, there is no reason why they should not avail themselves of modern drugs and medical treatments to help break themselves of the habit of drinking, but this does not absolve the society of its own obligations to stop the spread of alcoholism by persuasion, social pressure and if necessary by legal punishment as a deterrent.

There are three main elements in the success of this Islamic policy on alcohol:

1. *The impact of belief and understanding:* This has been discussed. The Muslim knows that by drinking he is not only harming his body and mind, but that he is also in rebellion against his Creator. This consciousness produces feelings of guilt and fear which deter him from becoming a drinker. It is also the divine origin of the injunction against alcohol which gives it its authority at state level.

2. *Public Pressure:* In an Islamic community alcohol is automatically not readily available as it is in the West. It is not served on social occasions, it is not advertised, it is not freely sold in shops and bars. The Muslim who takes to drinking at home will also find himself under pressure from his friends and relatives to stop it. He should also be aware that if his wife takes him to a Shari'a Court she can obtain divorce on proof of his drinking alcohol, whether or not his beats her or has committed any other offense.

3. *Punishment under the Law:* In non-Muslim countries, drunkenness and alcoholism are generally regarded as the concern of the individual. It is

therefore left to the individual to seek treatment as and when he decides to. As we have seen, this is usually, when he has already reached the end of the line—his life in ruins and his family shattered. In other words, treatment is often too late and cannot undo the harm already done. In Islam, drunkenness and alcoholism are seen to have effects on the whole society, through crime, accidents, illness, loss of work and family breakup. Its effects are just as profound as those of stealing and if anything more devastating. Therefore as Islamic society does not sit by and watch this process run its course; it can deal with it at the first sign under the law.

What has been said about the success of the Islamic measures against alcohol refers of course only to where they are applied. If any Muslim community fails to teach its children effectively to believe in Allāh and the Last Day, fails to prevent the free circulation of alcohol, fails to apply social pressure on those who start to drink, and fails to apply the punishment under the Sharīʿa, of course it cannot expect success in controlling alcoholism. We reap only what we sow. And if a farmer does not deal with weeds when they begin to show up, he should not be surprised when they spread far and wide and weaken or destroy his crops.

This applies to our situation in many parts of the Muslim world today. Many factors contribute to this—the spread of Western culture and social practices, Western educational systems, the secular state with its secular law and institutions. In some countries there is also the new factor of comparative affluence, ease of obtaining alcohol, advertisement of alcohol, and the example of non-Muslim and even of some Muslim fellow-citizens.

These three factors—incitement, opportunity and example—are mentioned by Kessel and Walton in their study of alcoholism as strong contributory factors in the prevalence of alcohol in any society. If these three factors—incitement, opportunity and example—contribute to the spread of alcohol, then obviously their reversal is required to obtain the control or abolition of alcohol.

1. *Discouragement of alcohol.* The opposite of incitement to drink alcohol is teaching, advice and campaign *not* to drink. This as we have mentioned begins with the education of young people in Islamic values including emphasis on the harm of alcohol, and its prohibition. Among young people, this can be done through schools and colleges, Muslim Students' Society functions, Islamic Study Circles and the general development of the spiritual life through reading, discussion and prayer. If a young person embarks on a course of spiritual development he will soon find that drinking is quite incompatible with his new understanding. He may also reflect on the seriousness of the punishment for drinking under the Sharīʿa, and on his accountability if he ignores such a clear warning. This appeal can be widened by writing for magazines and newspapers, and the use of radio and television to emphasize the dangers and harm of alcohol. At the government level Muslims may campaign for the abolition or restriction of the advertisement of alcohol. At a personal level it also involves advice to fellow-Muslims who may be drinking or involving themselves in the provision or serving of drink. All these are means of discouraging drinking.

2. *Reduction of opportunity to drink.* In any predominantly Muslim area there should be group pressure to reduce the availability of alcohol. For example Muslims may campaign and lobby against the siting of breweries in Muslim areas, since such occupations as working in a brewery are *haram* (forbidden) to Muslims, just like the brewery's product. Muslims may also lodge official complaints about the siting of bars in their vicinity. They should also make more effort to provide recreational facilities where alcohol is *not* served. At present almost every hotel, social club, sports club etc. serves alcohol. Why not establish some that are alcohol–free? Some state governors have discontinued the serving of alcohol at government cocktail parties. This is an encouraging step, to be noted by some Muslims who have taken to serving alcohol at naming ceremonies, weddings etc. , and also by students with regard to their Students' Union and other college activities. Are they involving themselves in the provision and sale of alcohol in any way? If so they have a duty to themselves and to others to discontinue it.

3. *What sort of example?* The good example shown by some state governors has already been commended. All Muslims who, due to their position in the public eye, are able to give an example to others—and this includes student leaders—should carefully consider their responsibility in respect of alcohol.

The Murrah Federal Building: Muslim Responses
Council on American-Islamic Relations

On April 19, 1995, The Murrah Federal Building in Oklahoma City was destroyed by a truck-bomb. Initial news reports assumed it to an act by "Muslim extremist terrorists." A Muslim man of Middle Eastern descent who happened to be leaving Oklahoma by airplane that morning was detained and interrogated extensively. Many American Muslims were themselves the victims of terrorism in the days that followed the tragedy. The Council on American-Islamic Relations (CAIR), based in Washington, DC, is a nonprofit, grassroots membership organization dedicated to presenting an Islamic perspective on issues of importance to the American public. In September, 1995, it published a 30-page report documenting the hate-crimes sustained by American Muslims in the aftermath of the Oklahoma City bombing, as well as their own responses to the tragedy.

The initial reaction among Muslims in the aftermath of the Oklahoma City bombing was pain and fear. Approximately one-in-four respondents reported that female family members were afraid to appear in public during the crisis. Another one-forth of the respondents said they feared for their children's safety.

Within hours of the first reports of the Oklahoma City blast, twelve Muslim organizations issued a joint statement condemning the bombing and asking for media restraint in reporting Muslim links to the incident. Other Arab and Muslim national and local organizations issued separate and/or joint statements condemning the bombing. The *Shura* Council (which consists of the Islamic Society of North America, the Islamic Circle of North America, The Ministry of Warith Deen Muhammad, and the National Community of Imam Jamil al-Amin) called on Muslims to offer supplication prayers during their weekly services on Friday, April 21. Although Muslim leaders were not included in the official memorial service, Muslim delegations from around the country, especially from the South Central region, attended the special memorial service organized by the Oklahoma Governor and his wife.

Material help followed words of condolences. Many of Oklahoma City's estimated 5,000 Muslims took part in the relief effort. The president of the city's American Muslim Association and his wife—a cardiologist and anesthesiologist—both volunteered at area hospitals the day of the explosion. From nearby Texas, Holy Land Foundation for Relief and Development, a national Muslim group based in Dallas, held a blood drive for explosion victims, donated $25,000 to the Red Cross and $5,000 to Oklahoma City's Disaster Recovery Scene. On April 23, some fifty foundation volunteers from different ethnic backgrounds flew to Oklahoma City to work with the Oklahoma City Food Bank and Feed the Children organization who accommodated families affected by the bombing.

Muslim contributions to the relief effort came from around the country. The International Islamic Relief Organization, headquartered in Washington, DC, opened a special fund for the bombing victims. A Muslim delegation met with the governor of Oklahoma and presented him with checks totaling $21,000 for the Victims Relief Fund. Islamic community centers nationwide (Dar al-Hijrah, Falls Church, Virginia; Dar al-Fitrah, North Texas, among others) organized blood drives on April 20 and April 21.

Some observers felt pity for Muslims who rushed to offer their blood after media reports blamed Middle Easterners for the bombing. Muslims, however, have far greater concerns than defensive reactions. Condemning the bombing and praying for the innocent victims, Muslims wanted to participate in the public move to ostracize extremist elements from all backgrounds and to reaffirm their commitment to the path of peaceful reform. Participating in the relief effort, the Muslim community leaders reacted in a way similar to leaders of other communities who were horrified by the bombing. In other words, Muslim organizations wanted to guide members of their community toward mainstream social action.

The Muslim response to the Oklahoma crisis did not go unrecognized. Frank Keating, the Governor of Oklahoma, in a letter thanking Muslim groups for their efforts on behalf of bombing victims, said: "I am immensely proud of Oklahomans of all races, creeds and faiths. They have come together in shared anguish and shared pride... May Allah bless you always." The governor also apologized in a CNN interview to Abraham Ahmad, the American Muslim Oklahoman who was initially and irrationally treated as a bombing suspect. Other American leaders and citizens, some in conjunctions with Muslims, sent letters to the editor in a number of cities publicly apologizing to Muslims for the early suspicions and hate crimes Muslims endured in wake of the bombing.

Love Thy Neighbors: Charity begins at home
Omar Afzal

The author wrote this article to encourage Muslims to broaden their definition of mission and outreach to include meeting the physical needs of those around them.

Every day I receive three, sometimes five or more, appeals for funds to take care of the needs of Muslims in distress in some far off lands. At other times, the requests are for building a mosque or a Muslim Community Center somewhere in North America. It shows the vitality and caring of Muslims living in North America. We vigorously try to establish our presence in this land and care about the needs of Muslims from many of our home countries. However, we seldom worry about the needy in our own neighborhood. Have we decided to close our eyes, or is our love and mercy reserved only for the Muslims in distant lands?

Many of us share the feeling that Muslims in North America are not doing enough for their neighbors. As a matter of fact, many feel that we are not shouldering our civic, social and political duties. How many of us volunteer even for the PTA when our children need us to help them get through the maze of school rules, curriculum or food requirements.

Every mosque and Muslim Community Center has a *dawah* [mission] or outreach program. But, these programs have been drastically limited. We enthusiastically shout slogans like *"Allāhu Akbār"* [God is greatest] if a searching soul finds her or her way to Allah by sheer chance and takes *shahādah* [bears witness to the faith] in our presence. Most of the time this happens without any real effort on our part. Muslims frequently go to nearby prisons to help incarcerated persons learn something about Islam. Sometimes we stand on a corner and distribute a few leaflets and pamphlets stressing Islam's universality and its approach to human problem solving, But, is this enough?

What about applying some of the Islamic solutions to the local problems of helping the elderly, emergency relief in disasters, fighting drug use and juvenile delinquency, neighborhood watch programs, soup kitchens, clothes and toys for the poor on *Eid* day and hundreds of other similar projects in your neighborhood? The dimensions of participation in the voluntary sector are limitless. Welfare, health care, poverty, education, and religious and cultural awareness require tremendous efforts and large sums of money to address a part of the problem.

I don't think Muslims can duplicate federal and state social welfare programs. Some Muslims argue that most Americans are far better off than the majority of people living in Muslim countries. US federal and state programs take care of many Americans with hundreds of social service programs. Private charities help some special groups. The Muslims in many countries are extremely poor and therefore have great need for the meager resources collected. This argument may have some validity, but we cannot justify our indifference to local needs.

Allah says: *"Don't you see the one who denies the Judgment. It is he who repulses the orphan, and does not encourage the feeding of the indigent. So woe to those who pray, [but] are neglectful of their prayers; those who want but to show off and refuse to give away for neighborly needs." (107:1-7)*

The Messenger (pbuh) instructed us to visit the sick, feed the hungry and free captives. At another point he (pbuh) was very emphatic about reminding us of our duties to our neighbors. He (pbuh) said, "By Allah, they are not believers (three times). The audience asked, Who are they? He replied, They are those whose neighbors are not safe from their exploits."

In another *Hadith* we find him (pbuh) informing us, "He is not a believer who fills his stomach and his neighbor goes hungry." In a similar statement he (pbuh) told us that the best charity is that you feed a hungry stomach.

According to a narration, Prophet Muhammad (pbuh) said, "He who likes that Allah and His Messenger (pbuh) love him should behave nicely with his neighbor."

Jibril [the angel Gabriel] (the blessings of God be upon him) repeatedly reminded the Messenger (pbuh) in such strong terms about the rights of one's neighbors that the Messenger (pbuh) reported that he thought one's neighbor would be given a share in one's inheritance. Where to look for a neighbor is solved by the Messenger (pbuh) as well. Someone asked him (pbuh) which one should he choose if he has two neighbors? He (pbuh) replied, "The one whose door is nearer to your house." The end purpose of neighborly love is to please Allah. Muslims must keep in mind that their mercy and charity may help their neighbors better learn about Islam and Muslims. This is a noble end by itself especially in North America where Islam and Muslims are maligned every day by the powerful media. We should do it without any other motive, however.

Wherever Muslims live in metropolitan or rural areas, they may not have to go very far to find out those who need their help. There are sick, elderly, homeless, abandoned and indigent people all around. There are many other sections of population in urban as well as rural neighborhoods who would welcome any assistance we may provide.

The first step is to convince your local Muslim group about the need for an outreach program. Select your targets carefully. Initiate new ideas and processes to gather the needed manpower and money. Start on a very small scale, doing only what you may easily achieve. For example, just visit the elderly in their homes. To gain their confidence, enter into meaningful conversations with your lonely elderly neighbors. Help them with their grocery shopping. See if they need help getting their medicine from the drug store. Maybe they cannot walk due to snow or distance. Shovel the snow from their porch or driveway. They may need you for dozens of things. Just running a few errands or filling out a few forms may be all that the elderly need to make their lives easier.

Develop a public policy statement and get support from local interest groups. There may be others in neighborhood churches and synagogues who are thinking similarly. Talk to them and learn from their experiences. Explore the possibility of doing something jointly. In many towns and cities, you will find public programs run by federal, state, or local governments. They need volunteers. Explore the areas where your group may help. Often charities have funds to help start up a voluntary group for specific purposes.

What is needed is a strong urge and motivation to fulfill the duties of a Muslim. You have the motivation to please Allah and follow His Messenger (pbuh). You must create the urge in your heart because it is the best way to reach out. Empty words and actions will not hold anyone's attention. It is your expression of neighborly love and Islamic character which attracts others to you.

Helping People Help Themselves: Mercy International USA
Mercy International News Staff

Founded in 1986 by American Muslims, Mercy International USA, Inc. (Mercy) is an non-profit relief and development organization dedicated to alleviating human suffering and building self-reliance by providing health care and promoting economic and educational growth around the world. Its motto—"Helping people help themselves"—emphasizes this agency's determination to restore dignity to the individuals and communities it assists. Headquartered in Plymouth, Michigan, it also maintains offices in West Covina, California; Zagreb, Croatia; Sarajevo, Tuzla, and Zenica, Bosnia; Magadishu, Somalia; Nairobi, Kenya; and Tirana, Albania. Mercy for International Relief Agency, Inc., is the sister organization headquartered in Canada. While the variety and range of its activities is extensive, the article given here examines Mercy's work in Bosnia.

Mercy International conducts well-organized relief programs in many of the world's trouble spots, including Albania, Somalia, and the former Yugoslavia. Its efforts in the face of the ongoing civil war in Bosnia-Herzogovena have centered on providing the war's survivors with the means to reestablish meaningful lives. Seeds and breeding animals enable families to farm, feed themselves, then return a portion of their produce to Mercy to help other families get back on their feet.

During the fall of 1995, Mercy distributed 99,000 pounds of wheat seed to families—a total of approximately 8,000 individuals—in the Zenica region. In return, Mercy received over 92,000 pounds of harvested wheat which was then distributed to the most vulnerable groups in the region, including handicapped persons, seniors, and the terminally ill. In early spring of 1996, a total of 39,000 family seed packs were distributed benefiting an estimated 180,000 people in the Tuzla region (including Brcko, Celic, Doboj East, Gradacac, Odzak, Zvornik, and the city of Tuzla), in Zenica (including Maglaj and Travnik), and in Sarajevo. Each of the seed packs contained beans, spinach, peas, cabbage, cauliflower, cucumber, leek, lettuce, parsley, sweet pepper, tomato, black zucchini, and red beet seeds. The project was coordinated by the Food and Agricultural Organization (FAO) and the United Nations High Commission for Refugees (UNHCR). The US Army First Brigade (IFOR) assisted in distributing seeds in the municipality of Odzak. "This just seemed like a good marriage of two groups who helped each other out," said Michael Yuknis, then Mercy's Tuzla Field Office Director.

A partnership between Mercy International and Kokaprodukt, a Bosnian poultry farm, made possible another relief project. During the first phase which lasted from May '95 to May '96, a total of approximately 1.6 million fresh eggs were produced and 85% of them were distributed to vulnerable groups at more than eighty distribution sites. Hospital patients, school children, orphans, displaced persons from Srebrenica, the elderly, and the truly indigent are among those who benefited from the egg distribution. The first phase of egg production also provided an economic stimulus to the region because 15% of the production remained with the poultry farm. This has allowed Kokaprodukt to continue operations without Mercy's direct involvement. During the various phases of this project, Mercy has cooperated with a number of charitable agencies including the UNHCR, Norwegian People's Aid, the Red Crescent Society, and other local charitable organizations. Until February of 1996, this program also included the daily preparation and serving of 1,300 egg and jam sandwiches to children and refugees. UNPROFOR's Second Pakistani Battalion was Mercy's partner in this sandwich distribution. The concluding phase came in June 1996, when 2,800 layer chickens were given to individual refugee families in Tuzla's Lakavac municipality; an additional 2,800 layer chickens remained with Kokaprodukt. A total of 43,000 persons in the Tuzla region benefited from this project, with 4,000 benefiting on a daily basis.

Recipients of the donations of wheat and eggs also received one-pound cans of meat at the same time. During the fall and winter of 1995–1996, 115,000 cans fed needy Bosnian refugees; another 41,500 cans were distributed in the spring of 1996. Meanwhile, Cunex, a local Bosnian company, helped launch Mercy International's rabbit project in October of 1995. Originally, the project was designed to have a two-year duration. However, due to the outbreak of an epidemic among some of the rabbits and the subsequent illness of the firm's owner, Cunex was forced to cease operations. Therefore, the second phase of the project, distribution to individual families, had to begin earlier than planned. A total of 668 rabbits (80% female and 20% male) were distributed to about eighty families in the Zenica region. These animals will supplement the protein needs of recipient families as well as allow them to begin their own small rabbit production businesses. Rabbits are extremely fast meat producers; a female rabbit reaches maturity at five to six months of age, and can then produce as many as forty offspring per year. This project will continue to help families for years to come because each recipient family will provide Mercy with the same number of rabbits as they receive. Mercy will then distribute these rabbits to new recipient families who will in turn provide Mercy with an equal number of rabbits for distribution to other families. Working with Spreca, another local Bosnian company, a cattle breeding program has been underway since December of 1995. The first phase was completed with the delivery of 1,000 doses of bull semen and medical supplies to the company in Kalisija in the Tuzla region. In return, Mercy will receive ten pregnant cows for distribution to families so that they may provide for their own dairy needs and supplement their income.

Always striving to stimulate local commerce and industry in the midst of conflict, Mercy International is helping to revive Sarajevo's once thriving honey production industry. In June 1996, the organization reached an agreement with the Beekeepers Association of Sarajevo (BAS) to provide each of that agency's one hundred members with two wooden beehives and 8.8 pounds of wax. (Beekeepers themselves must purchase the bee swarms and the necessary tools, either individually or through BAS.) In return, BAS will provide Mercy with 8,800 pounds of high-grade honey over a three year period. It will be packed in 6.6–11 pound plastic containers which Mercy will distribute to needy families.

While many of Mercy International's projects have focussed on food production and distribution, other health needs have also been addressed. In cooperation with Doctors Without Borders (MSF), the World Health Organization (WHO), UNHCR, and the Office of Foreign Disaster Assistance–Disaster Response Team (OFDA–DART), Mercy supported the renovation of a production center which, since its reopening in October 14, 1995, has produced intravenous solutions on a regular basis and in a sufficient quantity to cover demand in greater Sarajevo. Mercy continues to provide raw material for this. A pharmaceuticals project is also being carried out at the State Hospital in Sarajevo in cooperation with Pharmacists Without Borders (PSF). Mercy delivered all raw materials for pharmaceutical production and packaging, which began in February 1996, and will take care of the needs of Greater Sarajevo for three months. Eye drops, baby creams, antacid pills, and ultrasound gel are among the items being produced.

The work of Mercy International has received significant coverage both locally and nationally in print, radio, and television news media. Mercy's President Umar al-Qadi has been interviewed by NBC, CBS, and National Public Radio affiliates, and was one of the three panelists on PBS's News Hour with Jim Lehrer in January, 1996. The panel, which also included Kenneth Hackett, Executive Director of Catholic Relief Services, and Robert Daveccie, President of the International Rescue Committee, discussed prospects for a peaceful reconciliation of the Bosnian conflict and the rebuilding of the society.

As one of the relief organizations working in Bosnia, Mercy International was honored by Hillary Rodham Clinton at a White House ceremony on January 29, 1996. At that ceremony, the First Lady announced a multi-ethnic initiative aimed at treatment for victims of trauma in Bosnia, in which Mercy expects to participate. As a token of appreciation for her efforts in publicizing the needs of the Bosnian people, Umar al-Qadi presented Mrs. Clinton with an original painting by Bosnian artist, Aldin Hadzic.

United Muslim Movement Against Homelessness
The Message News Staff

The acronym for the relief organization introduced here spells the Arabic word for community: U.M.M.A.H. It is a volunteer agency funded by donations from the local Muslim community, and reaches out to the entire community of the homeless, regardless of race, creed, color, or religion. Its founding by Br. Khatib Akbar Jihad was inspired by an awareness of an increasing number of Muslims among New York's homeless, along with the realization that none of the city's mosques was yet operating a homeless shelter.

Imam Talib Abdur Rashid gave U.M.M.A.H. space to work at Harlem's Mosque of Islamic Brotherhood until it could afford a permanent headquarters. U.M.M.A.H. began as a Mobile Outreach Program distributing food, clothing, and referral information to New York's needy every Sunday afternoon, wherever the homeless could be found: on the streets, under bridges, in parks. It also went to men's shelters around the city.

Eventually, the United Muslim Movement Against Homelessness became part of a larger organization: ICNA Relief. Three months after the article below was published in its periodical, *The Message,* the Islamic Circle of North America reported that U.M.M.A.H. was averaging 200 servings at its free weekly meals in New York City, and was working toward expansion of its program to three days per week. The United Muslim Movement Against Homelessness is also one of the largest collectors and distributors of used clothing in New York City. It distributes trunk-loads of clothing along with the Sunday food program, and brings van-loads of clothing to city and private shelters in the five boroughs, and conducts an annual Toy Drive for Homeless Children in order to donate new toys to three family shelters.

The roots of homelessness in the United States can reasonably be traced to the displacement of the Native Americans by European colonial settlers. While many Native American nations were nomadic, the vast majority, particularly on the eastern seaboard and in the Midwest, were sedentary, with land-based, stationary settlements. The American settler movement, beginning in earnest in the 1840s, was the chief conveyor of homelessness among the indigenous populations. Tribe after tribe was either forcibly driven from their ancestral lands, confined to nonarable areas or physically exterminated by the western land-grab of American settlers. The policy of the federal government of the United States was to condone and even facilitate the excesses of the settlers against the tribes. After the Civil War, US troops assisted the settler movement with the use of unbridled brutality against the militarily overmatched Native Americans.

During the Great Depression of the 1930s, hundreds of thousands of otherwise financially stable individuals and families faced the prospect of homelessness. As banks foreclosed on properties and landlords evicted tenants for lack of payment, cardboard box houses began to proliferate in cities across America. However, because homelessness was not stigmatized during the Great Depression, the homeless were usually treated with compassion, rather than scorn, by the general populace and the media.

Not until the mid 1970s, did so many Americans suffer from a state of homelessness that was not of a temporary nature, but permanent. In 1975, the Federal government changed its regulations governing long-term confinement in mental institutions. The practical effect of this changed policy was to cast on the streets thousands of mentally disturbed persons who were unable to adequately provide for their housing and subsistence needs. Homelessness in America had now come out of the closet and literally positioned itself on the heat grates and alleyways of cities throughout the country. Unlike their counterparts during the Great Depression though, the "new" homeless were derisively characterized as bums, hoboes, and vagabonds. America of the 1970s was unwilling to extend fellow feelings and understanding to this latest transient population.

Credit, or blame, must be attributed to the 1980s administrations of Ronald Reagan for institutionalizing homelessness in America. Homeless shelters became regular features of the housing stock in the US as the government's trickle-down economic policies drove more and more Americans well below the poverty line and into homelessness.

It is conservatively estimated that close to two million men, women, and children are homeless in the United States today. No longer the exclusive domain of so-called bums, homelessness—and its corollary ills, hunger, disease, and emotional imbalance—now affect the working poor. Entire families now reside in homeless facilities with little prospect of acquiring their own residences in the foreseeable future. Homelessness has become a profitable, growth industry, particularly for motel and hotel operators in major urban centers. Many marginal hotel operations have discovered the financial feasibility of converting their facilities into "homeless hotels" rather than continuing to compete in the uncertain temporary housing market. In cities such as New York, hotel operators are paid from $1500 to $2000 a month for each homeless person housed in their facility.

The United States has over 12 million children going hungry or malnourished each year. Over 30 million persons suffer from hunger and are unable to meet the basic nutritional requirements, Hunger in the US has grown approximately 50 percent since the mid-1980s and currently affects one-eighth of the total population of the country. What are Muslims doing to address this problem?

Nearly four years ago, Br. Khatib Akbar Jihad felt a sense of mission to do something about the growing homeless problem that had reached near epidemic proportions. His sense of mission included doing something significant for the homeless while delivering guidance, direction, health and social services to a population of desperately needy people. Br. Khatib's "calling" resulted in the formation of the United Muslim Movement Against Homelessness (U.M.M.A.H.). Based in New York City, U.M.M.A.H., with Br. Khatib as its Director, became a subdivision of ICNA Relief in January, 1996. It has established the following mission statement:

> To raise up a community of people from the homeless population who are committed to reclaiming their rightful place of responsibility in society, enjoining what is right, forbidding what is wrong, while striving to uplift themselves and the communities in which they live.

The Muslim community in the New York metropolitan area has provided substantial cooperation and support to U.M.M.A.H. Its weekly mobile feeding program has depended heavily on donations from area mosques and individuals. Clothing is collected and stored in local mosques to be distributed, at no cost, to the homeless population. In addition to food and clothing distribution, U.M.M.A.H. sponsors an annual toy drive for the children of homeless parents. It provides services to the long-term homeless living in the streets as well as services to the homeless in shelters. Orientations are held for new volunteers each week. The Mobile Outreach Program, M.O.P., brings food, clothing, medical referrals, and needs assessment information to homeless people on the streets. Regular speaking engagements are done in shelters consisting of motivational lectures utilizing audio and video aids.

Spiritual nourishment, in the form of dawah materials, is given to the recipients of U.M.M.A.H.'s donations. U.M.M.A.H. further aims to provide a comprehensive program for homeless men. They believe that men must be elevated first to fulfill their positions as caretakers of the women and children. U.M.M.A.H. has intentions to secure a facility large enough to offer a loving and caring environment because of their belief that people who have suffered the devastation and frustration of poverty and homelessness, need to be in a nurturing environment.

Since becoming a part of ICNA Relief, Br. Khatib is hopeful that additional services such as Moral and Ethics Classes and Nutrition and Exercise Classes will be implemented. Unfortunately, homelessness is not likely to end any time soon in this country. By the Grace of Allah, there are some Muslims who do more than engage in philosophical discussions about the problem. They do something.

A Story of Two Ayeshas
Abdul Mālik Mujāhid

The author is the Āmir of the Islamic Circle of North America. He draws parallels between a 20th-century social activist who shares the name of the last and youngest of the wives of the Prophet Muḥammad. She, along with all of the Prophet's wives, are honored as the Mothers of the Believers. As with any word transliterated from one alphabet to another, Ayesha's name receives many different spellings other than the one Āmir Mujāhid has employed. For instance, *ʿAʾisha* (or *Aisha*) is frequently used.

This is the story of two Ayeshas living 1400 years apart. One is our mother Ayesha, may Allah be pleased with her. The other Ayesha is called "the Mother of Homeless" in Chicago, may Allah help her wherever she is.

I recently visited Br. Carl Al-Amin when he was hospitalized because of a kidney problem. I found an old *daee* [missionary] there, Br. Bilal Abdallah. As we sat talking, the discussion started about how long ICNA has been trying to establish a soup kitchen for the homeless in Chicago. As we talked about the dream, Carl forgot about the tubes sticking out of him. He got up and joined in as Bilal told us about Sister Ayesha. She works and lives in downtown Chicago. After paying her rent and other bills, Sr. Ayesha uses all her salary to purchase food supplies. Every day after work she cooks food in large quantities. She fills two large bags with warm sandwiches and starts distributing them to homeless and needy people in downtown Chicago. I was in a state of ecstasy. With most of the over seventy small and large mosques in Chicago doing little, Allah blessed this sister to actually do something meaningful. *Alhamdulilah.* [Thanks be to God.] Where can I find her? What is her phone number? Can she be the leader of ICNA's soup kitchen programs? Unfortunately, as much as Br. Bilal purposefully wanders about town, he had no idea.

This Chicago Ayesha was named after Ayesha, the Mother of Muslims, may Allah be pleased with her. She learned a lot from the Prophet (pbuh). Hadrat [holy person] Ayesha was one of the most significant teachers of Muslims. One day a woman came to her with her two daughters and asked for some food. Ayesha looked for food in the home and could only find a piece of date. Instead of keeping it for herself and the Prophet (pbuh), she gave it to the needy mother. Instead of the needy mother eating the date herself, she gave it to one of her daughters who shared it with her sister. Mothers of the ideal Islamic time were like that. They shared with the needy even if there was nothing left for themselves.

"They offer food to the needy, the orphan and the captive out of love for Him: We are only feeding you for Allah's sake. We want no reward from you nor any thanks. We fear a gloomy, dismal day from our Lord. Allah will shield them from that day's evil, and procure them splendor and happiness." (76:8-11)

I was finally able to track down Sister Ayesha of Chicago. She was doing more for the poor than any mosque. Her *īmān* [faith] speaks louder than big minarets. But, when I found her, things had happened. She was in the Muslim Community Center of Chicago waiting to get her application accepted for financial help. She needed $7000 to get an apartment for herself. She was kicked out of her last apartment because so many homeless people had been standing outside waiting for her to bring down food. She then lost her job as well. It was her third trip to see if that Center could help her. The Mother of Homeless was homeless herself. Was she discouraged? No way! She was lifted up with *sabr* [patience] when Br. Carl and I sat down to talk to her about starting a soup kitchen in Chicago. She is one true follower of Ayesha, the Mother of Muslims.

May Allah bless Sister Ayesha with the best of *dunyā* (this world) and the best of *ākhira* (hereafter). May Allah help us as individuals and as organizations to do our part in helping the poor and needy.

American Muslims Unite to Help Others
The Message News Staff

The Islamic Circle of North America has been holding an annual convention for over a quarter-century. Each year, the focus is different. The following article from ICNA's periodical documents a project which arose out of the 1995 gathering in Columbus, Ohio.

In Columbus, Ohio numerous Muslims were more interested in solutions than they were in problems. Over 300 of them decided to take the first step toward saving someone's life. They were all participants in the Bone Marrow Registration Drive, a joint project of the Islamic Medical Association (IMA) and the National Marrow Donor Program (NMDP). This drive was coordinated with other Community Outreach Projects, headed by Noreen Majeed, a McGill University student and ICNA Summer Intern.

Every year, 30,000 children and adults in the US are diagnosed with fatal blood diseases such as leukemia and aplastic anemia. The only hope for many of them is a bone marrow transplant. Marrow is the blood-like substance found in the large hollow bones of the body that helps to form the body's immune system. Without properly functioning marrow, even mild illnesses can be fatal. That is why a transplant is so critical. The first step toward the transplant is to have a simple blood test taken. At the convention, the Columbus Chapter of the American Red Cross, which serves as the local donor center for the NMDP, provided the staff to administer the test. There were 317 people that registered by having blood samples taken, far beyond anyone's expectations, *alhamdulilah* [thanks be to God]. These blood samples were then sent for tissue typing, which means they were tested to identify the unique genetic code of the blood. The results of these tests were stored in the NMDP registry.

When a person needs a bone marrow transplant, the first step is to test other members of the individual's family for compatibility. Unfortunately, matches are found only a third of the time. When no match is found within the family, the potential patient must rely on the generosity of strangers listed in the NMDP Registry. If an individual listed in the registry is found to be a match, that individual will be contacted as a potential donor. Even at this point the potential donor has the right to refuse to participate. If he or she agrees to continue the process, other tests are performed to ensure that the blood is safe and that the potential donor is in good physical and mental health.

In the hospital, while the donor is under general anesthesia, the marrow is taken from the back of the pelvic bone with a special needle. No incisions are made and no stitches are required after the procedure. The donor usually stays in the hospital overnight and is back to work two or three days later. The only side effect is soreness in the lower back that lasts about a week. In the process of getting a little sore, the donor has helped to save someone's life.

"We know that Allāh decides when life ends," said Dr. Farhat Khan, who has been diagnosed with a fatal blood disease. "Allāh, *subhanawata'ala,* [may God's supreme name be praised] also commands us to do whatever we can in order to save a life. *And whosoever saves a life, it is as if he has saved the life of all humankind.* (Qur'ān 5:32)" Dr. Khan is a strong advocate for the NMDP and really encourages Muslims to get involved. "As a physician, I used to see people with fatal diseases every day. I didn't think it would happen to me. Allāh, in His mercy, has given us the knowledge and technology to help people. It's just a matter of getting yourself registered and believing you can make a difference."

"I have literally spent years of my life in the hospital," said a teary-eyed ICNA President Abdullah Idris during the Community Outreach Project Inauguration. "We should step forward to help people with these physical problems. There is great reward in it for us, *Insha' Allāh* [God willing]." Upon this endorsement, Idrīs announced he would begin the process and get tested right away. With a strong show of unity, the second announcement of support came from former ICNA President Muhammad Yūnus.

May Ma, Western Regional Office Representative for the NMDP, came all the way from Los Angeles to educate the Muslim community about the marrow donation process and encourage us to take a step forward. The idea of launching a national campaign to get Muslims to become potential marrow donors began when Dr. Sheikh Abdul Rahman of the Islamic Association of Cincinnati set up a committee to begin local recruitment. The Cincinnati experience became the starting point as Cincinnati doctors Suleiman Sherif, Talat Rizvi, Rabia Hashmi, and Naeem Hashmi had already obtained 90 local Muslims to register with the NMDP. After this experience, Dr. Abdul Rahman approached IMA to take the project even further. "The IMA family of Muslim healthcare professionals is ready to help," said Dr. Khursheed Mallick, IMA Executive Director. "If we are serious about serving Allāh by serving humanity, this is one way we can get

involved." IMA immediately opened an account to raise funds for the manage-
ment of the project and is serving as the administrative liaison with the NMDP.

The Islamic Shura Council of North America members have also announced
their support and are looking into the possibility of coordinating drives at
conventions and conferences of each of the organizations within the Shura
Council. A national campaign was launched to get even more Muslims to become
registered with the NMDP. The campaign was appropriately titled, *American
Muslims Unite for Life.* As May Ma stated, "Muslims have an important role to
play. Marrow is genetic, so people usually only match someone within their own
racial or ethnic group." Right now most of the donors in the pool are Caucasian.
There is a desperate need for more donors who are African-American, Asia/
Pacific Islander, Hispanic, and American Indian. Since American Muslims are
largely comprised of African and Asian Americans, they are a natural choice to
help. "When Muslims register with the NMDP, they have a chance to help
themselves and help non-Muslims who need marrow transplants as well," said
Ma. "I am really looking forward to working with the Muslim community. The
ISNA Convention was the first step. IMA and NMDP, with the support of the
Islamic Shura Council of North America, are hoping to coordinate drives at
Islamic Centers all over the country.

ENDNOTES

1   Rahman refers to the following passages from the Qur'ān to illustrate his point: 3:14, 185,
197; 4:77; 10:23, 70; 13:26; 16:117; 28:60; 40:39; 42:36; 43:35; 57:20 as examples.

2   See the Qur'ān 70:25; also 51:19.

3   See Qur'ān 90:6.

4   See Qur'ān 30:39; 2:245; 5:12, 18; 64:17; 73:20.

5   Qur'ān 2:260-74. A "Medinan passage" is a chapter of the Qur'ān which is presumed to date
from the period of time during which the prophet Muhammad lived in Medina (622-630 CE).

6   'Ali's rendering of Sūra 2:15 is: "They ask thee what they should spend (in charity). Say:
Whatever ye spend that is good, is for parents and kindred and orphans and those in want and for
wayfarers. And whatever ye do that is good—Allāh knoweth it well."

Using This Anthology

This anthology was designed to provide literature for a course in Religion & Society, or Faith in Action, or even a general survey course in the world's religions. The best use of this material will depend on the length of the term, the amount of material a particular group of students can be expected to read between class meetings, the particular focus of the course, and the creativity of teacher and students alike. The following suggestions are not exhaustive, but may provide a springboard.

1. A course which investigates compassionate action in many faiths ought to be preceded by a survey course on the world's religions. If it is not realistic to require such a course as a prerequisite, then some time must be dedicated to a brief synopsis of the worldview and practices of each faith, either as an introductory unit, or by presenting the essentials of each religion just prior to assigning the readings pertinent to it. Any well-written world religions textbook will provide helpful supplement to this anthology. Several which have been well received by teenaged readers include:

    a. *Living Religions* by Mary Pat Fisher (Upper Saddle River, NJ: Prentice Hall, 1994)

    b. *World Religions in America* by Jacob Neusner (Louisville: Westminster/John Knox, 1994)

    c. *A Handbook of Living Religions* by John R. Hinnells (London: Penguin, 1984)

    d. *The World's Religions* by Huston Smith (San Francisco: Harper, 1991

2. While all students may be assigned all of each chapter of this anthology, it may be more effective to divide the material of each chapter among the members of the class. The students might then have them report to each other, or read aloud the excerpts they found most compelling. Some of the passages make effective dramatic readings. It is also useful to spend class time reading one of the entries aloud in its entirety, assigning paragraphs to various students.

3. This anthology was conceived to provide an academic component to a course which centers on community service. Consider, then, one of the following approaches—or a combination of the two.

    a. Each student in the course is to give a minimum of forty hours of community service, either before the course begins or concurrent with it. A journal should be kept which documents not only what was done, but the student's reflections on the experience. Journal excerpts may be read aloud in class as a springboard for discussion, or may form the basis of reflection papers.

    b. Choose one or more community service projects and participate in them as a class (or in teams, if the class is large). The possibilities include joining such formal occasional activities such as CROPWALK which raise money for a specific cause, or assisting in the work of an established project in your area such as Habitat For Humanity or a local soup kitchen, or devising an original project.

4. Several of the readings might be well illustrated by a poster or a portfolio. For instance, the class might work individually to find articles or create original artwork which illustrates:

    a. The Three Da's (p. 2)

    b. Three Kinds of Rain (p. 27)

    c. The Five Precepts according to Thich Nhat Hanh (p. 41)

    d. Gandhi's list of society's seven sins (p. 13).

    e. Maimonides' Ladder of Charity (p. 83)

    f. The Beatitudes as explained by Elias Chacour (p. 156).

    g. Appropriate recipients of zakāt (Sūra 9.60, p. 161)

5. Class discussions and short reflection papers are a helpful means for digesting this material. Often it is useful to combine the two by having students read their reflection papers to their classmates as a springboard for discussion. Some possibilities are:

    a. In reflecting on this article (or unit), what lessons did you find for yourself or for today's society?

    b. How did this article (or unit) help you rethink who can be a caregiver and who can be the recipient of service?

6. Write the home offices of major religious groups and ask for newsletters or other material which explain what this group does nationally and globally in the areas of compassionate action or social outreach. Contact representatives of local religious organizations and make the same inquiry.

7. Maps are an important resource in a course such as this, especially those which are designed to help us see our world differently. Make use of a world map or globe to locate places mentioned in the articles read. Consider using other map resources which help students look at the world from a variety of perspectives, such as:

   a. Western hemisphere map with South America on top[1]

   b. World map with Australia on top

   c. World map with country sizes drawn according to population

   d. World map with country sizes drawn according to natural resources or population[2]

   e. World map in equal area presentation (Peters Projection)[3]

8. Create a glossary of the specialized vocabulary you have discovered as you have encountered each religion.

9. Create a portfolio of news articles and other supplementary material on faith in action.

10. Write an essay on a question such as:

    a. Is the quality of the deed changed either by the motives of the doer or the attitude of the recipient? Draw upon your reading and experience to support your position.

    b. How would you describe the unique aspect of "call of service" within each faith? What is universal in this call? Draw upon your reading to document your answer.

    c. Choose reading from one of the even-numbered chapters, and find readings from its companion chapter of scriptural excerpts which support the point the author is making. Is there another position which could be drawn from those same passages? Explain.

    d. Draw comparisons and contrasts between articles from two different chapters.

11. Make use of games, dramatic readings, and other simple projects which help us see hunger and justice issues through a different lens. The Church World Service Unit of the National Council of Churches of Christ in the USA has many such resources for classroom activities. A catalogue may be obtained from CWS, P. O. Box 968, Elkhart, Indiana 46515. Bread for the World (1100 Wayne Avenue, Suite 1000, Silver Springs, Maryland 20910) and Interfaith Impact for Justice and Peace (110 Maryland Avenue NE, Washington, DC, 20002) are also good sources for material.

12. As a class, watch a film on the life of Gandhi, Mother Teresa, or some other such social activist. World religions video series often contain relevant material as well; many such series are available from educational film distributors.

1   *Turnabout Map* distributed by Laguna Sales, 4015 Orme Street, Palo Alto, CA 94306.
2   Maps b, c, and d are available from Poster Education, Box 8774, Asheville, NC 28814.
3   English version by Oxford Cartographers Ltd., Oxford, UK.

Bibliography

The following resources are in addition to those listed in the Guide to Sources beginning on page 204.

Books

'Ali, 'Abdullah Yusuf. *The Meaning of The Holy Qur'ān: New Edition with Revised Translation and Commentary.* (Brentwood, Maryland: Amana Corporation, 1989).

Barnett, James Monroe. *The Diaconate: A Full and Equal Order.* (Minneapolis: The Seabury Press, 1979).

Booty, John E. *The Servant Church: Diaconal Ministry and the Episcopal Church.* (Wilton, Connecticut: Morehouse-Barlow, 1982).

Brown, Robert McAfee & Sydney Thomson Brown, eds. *A Cry for Justice: The Churches and Synagogues Speak.* (New York: Paulist Press, 1989).

Bryant, M. Darrol & Frank Flynn, ed. *Interreligious Dialogue: Voice from a New Frontier.* (New York: Paragon House, 1989).

Coward, Harold. *Sacred Word and Sacred Text: Scripture in World Religions.* (Maryknoll, New York: Orbis Books, 1988).

Diehl, William J. *The Monday Connection: A Spirituality of Competence, Affirmation, and Support in the Workplace.* (San Francisco: HarperCollins, 1991).

Donders, Joseph. *The Global Believer.* (Mystic, Connecticut: Twenty-third Publications, 1986).

Eliade, Mircea, editor-in-chief. *The Encyclopedia of Religion.* (New York: Macmillan, 1987).

Ellis, Marc H. *Toward a Jewish Theology of Liberation.* (Maryknoll, New York: Orbis Books, 1987).

Falk, Randall M. & Walter J. Harrelson, *Jews & Cristians in Pursuit of Social Justice.* (Nashville: Abingdon Press, 1996).

Farman Farmaian, Sattareh, with Dona Munker. *Daughter of Persia: A Woman's Journey from Her Father's Harem Through the Islamic Revolution.* (New York: Crown, 1992).

Fernando, Anthony, with Leonard Swidler *Buddhism Made Plain: An Introduction for Christians and Jews.* (New York: Orbis Books, 1985).

Fisher, Mary Pat. *Living Religions.* (Upper Saddle River, New Jersey: Prentice Hall, 1994).

Foster, Richard J. *Study Guide for Celebration of Discipline.* (San Francisco: Harper & Row, 1983).

Greenleaf, Robert K. *The Servant as Religious Leader.* (Peterborough, New Hampshire: Windy Row Press, 1982).

Gremillion, Joseph, presenter. *Food/Energy and the Major Faiths.* (Maryknoll, New York: Orbis Books, 1978).

Hamilton, Clarence H., ed. *Buddhism: A Religion of Infinite Compassion: Selections from Buddhist Literature, Edited, with an Introduction and Notes.* (New York: The Liberal Arts Press, 1952).

Hessel, Dieter T. *Social Ministry.* (Philadelphia: Westminster Press, 1982).

Houghton, Alanson B., May B. Morris, & Kay K. Stricklin. *Private Choices: Public Consequences: A Discussion on Ethical Choices Using Gandhi's Seven Sins As Challenges and Guides.* (Cincinnati, Ohio: Forward Movement, 1992).

Hunt, Arnold D., Marie T. Crotty, & Robert B. Crotty. *Ethics of World Religions.* (San Diego, California: Greenhaven Press, 1976).

Ingram, Catherine. *In the Footsteps of Gandhi: Conversations With Social Activists.* (Berkeley: California: Parallax Press, 1990).

Kellner, Menachem Marc, ed. *Contemporary Jewish Ethics.* (New York: Hebrew Publishing House, 1978).

Kushner, Harold. *To Life! A Celebration of Jewish Being and Thinking.* (Boston: Little, Brown and Company, 1993).

Lemu, B. Aisha. *Islam and Alcohol.* (Alexandria, VA: Saadawi Publications, 1992).

Miller, William. *A Harsh and Dreadful Love: Dorothy Day and the Catholic Worker Movement.* (Garden City, New York: Image Books, 1974).

Miller, William D. *Dorothy Day: A Biography.* (San Francisco: Harper & Row, 1982).

Minor, Robert N., editor. *Modern Indian Interpreters of the Bhagavadgita.* (Albany: State University of New York Press, 1986).

Muslehuddin, Muḥammad. *Morality, Its Concept and Role in Islamic Order.* (Lahore, Pakistan: Islamic Publications, Ltd., 1984).

Poser, ed. *Diakonia 2000: Called to Be Neighbors: Official Report, WCC World Consultation on Inter-church Aid, Refugee, and World Service, Larnaca, 1986.* (Geneva: World Council of Churches, 1987).

Rouner, Leroy S., ed. *Human Rights and the World's Religions.* (Notre Dame, Indiana: University of Notre Dame Press, 1988).

Rowthorn, Anne. *Caring For Creation.* (Wilton, Connecticut: Morehouse-Barlow, 1989).

Rowthorn, Anne. *The Liberation of the Laity.* (Wilton, Connecticut: Morehouse- Barlow, 1986).

Sharma, Arvind, ed. *Neo-Hindu Views of Christianity.* (Leiden: E. J. Brill, 1988).

Sherwin, Byron L. *Toward a Jewish Theology.* (Lewiston, New York: Edwin Mellen Press, 1991).

Smart, Ninian & Richard D. Hecht, eds. *Sacred Texts of the World: A Universal Anthology.* (New York: Crossroad, 1982).

Smith, Huston. *The World's Religions.* (San Francisco: HarperSan Francisco, 1991).

Spangler, Ann, ed. *Bright Legacy: Portraits of Ten Outstanding Christian Women.* (Ann Arbor, Michigan: Servant Books, 1983).

Swidler, Leonard, ed. *Religious Liberty and Human Rights in Nations and in Religions.* (Philadelphia: Ecumenical Press, 1986).

Wigoder, Geoffrey, editor-in-chief. *The Encyclopedia of Judaism.* (New York: Macmillan, 1989).

Wilson, Andrew, editor. *World Scripture: A Comparative Anthology of Sacred Texts.* (New York: Paragon House, 1991).

PERIODICALS

Beckerlegge, Gwilym. "Social Service as *Sadhana:* Different perceptions of the nature of the continuity between the teachings of Sri Ramakrishna and Swami Vivekananda," *Religion and Society,* Vol. 33, No. 4 (December 1986).

Brown, Robert McAfee, "Toward a Just and Compassionate Society: A Christian View," *Cross Currents* (Summer 1995).

Dhavamony, Mariashsai. "Mother Teresa's Mission of Love for the Poorest of the Poor," *Studia Missionalia,* Vol. 39 (1990).

Gunaratne, Neville. "An Evaluation by a Buddhist of Mother Teresa's Boundless Compassion and Voluntary Poverty," *Dialogue,* Vol. 8, No. 1-3 (1981).

Tong, Fung-Wan. "Understanding of the Social Ethical Dimensions of Buddhism and Christianity," *Taiwan Journal of Theology,* No. 7, (1985).

Watson, JoAnn Ford. "Ministering in Mother Teresa's Home for the Dying Destitutes, Calcutta, India," *Ashland Theological Journal,* Vol. 21 (1989).

Acknowledgments

Grateful acknowledgment is extended to the following holders of copyright for permission to reprint passages from the following works:

Addison Wesley (Reading, Massachusetts)
Dorothy Day: A Radical Devotion, by Robert Coles (1987).

Alban Institute (Washington, DC)
"Mission on the Doorstep," by William G. Carter in *Action Information,* Vol. 18, No. 2 (March/April 1992).

Alfred A. Knopf (New York)
Buddhism: A Way of Life and Thought, by Nancy Wilson Ross (1980).

Amana Corporation (Brentwood, Maryland)
The Meaning of The Holy Qur'ān: New Edition with Revised Translation and Commentary, 'Abdullah Yusuf 'Ali, translator (1989).

Asiatic Society (Calcutta, India)
The Markandeya Purana, by F. E. Pargiter, translator (1904).

Association for Religion & Intellectual Life (New Rochelle, New York)
"The Language of Judaic Community: Commandment, Calendar, Commitment," by Shamai Kanter in *Cross Currents: The Journal of the Association for Religion & Intellectual Life,* Volume 6, No. 1 (Fall 1988).
"Toward a Just and Compassionate Society: A Jewish View," by Byron L. Sherwin, in *Cross Currents* (Summer 1995).

Behrman House (New York)
"Maimonides's Ladder of Charity," in *A Maimonides Reader,* Isadore Twersky, ed. (n.d.).
The Sayings of the Fathers, J. Hertz, ed. (1945): 2:13.

Bhaktivedanta Book Trust (Malmoe, Sweden)
Srimad Bhagavatam, Swami Prabhavananda, translator (1943).

Bibliotheca Islamica (Minneapolis, Minnesota)
Major Themes of the Qur'ān, by Fazlur Rahman (1989).

B'nai B'rith International (New York)
"Affirmative Actions: Young Jews and African–Americans learn how to get along," by Alyson Gold in *B'nai B'rith International Jewish Monthly* (1995).

Bruce Publishing Company (New York)
Religions of India: Hinduism, Yoga, Buddhism, by Thomas Berry (1971).

Buddhist Society (London)
"Buddhism and the Thai Refugee Camps," by Keno Visakha Kawasaki, in *The Middle Way: Journal of the Buddhist Society,* Volume 65 (November 1990).

Buddhist Text Translation Society (San Francisco)
A General Explanation of the Buddha Speaks, The Sutra in Forty-Two Sections by Hsuan-hua, Bhikshuni Heng Chih, translator (1977).

Chacour, Elias
We Belong to the Land (1990).

Christian Institute for Religion and Society (Bangalore, India)
  "Hinduism and Development: Three Case Studies," by Jan Peter Schouten in *Religion and Society*, Vol. 28, No. 2 (June 1981).

Clem, Gordon
  O God, My Heart Is Ready (1996).

Congressional Quarterly (Washington, DC)
  "Those Who Give: The Link Between Charity and Religion," in *CQ Researcher* (November 12, 1993).

Council on American-Islamic Relations (Washington, DC)
  A Rush to Judgment: A Special Report on Anti-Muslim Stereotyping and Hate Crimes Following the Bombing of Oklahoma City's Murrah Federal Building, April 19, 1995 (September, 1995).

Doubleday (Garden City, New York)
  Saints Are Now: Eight Portraits of Modern Sanctity, John J. Delaney, ed. (1981).

Farrar, Straus, & Giroux (New York)
  The Wisdom of Heschel by Abraham Joshua Heschel, selected by Ruth Marcus Goodhill (1975).

General Board of Church and Society of the United Methodist Church (Washington, DC)
  "You Give Them Something to Eat," by Ray Buchanan in *Christian Social Action* (November 1995).

Georgia Magazine (Atlanta, Georgia)
  "No More Shacks" by Kerra Davis (February 1993).

Gerald Duckworth & Company (London)
  Hadith, Neal Robinson, translator (1991).

Habitat For Humanity International (Atlanta, Georgia)
  A Decent House in a Decent Community for God's People in Need (1996).

Harold Ober Associates
  Vintage Muggeridge: Religion and Society, by Malcolm Muggeridge with Geoffrey Barlow, ed. (1985).

Harper & Row (New York & San Francisco)
  Celebration of Discipline: The Path to Spiritual Growth, by Richard J. Foster, 1988.
  Something Beautiful for God: Mother Teresa of Calcutta, by Malcolm Muggeridge (1971).

Hartford Seminary (Hartford, Connecticut)
  "Ramadan: Struggle, Compassion & Joy," by Ernest Hamilton in *PRAXIS* (n.d.).

Hinduism Today (Kapaa, Hawaii).
  "A spiritual response to the environment," by Jagmohan, n.v. (n.d.).
  "Amazing! Such service all belongs to God," by V. V. Gokhale, Volume 17, No. 7 (July 1995).
  "Building lives and villages after Maharashtra earthquake," by Sujata Anandan, Volume 16, No. 3 (March 1994).
  "Redefining Hindu charity," by Shrikumar Poddar, Volume 16, No. 3 (March 1994).
  "Swamini steers two Chinmaya Mission ashrams into Youth Training and ecological recovery," by Lavina Melwani, Volume 17, No. 5 (May 1995).

Indiana University Press (Bloomington, Indiana)
  Vedanta for the West: The Ramakrishna Movement in the United States, by Carl T. Jackson (1994).

Islamic Circle of North America (Jamaica, New York)
  "Challenges, Not Obstacles: How American Muslims Unite to Help Others," in *The Message*, Volume 18, No. 8 (February 1995).
  "Compulsory," by Shamal Zamaluddin in *The Message*, Volume 17, No. 9 (February 1994).
  "Love Thy Neighbors," by Omar Afzal in *The Message*, Volume 20, No. 8 (February 1996); "United Muslim Movement Against Homelessness," *Ibid.*; "A Story of Two Ayeshas," by Abdul Malik Mujahid, *Ibid.*
  "Where's the Beef?" in *The Message*, Volume 20, No. 11 (May 1996).

Jewish Publication Society (Philadelphia)
  TANAKH: The Holy Scriptures: The New JPS Translation According to the Traditional Hebrew Text (1988). (All biblical passages except those credited to OUP below.)

KAZI Publications (Chicago)
  What Everyone Should Know About Islam and Muslims, by Suzanne Haneef (1982).

Library of Tibetan Works and Archives (Bangalore, India)
  A Guide to the Bodhisattva's Way of Life, Stephen Batchelor, translator (1979).

Little, Brown and Company (Boston)
  To Life! A Celebration of Jewish Being and Thinking, by Harold Kushner (1993).
Mercy International–USA (Pymouth, Michigan)
  Helping People Help Themselves (*Mercy News,* July 1996).
New York Times (New York)
  "A Yom Kippur Plea" (9/22/90); "Rolling up sleeves to help Soviet emigrés" (3/4/90); "To stay young: walk, feed birds, help old people" (2/21/90).
Nilgiri Press (Tomales, California)
  The Bhagavad Gita for Daily Living, Eknath Easwaran, ed. (1985).
Orbis Books (Maryknoll, New York)
  Buddhism Made Plain: An Introduction for Christians and Jews by Anthony Fernando with Leonard Swidler (1985).
Oxford University Press (New York)
  The Dhammapada, John Ross Carter, translator (1987).
  "Make Us Worthy Lord," by Mother Teresa of Calcutta in *The Oxford Book of Prayer,* George Appleton, general editor (1985).
  The Moral and Political Writings of Mahatma Gandhi, Raghavan Iyer, editor (1986).
  The New Oxford Annotated Bible with the Apocryphal/Deuterocanonical Books, New Revised Standard Version, Bruce M. Metzger and Roland E. Murphy, editors (1991): Lev. 18b; Deut. 24:10–15 & 32:36; Isa. 49:13; Ps. 10:2, 22:26, 37:14, 41:1-2a, 112:5–6. 146; Prov. 14:21 &31, 19:17, 21:13, 22:2, 22:9, 22:16, 22:22–3, 28:3 & 6, 29:7 & 14; Lam. 3:31–33; II Chr. 30:7–9, 36:15; and all New Testament passages.
  "Social Justice," by Ibrahim Abu-Rabiʿ in *The Oxford Encyclopedia of the Modern Islamic World,* John L. Esposito, editor in chief (1995).
Pali Text Society (Oxford, England)
  Astasahasrika Prajnaparamita Sutra Edward Conze, translator.
  Dohakosha, Edward Conze, translator (1954).
  Itivuttaka from *The Minor Anthologies of the Pali Canon, Part 2, Udana: Verses of Uplift and Itivuttaka: As It Was Said,* F. L. Woodward, translator (1935). *Vinaya-Pitaka,* I. B. Horner, translator (1938-67).
  Khuddaka Patha, Bhikkhu Nanamoli, translator (1960).
  Vimanavatthu from *The Minor Anthologies of the Pali Canon, Part 4, Vimanavatthu: Stories of the Mansions, and Petavatthu: Stories of the Departed,* I. B. Horner & H. S. Gehman, translators (1974).
Pannikar, Raimundo
  Rig Veda 1.125.5
Pantheon/Random House (New York)
  The Ethics of the Talmud: Sayings of the Fathers, R. Travers Herford, ed. (1925): Abot 1:2, 14; 2:5, 21; 4:1; 5:10.
Parallax Press (Berkeley, California)
  "Generosity," from *For A Future to be Possible* by Thich Nhat Hanh (1993).
  "Please Call Me By My True Names," by Thich Nhat Hanh, from *The Path of Compassion: Writings on Socially Engaged Buddhism,* Fred Eppsteiner, ed. (1988).
Paulist Press (New York)
  Zohar: Book of Enlightenment, Daniel Chanan Matt, translator.
Penguin Press (London)
  "November Third," by Miyazawa Kenji from *The Penguin Book of Japanese Verse* (n.d.).
  Rig Veda, W. D. O'Flaherty, translator, (All *Rig Veda* passages except 1.125.5)
Princeton University Press (Princeton, New Jersey)
  The Qurʾān, Ahmed ʾAli, translator (1988).
Saadawi Publications (Alexandria, Virginia)
  Islam and Alcohol, by B. Aisha Lemu (1992).
Shambhala Press (Boston)
  The Flower Ornament Scripture: A Translation of the Avatamsaka Sutra (1984-7).
Sheed and Ward (Kansas City, Missouri)
  "A Poem," by Michel Quoist from *Prayers for Life.*

Spangler, Ann (editor)
  Bright Legacy: Portraits of Ten Outstanding Christian Women (1983).

Swearer, Donald
  Dialogue: The Key to Understanding Other Religions (1977).

United States Catholic Conference, Inc. (Washington, DC)
  A Pastoral Message: Economic Justice for All, by National Council of Catholic Bishops, Monsignor Daniel F. Hoye, General Secretary (1986).

University of Chicago Press (Chicago)
  The Talmud of the Land of Israel: A Preliminary Translation and Explanation, Roger Brooks, translator, Volume 2; Jacob Neusner, general editor (1990): Peah 1:1, 4:13.

Westminster Press (Philadelphia)
  Buddhism and Christianity: Some Bridges of Understanding, by Winston L. King (1962).

World Council of Churches (Geneva, Switzerland)
  The Meaning and Nature of Diakonia, by Paulos Mar Gregorios (1988).

Vedanta Society of Southern California (Hollywood, California)
  The Upanishads: Breath of the Eternal: The Principal Texts Selected and Translated from the Original Sanskrit. Swami Prabhavananda and Frederick Manchester, translators (1957).

Yale University Press (New Haven, Connecticut)
  The Fathers According to Rabbi Nathan, Judah Goldin, translator (1955).
  The Midrash on Psalms, William G. Braude, translator (1959).
  The Mishnah, Jacob Neusner, translator: Peah 1:2; 4:4, 5, 10.
  Sifre: A Tannaitic Commentary on the Book of Deuteronomy, Reuven Hammer, translator (1986).

Every effort has been made to trace the copyright holders of all material contained in this anthology. However, if any have been overlooked inadvertently, CRIS will be pleased to make the necessary arrangements at its earliest opportunity.

Guide to Sources

Hinduism

Anandan, Sujata. "Building lives and villages after Maharashtra earthquake," in *Hinduism Today.* Volume 16, No. 3. (March 1994).

Easwaran, Eknath, ed. *The Bhagavad Gita for Daily Living.* (Tomales, California: Nilgiri Press, 1985).

Gandhi, Mohandas K. "Religion and Social Service" from *The Moral and Political Writings of Mahatma Gandhi, Volume One: Civilization, Politics, and Religion,* Raghavan Iyer, ed. (Oxford: Clarendon Press, 1986).

Gandhi, Mohandas K. "Ethical Religion: Morality & Society" & "The Spirit of Service" from *The Moral and Political Writings of Mahatma Gandhi, Volume Two: Truth and Non-Violence,* Raghavan Iyer, editor (Oxford: Clarendon Press, 1986).

Gokhale, V. V. "Amazing! Such service all belongs to God," *Hinduism Today,* Volume 17, No. 7 (July 1995).

Jackson, Carl T. *Vedanta for the West: The Ramakrishna Movement in the United States.* (Bloomington, Indiana: Indiana University Press, 1994).

Jagmohan. "A spiritual response to the environment," *Hinduism Today,* n.v. (n.d.).

Melwani, Lavina. "Swamini steers two Chinmaya Mission ashrams into Youth Training and ecological recovery," *Hinduism Today,* Volume 17, No. 5. (May 1995).

O'Flaherty, W. D., tr. *Rig Veda.* (London: Penguin Press, n.d.) (All *Rig Veda* passages except 1.125.5).

Pannikar, Raimundo. *Rig Veda* 1.125.5.

Pargiter, F. E. , tr. *The Markandeya Purana.* (Calcutta, India: Asiatic Society, 1904).

Poddar, Shrikumar. "Redefining Hindu charity," *Hinduism Today,* Volume 16, No. 3 (March 1994).

Schouten, Jan Peter. "Hinduism and Development: Three Case Studies," in Religion and Society, Vol. 28, No. 2. (June 1981). Christian Institute for Religion and Society (Bangalore, India).

Swami Prabhavananda and Frederick Manchester, trs. *The Upanishads: Breath of the Eternal: The Principal Texts Selected and Translated from the Original Sanskrit.* (Hollywood, California: Vedanta, 1957).

Swami Prabhavananda, tr. *Srimad Bhagavatam.* (Malmoe, Sweden: Bhaktivedanta Book Trust International).

Buddhism

Batchelor, Stephen, tr. *A Guide to the Bodhisattva's Way of Life.* (Dharamsala, India: Library of Tibetan Works and Archives, 1979).

Berry, Thomas. *Religions of India: Hinduism, Yoga, Buddhism.* (New York: Bruce Publishing Company, 1971).

Carter, John Ross, tr. *The Dhammapada.* (New York: Oxford University Press, 1987).

Conze, Edward, tr. *Sikshasamuccaya.* (Oxford, England: Bruno Cassirer, Ltd., n.d.).

Conze, Edward, tr. *Astasahasrika Prajnaparamita Sutra.* (Oxford: Pali Text Society, n.d.).

Conze, Edward, tr. *Dohakosha.* (Oxford: Pali Text Society, 1954).

Fernando, Anthony with Leonard Swidler. *Buddhism Made Plain: An Introduction for Christians and Jews.* (Maryknoll, New York: Orbis Books, 1985).

Hanh, Thich Nhat. "Generosity," from *For A Future to be Possible.* (Berkeley, California: Parallax Press, 1993).

Hanh, Thich Nhat. "Please Call Me By My True Names," from *The Path of Compassion: Writings on Socially Engaged Buddhism,* Fred Eppsteiner, ed. (Berkeley, California: Parallax Press, 1988).

Horner, I. B. & H. S. Gehman, trs. *Vimanavatthu* from *The Minor Anthologies of the Pali Canon, Part 4, Vimanavatthu: Stories of the Mansions, and Petavatthu: Stories of the Departed.* (Oxford, England: Pali Text Society, 1974).

Horner, I. B. , tr. *Vinaya-Pitaka.* (Oxford, England: Pali Text Society, 1938-67).

Hsuan-hua. *A General Explanation of the Buddha Speaks, The Sutra in Forty-Two Sections.* Bhikshuni Heng Chih, tr. (San Francisco: Buddhist Text Translation Society, 1977).

Kawasaki, Keno Visakha. "Buddhism and the Thai Refugee Camps," in *The Middle Way: Journal of the Buddhist Society,* Volume 65. (London: Buddhist Society, November 1990).

Kenji, Miyazawa. "November Third," from *Penguin Book of Japanese Verse.* (London: Penguin Press, n.d.).

King, Winston L. *Buddhism and Christianity: Some Bridges of Understanding.* (Philadelphia: Westminster Press, 1962).

Nanamoli, Bhikkhu, tr. *Khuddaka Patha.* (Oxford, England: Pali Text Society, 1960).

Ross, Nancy Wilson. *Buddhism: A Way of Life and Thought.* (New York: Alfred A. Knopf, 1980).

Swearer, Donald K. *Dialogue: The Key to Understanding Other Religions.* (Philadelphia: Westminster Press, 1977).

The Flower Ornament Scripture: A Translation of the Avatamsaka Sutra. (Boston: Shambhala Press, 1984-7).

Woodward, F. L., tr. *Itivuttaka* from *The Minor Anthologies of the Pali Canon, Part 2, Udana: Verses of Uplift and Itivuttaka: As It Was Said.* (Oxford, England: Pali Text Society, 1935).

Judaism

"A Yom Kippur Plea" *New York Times.* (9/22/90).

Braude, William G., tr. *The Midrash on Psalms.* (New Haven, Connecticut: Yale University Press, 1959).

Brooks, Roger, tr. *The Talmud of the Land of Israel: A Preliminary Translation and Explanation,* Volume 2, Jacob Neusner, general editor. (Chicago: University of Chicago Press, 1990): Peah 1:1, 4:13.

Gold, Alyson. "Affirmative Actions: Young Jews and African-Americans learn how to get along," in *B'nai B'rith International Jewish Monthly.* (New York: B'nai B'rith International, 1995).

Goldin, Judah, tr. *The Fathers According to Rabbi Nathan.* (New Haven: Yale University Press, 1955).

Hammer, Reuven, tr. *Sifre: A Tannaitic Commentary on the Book of Deuteronomy.* (New Haven: Yale University Press, 1986).

Herford, R. Travers, ed. *The Ethics of the Talmud: Sayings of the Fathers.* (New York: Pantheon/Random House): Abot 1:2, 14; 2:5, 21; 4:1; 5:10.

Hertz, J., ed. *The Sayings of the Fathers.* (New York: Behrman House, 1945): 2:13.

Heschel, Abraham Joshua, selected by Ruth Marcus Goodhill. *The Wisdom of Heschel.* (New York: Farrar, Straus, & Giroux, 1975).

Hurwitz, Hyman tr. "The Twofold Charity of the Benevolent Physician" from *Hebrew Tales.* (London: Morrison and Watt, 1826).

Kanter, Shamai. "The Language of Judaic Community: Commandment, Calendar, Commitment," in *Cross Currents: The Journal of the Association for Religion & Intellectual Life,* Volume 6, No. 1. (Fall 1988). (New Rochelle, New York: Association for Religion & Intellectual Life).

Kushner, Harold. *To Life! A Celebration of Jewish Being and Thinking.* (Boston: Little, Brown and Company, 1993).

Matt, Daniel Chanan, tr. *Zohar: Book of Enlightenment.* (New York: Paulist Press, n.d.).

Neusner, Jacob, tr. *The Mishnah.* (New Haven, Connecticut: Yale University Press, n.d.): Peah 1:2; 4:4, 5, 10.

"Rolling up sleeves to help Soviet emigrés" *New York Times.* (3/4/90)

Sherwin, Byron L. "Toward a Just and Compassionate Society: A Jewish View," in *Cross Currents.* (Summer 1995). (New Rochelle, New York: Association for Religion & Intellectual Life).

TANAKH: The Holy Scriptures: The New JPS Translation According to the Traditional Hebrew Text. (Philadelphia: Jewish Publication Society, 1988): (All biblical passages except those credited to OUP.).

"Those Who Give: The Link Between Charity and Religion," in *CQ Researcher.* Volume 3, No. 42 (November 12, 1993), p. 1002. (Washington, DC: *Congressional Quarterly*).

"To stay young: walk, feed birds, help old people," in *New York Times.* (2/21/90).

Twersky, Isadore, ed. "Maimonides's Ladder of Charity," in *A Maimonides Reader.* (New York: Behrman House, n.d.).

Christianity

A Decent House in a Decent Community for God's People in Need. (Atlanta, Georgia: Habitat For Humanity International, 1996).

Buchanan, Ray. "You Give Them Something to Eat," in *Christian Social Action.* (November 1995). (Washington, DC: General Board of Church and Society of the United Methodist Church).

Carter, William G. "Mission on the Doorstep" in *Action Information,* Vol. 18, No. 2. (Washington, DC: Alban Institute, March/April 1992).

Chacour, Elias with Mary E. Jensen. *We Belong to the Land.* (New York & San Francisco: Harper & Row, 1990).

Coles, Robert. *Dorothy Day: A Radical Devotion.* (Reading, Massachusetts: Addison Wesley, 1987).

Davis, Kerra. "No More Shacks," *Georgia Magazine.* (February 1993).

Delaney, John J., ed. *Saints Are Now: Eight Portraits of Modern Sanctity.* (Garden City, New York: Doubleday, 1981).

Foster, Richard J. *Celebration of Discipline: The Path to Spiritual Growth.* (New York & San Francisco: Harper & Row, 1988).

Gregorios, Paulos Mar. *The Meaning and Nature of Diakonia.* (Geneva, Switzerland: World Council of Churches, 1988).

Metzger, Bruce M. and Roland E. Murphy, eds. *The New Oxford Annotated Bible with the Apocryphal/ Deuterocanonical Books.* New Revised Standard Version. (New York: Oxford University Press, 1991): Lev. 18b; Deut. 24:10-15 & 32:36; Isa. 49:13; Ps. 10:2, 22:26, 37:14, 41:1-2a, 112:5-6. 146; Prov. 14:21 &31, 19:17, 21:13, 22:2, 22:9, 22:16, 22:22-3, 28:3 & 6, 29:7 & 14; Lam. 3:31-33; II Chr. 30:7-9, 36:15; and all New Testament passages.

Mother Teresa of Calcutta. "Make Us Worthy Lord," in *The Oxford Book of Prayer.* George Appleton, general editor (New York: Oxford University Press, 1985).

Muggeridge, Malcolm. *Something Beautiful for God: Mother Teresa of Calcutta.* (New York & San Francisco: Harper & Row, 1971).

Muggeridge, Malcolm with Geoffrey Barlow, ed. *Vintage Muggeridge: Religion and Society.* (Grand Rapids, Michigan: William B. Eerdmans, 1985).

National Council of Catholic Bishops, Monsignor Daniel F. Hoye, General Secretary. *A Pastoral Message: Economic Justice for All.* (Washington, DC: United States Catholic Conference, Inc., 1986).

Quoist, Michel. "A Poem," from *Prayers for Life.* (Kansas City, Missouri: Sheed and Ward, n.d.).

Spangler, Ann, ed. *Bright Legacy: Portraits of Ten Outstanding Christian Women.* (1983).

Swearer, Donald K. *Dialogue: The Key to Understanding Other Religions.* (Philadelphia: Westminster Press, 1977).

Islam

A Rush to Judgment: A Special Report on Anti-Muslim Stereotyping and Hate Crimes Following the Bombing of Oklahoma City's Murrah Federal Building, April 19, 1995. (Washington, DC: Council on American-Islamic Relations, September, 1995).

Abu-Rabiʿ, Ibrahim. "Social Justice," in *The Oxford Encyclopedia of the Modern Islamic World,* John L. Esposito, editor in chief. (New York: Oxford University Press, 1995).

Afzal, Omar. "Love Thy Neighbors," in *The Message,* Volume 20, No. 8. (February 1996). (Jamaica, New York: Islamic Circle of North America).

ʾAli, ʾAbdullah Yūsuf, tr. *The Meaning of The Holy Qurʾān: New Edition with Revised Translation and Commentary.* (Brentwood, Maryland: Amana Corporation, 1989).

ʾAli, Ahmed, tr. *The Qurʾān.* (Princeton, New Jersey: Princeton University Press, 1988).

"Challenges, Not Obstacles: How American Muslims Unite to Help Others," in *The Message,* Volume 18, No. 8. (February 1995). (Jamaica, New York: Islamic Circle of North America).

Hamilton, Ernest. "Ramadan: Struggle, Compassion & Joy," in *PRAXIS.* (Hartford, Connecticut: Hartford Seminary, n.d.).

Haneef, Suzanne. *What Everyone Should Know About Islam and Muslims.* (Chicago: KAZI Publications, 1982).

"Helping People Help Themselves: Mercy International USA, Inc.," *Mercy News* (Plymouth, Michigan July 1996).

Lemu, B. Aisha. *Islam and Alcohol.* (Alexandria, Virginia: Saadawi Publications, 1992).

Mujahid, Abdul Malik. "A Story of Two Ayeshas," in *The Message,* Volume 20, No. 8. (February 1996), Jamaica, New York: Islamic Circle of North America).

Rahman, Fazlur. *Major Themes of the Qur'an.* (Minneapolis, Minnesota: Bibliotheca Islamica, 1989).

Robinson, Neal, tr. *The Sayings of Muḥammad.* (London: Gerald Duckworth & Company, 1991).

"United Muslim Movement Against Homelessness," in *The Message,* Volume 20, No. 8. (February 1996).

"Where's the Beef?" in *The Message,* Volume 20, No. 11. (May 1996). (Jamaica, New York: Islamic Circle of North America).

Zamaluddin, Shamal. "Compulsory," in *The Message,* Volume 17, No. 9. (February 1994). (Jamaica, New York: Islamic Circle of North America).